Island Gospel

AFRICAN AMERICAN MUSIC IN GLOBAL PERSPECTIVE

Portia K. Maultsby, Series Editor
Archives of African American Music and Culture
Indiana University

A list of books in the series appears at the end of this book.

Island Gospel

Pentecostal Music and Identity in Jamaica and the United States

MELVIN L. BUTLER

UNIVERSITY OF ILLINOIS PRESS
Urbana, Chicago, and Springfield

Publication of this book is supported by a grant from
the Bruno Nettl Endowment for Ethnomusicology.

Library of Congress Cataloging-in-Publication Data
Names: Butler, Melvin, author.
Title: Island gospel: Pentecostal music and identity in Jamaica and the United
    States / Melvin L Butler.
Description: Urbana: University of Illinois Press, 2019. | Series: African American
    music in global perspec | Includes bibliographical references and index. |
    Summary: "This book offers fresh insight into the musical world of Jamaican
    Pentecostals in all of its complexity. Drawing on deep immersion in both
    American and Jamaican musical context and performing communities, Melvin
    Butler explores how Jamaican Pentecostals, both in the United States and back
    home on the island, use music to express devotion to both faith and nation,
    and how they seek to reconcile their religious and cultural identities, especially
    when the latter are closely tied to iconic "secular" musics such as ska, reggae,
    and dancehall. Butler deploys the concept of flow to evoke both the experience
    of Spirit-influenced performance and the transmigrations that fuel a
    controversial sharing of musical and ritual resources between Jamaica and the
    United States. Seeking to make sense of the ways in which these Pentecostals
    use music to cross and construct boundaries between local and foreign ways
    of worshiping God, Goodbye World connects the porous boundaries and
    vibrant flows of black religious worship in the United States with those found
    throughout the African diaspora. This book tells a story—or rather, many
    stories—of how musical and religious flow engenders a sense of belonging
    among Jamaican people of faith"— Provided by publisher.
Identifiers: LCCN 2019025470 (print) | LCCN 2019025471 (ebook) | ISBN
    9780252042904 (cloth) | ISBN 9780252084720 (paperback) | ISBN
    9780252051760 (ebook)
Subjects: LCSH: Church music—Pentecostal Churches. | Church music—Jamaica. |
    Church music—United States.
Classification: LCC ML3178.P4 B87 2019 (print) | LCC ML3178.P4 (ebook) | DDC
    780.88/28994—dc23
LC record available at https://lccn.loc.gov/2019025470
LC ebook record available at https://lccn.loc.gov/2019025471

For Lori

Contents

Preface

During a recent chat with a young Jamaican preacher living in the United States, I mentioned that I was writing a book about music and identity in black Pentecostal churches. I wanted to get his take on an issue central to my work—namely, the idea that Jamaican Pentecostal worshippers—or "saints," as they call themselves—use music as a way to localize their faith and define themselves as holy and distinct from cultural outsiders. His response suggested that I was on the right track. "Yeah, man! Jamaicans have married their Christianity to their culture." Continuing in the third person, he added, "They reject certain music just because it doesn't sound Jamaican. They tell you, 'That's not the sound of Zion. That's not the Holy Ghost.'" The irony of the preacher's critique was not lost on either of us. Although he himself was a Jamaican Pentecostal Christian, he spoke in a way that distanced what "they" say from his own more liberal stance. "I used to think that way too!" he laughed. But his travels to and from Jamaica and other parts of the world had instilled in him a much less restrictive view concerning music's relation to holiness. He now embraced a wide gamut of gospel music styles. For him, they were all good—hip-hop–influenced African American gospel from the United States, traditional hymns composed in the early twentieth century, and old Jamaican choruses that his grandmother used to sing. He had come to accept, as have many of the Jamaicans with whom I have spoken, that the boundaries of musical holiness and Pentecostal identity are never stuck in place. Despite claims of collective distinctiveness, Jamaican Pentecostal musical practices reflect and shape identities that intersect with a variety of cultural and religious groups.

This book explores these intersecting identities and contradictory discourses through the lens of gospel music making. It benefits from my conversations with an array of critical thinkers whose pews and classrooms I share. It draws inspiration from the work of scholars housed in departments of music, anthropology, religion, and performance studies. Interdisciplinary flow emboldens me to grapple with what it means to be a boundary-crossing researcher, performer, and consumer of black gospel music. There is, within the pages that follow, lots of grappling of this sort. I imagine this comes as no surprise, as reflexivity has now become commonplace in ethnomusicological writing. I find it most instructive to tell *my* story when it is relevant to the stories I tell about others. So here at the outset, allow me to explain how this project has emerged from my efforts to navigate boundaries in my academic life and within the musical and spiritual landscapes of my upbringing.

While growing up in Kansas during the 1970s and '80s, I heard plenty of African American gospel music. Recordings by artists such as Tramaine Hawkins, James Cleveland, the Mighty Clouds of Joy, and Shirley Caesar were part of the soundscape of my youth. But Jamaica and its music were not even a blip on my radar, and I had only limited exposure to any sort of black gospel music in a live setting, much less in a Pentecostal worship service. Some of my earliest memories are of the recommissioned yellow school bus that carried my four siblings and me to Bethel Glen Church of the Nazarene, whose working-class members were, except for us, all white. Worship was cool and controlled, nothing like that of the hand-clapping, foot-stomping Pentecostal churches I would later discover. Singing at Bethel Glen was accompanied by a pianist who read music politely from the church hymnal, and there was little in the way of bodily movement from those in the congregation. As I approached my teen years and grew with more confidence into my cultural identity as an African American, I felt drawn toward the lively gospel music featured in the Pentecostal churches "over on the black side of town." The congregation of Madden Temple Church of God in Christ seemed uninhibited in worship, and I was captivated by the intensity of the tambourines, drums, guitar, and, of course, the Hammond B3 organ. This arsenal of instruments was augmented by the euphoria of voices, hands, and feet making a joyful noise unto the Lord.

I became a regular participant in this kind of spiritually charged setting once I moved to Boston to attend Berklee College of Music. By the early 1990s, I was a baptized member of a Caribbean-majority Pentecostal church where the singing styles and rhythmic interpretations contrasted with what I had heard in black churches back home. While in college, I also started working professionally as a saxophonist, and as a supplement to my jazz gigs, I joined a reggae band and began performing with Jamaicans, Trinidadians, Barbadians, and others from the English-speaking Caribbean. It was fun making music on both sacred and secular stages, hopping back and forth from nightclub to church service without experiencing private conviction or public scorn. But the risks and repercussions of these boundary-crossing escapades became all too evident when a preacher chastised me for playing jazz and predicted that my sustained attachment to such "worldly" music would lead me down a path to eternal damnation. This alarming sentiment is shared by Pentecostal pastors who implement strict codes of conduct that prohibit musical pleasure outside the context of worship.

Despite the obvious stylistic overlap of "sacred" and "secular" black musical forms, there is a well-documented history of perceived incompatibility between the music of African American churches and genres such as blues, jazz, R&B, and rap, which some Christians have labeled "the devil's music." Moreover, debates concerning what Timothy Rommen (2007) refers to as "the ethics of style" occur frequently within African diasporic Christian communities. Even though I was aware of these controversies, the preacher's stern rebuke stung. I remember feeling conflicted for a while, torn between my faith and my music. But in the end, I came to see this as a false choice. I was not about to set my beloved jazz cassettes ablaze in a heaping ritual bonfire, as some Pentecostal converts claimed to have done. Instead, I rebelled against the notion that such a dramatic renunciation was necessary, and with some mild trepidation I embarked upon a career that involves flowing between different fields of musical engagement.

After relocating to New York City in the mid-1990s I sought out new musical opportunities, frequenting local jam sessions and touring with a variety of artists. I also joined a Pentecostal church in Brooklyn and eventually became the organist and choir director, tasked with sustaining a worship environment that affirmed both African American and Caribbean musical preferences. As a doctoral student in New York University's ethnomusicology program, I began to realize that my frustration with the bifurcation of musical categories could be fruitful. It dawned on me that my personal struggle against rigid narratives of musical morality could be a springboard to greater insight regarding the ritual strategies of flow deployed by Jamaican Pentecostals in the United States and back home on the island. How and why does music matter to them? In what ways do they use music to express devotion to both faith and nation? To what extent do they express a desire to reconcile their religious and cultural identities, especially when the latter are closely tied to iconic "secular" musics such as ska, reggae, and dancehall? This book pursues these lines of inquiry by bearing witness to the creative capacities and contradictions of Pentecostal believers throughout Jamaica and its diaspora. These religious practitioners sit at the crossroads of musical meanings that both confirm and challenge their beliefs.

This project also strives to make sense of the musical and ritual techniques Jamaican Pentecostals employ to construct and collapse boundaries between local and foreign ways of worshipping God. While gospel musics from the United States and Jamaica are ostensibly creative tools for expressing devotion and praise, they are also expressive strategies through which believers position themselves within religious, national, and cultural frames of practice. In so doing, they draw lines in the sand and make heartfelt claims about who they are and who they are not. Musical research is perhaps my way of sitting atop these sorts of divisions while pondering the identity-forming activities taking place on either side of them. Such fence sitting is, I suggest, precarious and playful. It requires the courage to recognize flow across the social and symbolic boundaries that believers maintain as well as a mischievous refusal to resolve the inconsistencies between fiery proclamations of faith and the fickle practices of everyday life.

Readers of this ethnography will no doubt "hear" within it a mixture of divergent voices. By this I mean that there are moments in which I allow the words of my consultants to speak for themselves. But I strive also to make clear where my analytical take stands apart from the descriptions and testimonies of those I encounter. If the boundaries blur between these multiple perspectives, it is because I experience myself as part of the community I study. At any rate, I never go so far as to yield the authorial stage. It is my job as a scholar to determine the cast of characters, decide which voices merit amplification, and select the scripts of commentary to be included in this final product.

I am keenly aware that Christians who write about Christian music are sometimes assumed to be too close to our units of study to remain "objective." My conversations with fellow scholars of faith suggest that we find ourselves encumbered with the weight of an extra-heavy burden to prove that we possess the intellectual and critical tools to bear on the material at hand. We have been trained to avoid any hint of "celebratory" academic writing, lest we fail at our scholarly mission or, even worse, heighten the fears of those who suspect we have some hidden agenda to proselytize our students and colleagues. But a different set of assumptions follows my work when I present it before theologically oriented scholars. In those arenas, it is not uncommon for readers to question my faith commitment. They may consider me too spiritually dispassionate or insufficiently concerned with explicating the religious points of view under consideration. These are, as it turns out, critiques I can live with. They are emblematic of my own flowing to and from the unstable identities that distinguish me from other writers on this topic. Although I am both a scholar and a believer, I want readers to know that I have no ulterior motive. My goal is to provide an honest and thorough representation of what I have found. I hope, too, that *Island Gospel* proffers an analysis of Pentecostal music making that is rich, informative, and accessible to a diverse cohort of curious readers who pick up this text.

Ethnomusicology, as I have come to appreciate it, lends itself to the nurturing of a malleable self-definition. It is, among other things, an area of inquiry that absorbs ideas from a widening range of academic disciplines. Like most scholars of music and culture, I enjoy the flexibility to approach the study of music making from multiple angles. I am also sensitive to the shifting epistemological foundations on which our knowledge of people making music relies. Jamaican Pentecostals are not frozen in place and time. The musical world they inhabit intersects with my own, and it likewise abounds with conflict and ambiguity. As I demonstrate in these pages, the human beings within this world are every bit as complicated as those outside of it. They modify their beliefs and musical practices, they adapt to varying local and global circumstances, and they change their minds about things.

Island Gospel aspires to show that the boundaries of Jamaican Pentecostal identity are neither solid nor stable. They are drawn with conviction and sincerity but are eventually washed away by the winds and waters of time. In the Caribbean and the United States, Jamaican Pentecostals worship within and across these boundaries while refashioning them in myriad forms according to their particular musical, theological, and cultural contexts. This book offers new insight into the musical world of Jamaican Pentecostals in all of its complexity. I hope readers come away from it with a deeper understanding of that world and also of the playful precariousness of scholarly endeavors involving the study of people making religious music.

Acknowledgments

When I started writing *Island Gospel*, I had no idea that it would take quite as long as it has. Nor did I foresee having to rely on contributions from a pool of individuals so deep, their names would fill an additional chapter. Having reached the culmination of this humbling process, I take joy in paying tribute to at least some of those who helped me along the way. For their enthusiastic support, I first thank the director of the University of Illinois Press, Laurie Matheson, and outreach and development coordinator, Julie Laut, along with my project editor, Jennifer Argo, copyeditor, Julie Gay, and everyone who worked behind the scenes to bring this book to publication. I must also thank Mellonee Burnim and Portia Maultsby for expressing interest in my manuscript for their African American Music in Global Perspective series. I met these two prodigious figures in black music scholarship as a wide-eyed graduate student, and over the past two decades they took me under their wing and eventually pulled out of me a book I didn't know I could write. Dr. Burnim was magnanimous with her time and instrumental in helping me to refine my arguments. Long before taking on this project, she dispensed doses of affirmation and tough love that have made me a more rigorous and resilient scholar. Likewise, Dr. Maultsby spent I-don't-know-how-much time perusing drafts and providing suggestions for improvement while also urging me to press on with my writing when I felt like giving up. I am grateful for her patience and calm and honored by her faith in my ability to finish.

I also thank my former professors at New York University, who steered me through the embryonic stages of my scholarly development and shaped my work with criticisms that have proved remarkably constructive. Gage Averill shared his wealth of expertise in ethnomusicology through coursework and independent study. He offered sage advice throughout the processes of field-work and writing and has since remained a trusted advisor and friend. Stanley Boorman's demanding historical musicology classes taught me stamina, and his extraordinary eye for detail was a tremendous asset. Constance Sutton, who passed away in 2018, taught me the basics of anthropological research and invited me to her home in Washington Heights for conversations that trans-formed my understanding of Caribbean culture. I also thank Kyra Gaunt, who joined NYU's faculty at a pivotal stage of my research and writing. She chal-lenged me to embrace critical reflexivity in ethnographic work and became my "big sister" in academia just when I needed one. David Burrows, Mercedes Dujunco, and Edward Roesner offered unforgettable lessons in musicological analysis, and the interdisciplinary seminars I took with Barbara Browning, J. Michael Dash, Richard Schechner, and John Szwed opened my eyes to new theoretical horizons. Several doctoral students at NYU and Columbia Univer-sity also gave me feedback on my work. I thank especially Mark Burford, Scott Currie, Amanda Minks, Daniel Neely, and Monica Hairston O'Connell.

A Thurgood Marshall Dissertation Fellowship at Dartmouth College facili-tated my early research and writing. Ted Levin and Steve Swayne made me feel at home in the Music Department when I arrived in fall 2004, and Walt Cun-ningham and the Dartmouth Gospel Choir uplifted me during the wearisome winter months in Hanover, New Hampshire. For fun and productive conver-sations over lunch, I thank Judith Byfield, Lourdes Gutiérrez-Nájera, Clarence Hardy, and Anne Harper Charity Hudley. An additional fellowship at the Yale Institute of Sacred Music in 2012-2013 afforded me precious time and space to refine my ideas. Deborah Justice, David Stowe, and Michael Veal engaged with my work with particular attentiveness, and Harold and Rachel Brooks, along with the members of Beulah Heights First Pentecostal Church, extended to me wonderful hospitality in New Haven, Connecticut.

I owe special thanks to my cadre of colleagues at the University of Vir-ginia and the University of Chicago who enriched my professional academic life with their camaraderie and support. Matthew Burtner, Ted Coffey, Valerie Cooper, Scott DeVeaux, Robert Fatton, Cynthia Hoehler-Fatton, Claudrena Harold, Michelle Kisliuk, John Mason, Fred Maus, Deborah McDowell, Mar-lon Ross, Jalane Schmidt, Corey D. B. Walker, and Richard Will made palpable contributions to my well-being that enabled me to thrive from the moment I arrived in Charlottesville as a newly minted assistant professor. From 2008 to 2016 I benefited from research funding provided by the Humanities Division and the Department of Music at the University of Chicago. I recognize and thank all of my former musicology colleagues there, especially Philip Bohlman, Martha Feldman, Travis Jackson, Kaley Mason, and Steven Rings for their concern and mentorship. Thanks also to my student advisees, Lauren Eldridge and Alisha Lola Jones, for enlivening me with their fresh ideas and unwavering moral support.

My colleagues at the University of Miami, where I arrived in fall 2016, supplied intellectual energy and good cheer that fueled the later stages of my writing. In the acclaimed Frost School of Music, I have been privileged to join forces with fellow musicologists David Ake, Marysol Quevedo, Frederick Reece, Deborah Schwartz-Kates, Annie Searcy, Brent Swanson, and Nancy Zavac. Thanks also to Shelly Berg, Juan Chattah, Valerie Coleman, Charlton Copeland, John Daversa, Donette Francis, Kendee Franklin, Kysha Harriell, Osamudia James, Leslie Knecht, Michelle Maldonado, Kate Ramsey, Vanessa Van Dyke, and Nora Villegas for making it easier to flourish on campus and in the broader Coral Gables community.

I would be remiss not to express my appreciation to a number of other scholars, musicians, and friends who have also contributed in meaningful ways to this project. Kenneth Bilby, E. Patrick Johnson, Michael Largey, Elizabeth McAlister, Guthrie Ramsey, Teresa Reed, and Timothy Rommen have been indefatigable listeners and critics since the late 1990s, and their influence on how I think about black music and religion is enormous. For their words of encouragement during the writing process, I also salute Jafari Allen, Paul Austerlitz, Brian Blade and the Fellowship Band, Kimasi Browne, Johann Buis, Judith Casselberry, Judah Cohen, Robert Darden, Daniel Desormeaux, Jacqueline DjeDje, Jonathan Dueck, Jane Florine, Eileen Hayes, Monique Ingalls, John L. Jackson, Birgitta Johnson, Tammy Kernodle, Cheryl Keyes, Horace Maxile, Claudine Michel, Yolanda Pierce, Deborah Smith Pollard, Emmett Price III, Marc Prou, Lena Sheffield, and Gina Ulysse.

My fieldwork in Jamaica was funded by a Fulbright International Institute of Education Fellowship. The School of Graduate Studies and Research at the University of the West Indies at Mona granted me a student visa that enabled me to spend most of 2002 in Spanish Town and on the northern coast. I could never have carried out my research without the benevolence of men and women from all over the island. Marjorie and Bertie Lemard provided food and shelter during a crucial phase of my stay. Pastor Paul Orie gave me wise counsel and received me into his congregation with open arms. Dr. Patricia Holness went out of her way to connect me with Pentecostal clergy, such as Pastor Hermine Bryan, whose home in Spanish Town was an oasis of tranquility that greatly facilitated my fieldwork in St. Elizabeth Parish and allowed me to stay healthy and focused. I must also thank the numerous Jamaican musicians and ministers who motivated me to complete my research. Cranston Forbes, Samantha Gooden, Tyrell Lewis, Winston and Donna-Marie Rowe, Dennis Rushton, Sammy Stewart Jr., and C. Everton Thomas were especially gracious with their time and talent.

In the United States several Christian clergy have ministered to me in more ways than I could ever recount. Elder Francisco Tolentino kept me afloat while I was an undergraduate student, and it was as a member of his Boston congregation that I first met Pentecostals from the Caribbean. My church family at Emmanuel Temple in Brooklyn, New York, along with the broader cohort of believers in the New York–Ontario District of the Pentecostal Assemblies of the World Inc., sustained me during my graduate-school years. Pastor Tommy L. Seals and Dr. Delores Seals gave me a platform on which to hone my talents and taught me by example what it means to be a Spirit-filled follower of Jesus Christ. I also owe a huge debt of gratitude to Dr. Samuel Wright Jr., Bishop Horace E. Smith, Bishop S. Robert Stewart, and Pastor Kevin Fischer, whose ministries have instilled in me lessons of faith that I will always treasure. For uncommon acts of kindness they don't even remember, I thank Janet Broadus, Mark A. Brown, Grace Chambers, Joey Floyd, Anthony and Edith Ismael, Ray and Keitha Johnson, Errol and Judith O'Savio, Derek and Sharon Pierson, Jennifer Simpson, Phillip and Nicole Starks, Kino and Jessie White, and Raymond and Janet Williams.

I reserve my deepest expressions of gratitude for my family members. To my beautiful wife, Lori Ann Butler: Thank you for your fearless devotion and for walking right beside me through every storm. Your love and light rescued me, and without your self-sacrifice this book would be inconceivable. To my amazing son, Stanley: I got you! Thank you for making daddy so proud and for sharing hugs that fill me with hope and joy. To my dear mother, Karen Rush: Thank you for being my superhero and for believing in me when no one else did. Against all odds, you raised me with unbelievable care and gave me the moral and intellectual foundation to succeed. Thanks also to my brother, Orville "Eddie" Butler Jr., for his adventurous spirit and unflappable sense of humor; to Libe Rush, for his fatherly wisdom, work ethic, and warmth; and to Lee Earnest

Byers, Jerome Byers, and Angela Byers Pitts for their support through the years. For nourishing me with love and prophetic teachings, I give honor to my mother-in-law, Pastor Betty J. Roberts, and to my father-in-law, the late Bishop Edward C. Roberts. Although he did not live to see this book's completion, he left a legacy of moral and educational excellence that has profoundly impacted my study of Pentecostalism. I also thank the rest of my North Carolina kinfolk and the members of Calvary Christian Church of the Apostolic Faith in Charlotte. Finally, I thank the Lord God, who makes all things possible and without whom I can do nothing.

Island Gospel

Introduction

Throughout Jamaica and its diaspora, Pentecostals use music to declare what they believe and where they stand in relation to religious and cultural outsiders. In worship services that celebrate deliverance from sin and unlock pathways to the Holy Spirit, they sing and dance to rhythms and repertories that evoke feelings of home. A sense of collective distinctiveness is reinforced by the shared experience of religious transcendence, nostalgic narratives of the past, and the patrolling of stylistic boundaries between the church and the wider world. Jamaican Pentecostals describe themselves as being "in the world, but not of the world." By this they mean that while they are physically located within the larger society, they strive, as do other Christian practitioners, to be spiritually set apart from it by upholding their particular code of conduct. Distinguishing oneself from the world entails an ongoing process of renunciation. It is a lifelong walk of faith—an act of trust and obedience—wherein a believer bids farewell to prior attitudes and behaviors while embracing a new identity as a transformed child of God. This book aims to show how music, as a form of social and ritual boundary crossing, complicates these theological affirmations and uncovers the shifting foundations of Jamaican Pentecostal identity.

The lyrics of the traditional Jamaican chorus "Goodbye World" reflect the idea of a boundary between "God's way" and the "world" of sin.

> Goodbye, world. I'll stay no longer with you.
> Goodbye, pleasures of sin. I'll stay no longer with you.

I made up my mind to go God's way the rest of my life.
I made up my mind to go God's way the rest of my life.

This chorus is one of many examples of how boundaries are performed through gospel music in Pentecostal worship services. Yet my ethnography demonstrates that Pentecostals destabilize us–them dichotomies by appropriating popular musics and media from Jamaica and the United States, which circulate in transnational networks and travel across lines of sacred and secular demarcation. In this book I examine these boundary crossing phenomena and assess their impact on Jamaican congregations and the music they make. In other words, I emphasize the ritual strategies of flow through which believers navigate the crossroads of local and global practice. This dynamic process involves what Marc Gidal refers to as "musical boundary-work," a term that denotes "the use of music to reinforce, bridge, or blur boundaries, whether for personal, social, spiritual, or political purposes" (2016, 5). This concept of musical boundary-work also applies to the multiple ways that Jamaican Pentecostals create and consume gospel music during worship services, as well as to the discourses of music-making that shape, and are shaped by, their ritual and everyday practices.[1] While embracing certain types of musical transmission, church leaders are careful to monitor the access points through which outside influences enter their congregations. Highlighting social constructions of Jamaican religious and cultural identity, particularly a "sense of belonging to a specific social group, society or place" (Migge 2010, 1499), I argue that music is a vital mechanism for regulating spiritual and cultural flow. It is a creative yet controversial resource for Pentecostals who strive to maintain both the sanctity and fluidity of their evolving tradition.

Pentecostals represent a subgroup of Christian followers who emphasize ritual manifestations of the Holy Spirit and teach that one's church membership hinges on becoming "saved" or "born again." These members are then delivered from the penalty and power of sin and initiated into a global community of "saints" who have been baptized in water and filled with the Holy Spirit. For Pentecostals the appellation "saints" signifies those "believers who have professed Christ as their personal savior, been saved by His holy power, and now walk the 'set apart' path of sanctification" (Hinson 2000, 2). Collectively referred to as "the Church," this baptized body of believers comprises those who have been "called out" and divinely distinguished from a "sinful" mode of existence associated with pre-conversion life. In the above chorus, saying goodbye to the world does not involve a physical removal from the earth or the island of Jamaica. On the contrary, saints are encouraged to make the most of life by excelling in education, working hard, voting in political elections, and taking advantage of financial opportunities to prosper for the benefit of family and church. During my time in Jamaica, I found that "the world" means different things to different people. The world is sometimes understood to be the realm of the secular or profane. In other cases, the world is seen as those aspects of the country that are viewed as iconic representations of "Jamaican culture," such as Rastafarianism and reggae music. The holy–worldly dichotomy is richly layered, and it is mapped onto oppositional constructions of church and dancehall, self and other, and local and foreign. Some Pentecostals describe the world as "American culture," specifically characterizing African American gospel music as a worldly influence that threatens to degrade the "holiness" of Jamaican Christian worship. Pentecostal saints thus have multiple ways of distinguishing themselves from the world of unbelievers. Their strategies of worship suggest that music is, as Simon Frith argues, "a key to identity because it offers, so intensely, a sense of both self and others, of the subjective in the collective" (1996, 110).

Gospel Music, Worship, and Flow

The Center for Black Music Research defines gospel music as "African-American Protestant vocal music that celebrates Christian doctrine in emotive, often dramatic ways."[2] Mellonee Burnim refers to it as "the twentieth-century form of African American religious music that evolved in urban cities following the Great Migration of Blacks from the agrarian South in the period surrounding World Wars I and II" (2015, 189). But in the Caribbean the meaning of the term "gospel music" is less reliant on experiences unique to African American history and culture (Best 2004, 55), and the message of the music matters more than any culturally specific aesthetics of performance. Gospel music is understood to encompass ritual and recorded musics that convey the "good news" of Jesus Christ to listeners around the world in a plethora of styles. By this definition, "gospel music" includes acts of musical worship during church services as well as recorded songs that are distributed commercially as part of a global gospel music industry. It is this broader and more flexible definition that I wish to mobilize for analysis in the Jamaican Pentecostal context.

In this book I thus recognize "gospel music" as an umbrella category of Christian expression rendered through a variety of musical and rhetorical strategies. By attending to the *discourses* of gospel music, I mean to underscore the genre's multiple meanings and the fragility of the boundaries that Jamaican Pentecostals construct around it.[3] When Pentecostals use racial, ethnic, or cultural modifiers in reference to the genre (for example, "white," "black," or "Jamaican" gospel music), it is usually to distinguish older styles from newer ones, to comment on the ritual appropriateness of a given style, or to signal aesthetic differences between a Jamaican worship ideal and an "African American" one deemed more "modern" (see chapter 5). In any case, I consider that the analytical benefits of accepting the interpretational fluidity of "gospel music" outweigh the advantages of clinging to a definition that applies exclusively to African American cultural and religious contexts. This is not to overlook the fact that Jamaican and African American practitioners have a genuine stake in the matter. Churchgoers tend to regard gospel music as an expression of their particular cultural identity, and scholars have long marked the boundaries of "gospel music," in particular, according to a set of criteria that are historically and culturally specific.[4] But ceding discursive space to the overlap between "African American"- and "Jamaican"-derived styles and repertories yields a richer understanding of gospel music as a transnationally constituted genre that thrives both within and beyond local spaces.

It is undeniable that the heavy flow of African American music from the United States has had a tremendous influence on the sound and meaning of Jamaican genres and styles. There are Pentecostal churches in Kingston in which I was amazed by how closely the gospel singing resembled what I have heard in black churches in the United States. In Jamaican "country" churches such as Mercy Tabernacle (chapter 2) and Riversdale Pentecostal Church (see chapter 3), however, those songs pick up a Jamaican accent, so to speak. Initial *h* sounds are sometimes added or omitted, the letter *t* is pronounced, and there is a stronger preference for localized forms of "country gospel," a genre shaped by American country-and-western music and "southern gospel" recordings by white artists such as the Gaither Vocal Band (Mills 1998). But this "Jamaicanizing" of gospel music does not always preclude gospel music from being regarded as a foreign import. Several Jamaicans with whom I spoke define it by naming traditional African American gospel singers such as Mahalia Jackson, James Cleveland, and Shirley Caesar. Those versed in contemporary gospel music mention artists such as Tye Tribbett, Tasha Cobbs, Yolanda Adams, Tamela Mann, and Kirk Franklin.

Pieces such as "Goodbye World," however, are part of a vast repertory of "Jamaican songs" or "choruses" regarded as the product of island soil.[5] These songs and choruses fit under the wide canopy of "Jamaican gospel music," a generic category flexible enough also to incorporate "southern gospel" artists and harder-edged "gospel reggae" recorded by Jamaican dancehall artists-turned-gospel-singers such as Chevelle Franklyn, Papa San, and Stitchie.

However, the sacredness of gospel reggae is called into question by those who regard musics influenced by the dancehall genre as too worldly to merit the "gospel" label. Controversies regarding secular and sacred dancehall artists stem from the fact that these artists sometimes use the same underlying instrumental tracks in recordings and live performances. Employing what Dick Hebdige (1987) refers to as a "cut 'n' mix" technique, dancehall producers extract the instrumental parts known as the "riddim" from the vocal part. These riddim tracks then become foundational sonic material over which lyrics are sung or rapped by any number of performers. Debates involving what Melinda Weekes refers to as a "tussle across shifting sacred and secular definitions" (2005, 61), which have long raged among African American churchgoers and gospel music aficionados in the United States, thus find easy analogues in Jamaica and elsewhere in the Caribbean, especially in contexts of Pentecostal worship.[6]

The notion of "worship" is so commonplace among Pentecostal churchgoers that its definition tends to be taken for granted. Most of the Jamaican believers I know use it as part of the compound phrase "praise and worship" either to signify any genre of congregational church music or to specify the rock-influenced style of music recorded by contemporary Christian artists such as Hillsong United. But the nouns "praise" and "worship" are sometimes taken separately and differentiated according to musical style. In this sense, praise is understood to be up-tempo music that encourages dancing and hand clapping. By contrast, worship requires a more contemplative mode of musical participation, the purpose of which is to stir the heart of God and give him greater pleasure (see chapter 3). This stylistic distinction between "praise" and "worship" appears in other religious traditions as well (see, for example, Dueck 2011, 244–45). During worship, Pentecostals may close their eyes and lift their arms while singing songs or speaking in tongues as a means of expressing adoration toward God. When a Spirit-filled saint engages in this type of ritual activity with nothing but an earnest desire for intimacy with God, she is said to be worshipping "in the beauty of holiness." Pentecostals describe it as the most effective way to please God and foster communion with the Holy Spirit.[7] Those who hold this view do not argue that praise is insignificant. Rather, they see it as the indispensable means through which a transcendent state of worship, wherein participants are spiritually transformed by the presence and power of God, becomes attainable. Throughout these chapters, "worship" refers to a range of performative acts rendered by believers to express adoration to and for God. The stylistic boundaries of "musical worship" are likewise expansive enough to contain multiple ways of seeking divine favor through ritual song. I hope to keep alive a sense of the fluidity of Jamaican Pentecostal practice and the variability of musical worship styles that believers perform as they reposition themselves along congregational, generational, and cultural lines.

In this book, "flow" is a heuristic device that works as both an overarching conceptual metaphor and a way of connoting the transmission of people, ideas, and media within Jamaica and from abroad. Several types of flow are paramount to my discussion. *Cultural* flow concerns a variety of shifting practices and ideas—what Turino (2008) refers to as "habits" that reside within individuals and groups at any given time. To speak of "culture" not as a static entity but rather in terms of "cultural" flows is one way to emphasize the processual nature of Pentecostal identities based on "the idea of situated difference, that is, difference in relation to something local, embodied, and significant" (Appadurai 1996, 12). The transmission of sounds and images to and from the United States also involves Appadurai's well-worn dimensions of global cultural flow: ethnoscapes, technoscapes, finanscapes, mediascapes, and ideoscapes (33). All five of these "scapes" represent channels of flow through which local and global arenas of Pentecostal worship are being transformed over time as technologies bring styles of church music in ever closer proximity. This "condition of neighborliness" (29), however, has perhaps never represented the "new" state of affairs that Appadurai made it out to be. Neither has it sounded the death knell for a staunch Jamaican cultural nationalism that influences how Pentecostals choose to express their identities and make music in a particular time and place.[8]

Spiritual flow centers on the ways that Pentecostals discuss the movement of divine presence and power. Mihaly Csikszentmihalyi's classic theory of flow as optimal experience (1990) informs my discussion of worship as an "autotelic" activity. In many respects, it is its own reward. This is not to say that Pentecostal music-making has no extrinsic objective. Believers seek to render collective adoration to God while distinguishing, edifying, and expanding a particular Christian cultural formation. But as Pentecostals sing and dance in the Spirit, they also seek individual experiences of flow and transcendence. It is in this sense that the means justifies the ends. To a certain extent, the broader goals "lose their substance and reveal themselves as mere tokens that justify the activity by giving it direction and determining rules of action. But the doing is the thing" (Csikszentmihalyi 1975, 37).

Finally, *migratory* flow concerns the back-and-forth travels of Jamaicans, a significant portion of whom reside more or less permanently in the United States or England. There is, related to flow, talk of "movement" in the form of travel between congregations, denominations, and religious groups. These flows and movements make it clear that the development of Pentecostalism in

Jamaica, along with the musical forms through which this faith is practiced, is inseparable from a legacy of North American and Jamaican interaction.[9] There is also the "move of the Spirit" that occurs when believers invite divine presence to manifest. There is movement across sacred–secular boundaries, particularly between the church and the dancehall. And there is the physical movement of worshipping bodies, dancing, jumping, swaying, and bouncing to the beat of gospel music or the rhythm of the silent Spirit, which animates believers' minds and bodies. By tracing the development of Protestant and Pentecostal Christianity in Jamaica, we see that contemporary flows of people and expressive cultures are a continuation of boundary-crossing endeavors that have shaped Jamaican and African American musical and religious spheres for centuries.[10] I turn now to a brief discussion of the history of Jamaican's religious landscape and the migratory flows that have shaped contemporary Pentecostalism on the island.

Historical Developments

Twenty-first-century Pentecostalism in Jamaica is the product of centuries of cultural flow, much of which involved African American migration from the United States. Frey and Wood note that since the eighteenth century, African American migrants have "contributed decisively to the shaping of an Afro-cultural world that embraced the American South and a number of Caribbean islands" (1998, 130).[11] The endeavors of blacks migrating from the United States to Jamaica in the 1780s reveal "both the transatlantic and the inter-American dimensions of the religious transformation" of Anglophone Caribbean nations (131).[12] African Americans George Leile and Moses Baker are pivotal figures in the history of Jamaican religion. Leile, a formerly enslaved man from Georgia, and Baker, a member of colonial New York's free black community, brought with them their Christian faith, and together they planted the first highly successful missionary enterprise on the island (Pulis 1999, 192–93; Simpson 1978, 42). Leile and Baker also helped to prepare the way for white Baptist missionaries from England, who did not launch full-fledged missionary endeavors in Jamaica until some thirty years after black Baptist churches were established (Burton 1997, 37).

The nineteenth century saw even more dramatic developments in Jamaica's religious landscapes. Evangelical revivals that first swept through the United States and Britain in 1858 and 1859 had perhaps the strongest repercussions. Missionaries from the Church of Christ watered the seeds of a revival that had started on the East Coast of the United States (Austin-Broos 1997, 55) and would flourish in Jamaica throughout the remaining decades of the nineteenth century. Protestant Christianity became an intractable element within Jamaican ritual practice. Most scholars agree that the revival atmosphere of the early 1860s led to the formation of religious cults such as Pocomania and Revival Zion, which have continued to thrive in Jamaica through the twentieth and early twenty-first centuries.[13] Rather than privileging the missionary ideals of ethical rationalism and strict discipline, Revivalists placed a great emphasis on divine healing, not only from physical ailments but also from the "sickness" of sin. Revivalists' emphasis on the accessibility of Jesus and the healing power of the Holy Spirit would become prominent characteristics of twentieth-century Pentecostal practice. Other similarities include the predominant role of women despite mostly male leadership and the use of music to invite manifestations of the Holy Spirit.

Jamaica's socioreligious order in the early twentieth century was characterized by a transition from an older Revivalism to a Methodist Holiness movement and to a newer, more modern Pentecostalism taught primarily by missionaries from the United States. The 1906 Azusa Street revival in Los Angeles, California, became "the central mythic event" and "symbolic point of origin" for Pentecostals in the United States. It was, however, only one of several "fusillades of revival" (Creech 1996, 407–8) that precipitated a global resurgence of Pentecostalism. The twentieth century witnessed the birth of a number of Pentecostal organizations that continue to thrive in Jamaica, of which two basic types emerged: trinitarian groups (such as the Assemblies of God, the Church of God, and the Church of God in Christ) and apostolic organizations (such as the United Pentecostal Church and the Pentecostal Assemblies of the World). All of these organizations established missions in Jamaica by the middle of the twentieth century and have remained global in reach.[14]

The twentieth-century influx of missionaries, doctrines, and Christian ideologies coincided with a much higher premium on spiritual sanctification and moral discipline. Preachers began to exhort more vigorously on the dangers of fornication, stressing the role of the woman as the "weaker vessel" who is supposedly inclined, because of her natural "feminine wiles," to tempt a man and cause him to fall into sin (Austin-Broos 1997, 81, 165–66). Misogynistic ideas like these are still alive and well among Pentecostals, although younger saints tend to consider this "feminization of sin" more problematic (166, 194). Diane Austin-Broos explains how women are vessels for Spirit infilling and also serve as the human channels through which others in the community are born again. The widespread recognition of women's roles in "birthing saints" has historically worked to offset assertions, mostly but not exclusively by men, that women have a greater propensity to cause spiritual downfall (231). By virtue of their numerical majority and roles as spiritual midwives, women have been able to achieve positions of collective power within Pentecostal churches. Although the relatively small number of women in pastoral roles attenuates the scope of this power, churchgoers frequently comment on the indispensability of women as "defenders of the faith" who articulate through song and speech the central tenets of Pentecostal belief. My fieldwork afforded me the opportunity to sit at the feet of both women and men who are the most active and influential members of their congregations. The narratives in this book illustrate only a tiny fraction of what I learned in their presence.

Methodological Considerations

The research on which this book is based began in New York City, where I lived from 1994 to 2004. Conducting my preliminary fieldwork there afforded me access to what Constance Sutton calls "a Caribbean cross-roads," where Jamaicans are part of a "continuous and intense bi-directional flow of peoples, ideas, practices, and ideologies between the Caribbean region and New York City" (1987, 20). These transnational flows form a "transmission belt that reworks and further creolizes Caribbean culture and identities, both in New York and the Caribbean" (20). During my decade in New York City, I worshipped every Sunday at Emmanuel Temple, an eighty-member apostolic Pentecostal church in Brooklyn. Like the Crown Heights section of the borough in which it is located, Emmanuel Temple contained a relatively high concentration of black ethnicities from the Anglophone Caribbean (Conway and Bigby 1994, 72). Nearly one-third of Emmanuel Temple's congregation was composed of migrants from Jamaica. As I became increasingly involved in the church's musical activities, I was asked to assume the roles of organist and choir director. My experiences at Emmanuel Temple, along with the services I attended at the New York–based Jamaican Pentecostal church Wondrous Love, stimulated my interest in reconciling differences, and I sought to understand how seemingly incompatible styles of music coexisted within black congregations perceived by outsiders to be homogeneous (Butler 2000). Emmanuel Temple also served as the home base from which I would launch a deeper study (Butler 2005) of Pentecostal church music and its influence on the transnational societies within which people practice their faith.

In addition to Emmanuel Temple and Wondrous Love in New York, there are six Pentecostal churches in Jamaica whose members provided the crucial "data" upon which my ethnographic analyses are based: Mercy Tabernacle, Riversdale Pentecostal Church, All Saints Apostolic Church, Lighthouse Assembly,

Bethel Apostolic Church, and Faith Fellowship. In 2002 I spent ten months on the island conducting fieldwork in these congregations while dividing my time between the North Coast and Spanish Town, near the capital city of Kingston. After returning to New York I maintained contact with Jamaicans on the island and in New York. I was also able to return to Jamaica for one-week stays each summer from 2006 to 2008 to perform as a saxophonist with gospel pianist Dennis Rushton. Through conducting interviews, holding innumerable informal conversations, recording hymns and choruses, videotaping church services, and worshipping with Jamaican Pentecostals, I have been taught a great deal about the role of music in Pentecostals' lives. I have also seen up close how easily musical style can become a source of controversy.[15]

As this book explains, Pentecostal identities are shaped through conceptual and stylistic distinctions between sacred and secular musical genres.[16] Like the believers I discuss, I am no stranger to these oppositional categorizations. A dissonance between my spiritual and professional aspirations is precisely what sparked this research. On several occasions while living in New York, I found myself playing in a jazz club on Saturday night and ministering with the church choir on Sunday morning. No less daunting is the ongoing task of reconciling my religious faith with the exigencies of academic education. This delicate maneuver entails an ongoing process of learning to accept certain epistemological tensions.[17] I embrace these tensions as useful and edifying. Without them, I would have acquired much less insight into the various ways that crossing religious and cultural boundaries can become a transformative endeavor.

Throughout these pages my writing reflects an ongoing concern with the challenge of navigating everyday "fields" of performance. Much of this "field" work has entailed concerts and recording sessions with Caribbean bands and a slew of after-hours jam sessions and jazz engagements throughout the United States, Europe, and Japan. But this book benefits most directly from the twenty-five years I have spent in African American and Jamaican Pentecostal churches as a saxophonist, organist, minister of music, and, more recently, an ethnomusicological researcher. Scholars have long recognized the flaws of traditional ethnographic writing wherein tales of the researcher's "arrival" exaggerate the social isolation of a particular field site.[18] Less obvious are the ways that highlighting the subjective experiences of the researcher and his or her "informants" can unnecessarily refortify a conceptual boundary between "home" and "field." Even if we "toss out older assumptions about fieldwork" with its stale exoticisms, as Cooley and Barz suggest (2008, 13), and embrace "the new fieldwork" with its appreciation for genres and traditions closer to home, "the field" as a temporally and spatially bounded research site refuses to wither. It is what Vered

Amit describes as "a strangely persistent bubble of isolation in an otherwise earnestly contextualized (at least in principle) situation" (2000, 16). While I was making music with Jamaican churchgoers, my fieldwork at times became indistinguishable from my "homework,"[19] as I came to experience Jamaican Pentecostals as creative co-members of a global community of practice. I also remained aware that the ethnographic fields I was constructing were embedded within broader transnational fields connecting me to the Jamaican Pentecostals I studied, to the United States, and to other parts of the globe. Presenting Jamaican Pentecostal practice in relation to my identity as an African American scholar of faith, this book sheds light on the transformative dimensions of fieldwork, homework, and Spirit-influenced music in ritual contexts.

Those of us who conduct ethnographic research have long considered "participant observation" a reliable method for gaining an in-depth understanding of human cultural practices. Anthropologist James Spradley explains that the participant observer "seeks to become explicitly aware of things usually blocked out," in contrast to the "ordinary participant" who typically experiences social interactions in an "immediate, subjective manner" (1980, 55–56). Reconceptualizing fieldwork as "observant participation," Barbara Tedlock (1991) celebrates a shift of emphasis away from "coolly dispassionate" observation and toward the participatory aspects of field experience. She thus recoups some of the immediate, subjective experiences of fieldwork as valuable sources of insight. As both a "participant observer" and an "observant participant," I gained a holistic understanding of how musical worship unfolds in Jamaican Pentecostal services, where a premium is placed on what Turino refers to as "participatory performance" (2008, 59). Adopting this participatory stance required that I allow myself to be fully engaged with congregants in worship, joining with them to employ a range of sonic and bodily actions intended to facilitate spiritual transformation. In a conventional sense, I thus aspired toward what Kay Shelemay describes as "truly participatory participant-observation" (2008, 143), but my fieldwork also necessitated a heightened awareness of my "self," not only as a scholar and performer of music but also as a devout and curious "observer" of Pentecostal Christianity in more ways than one.

Throughout my time in Jamaica, I found it comforting to think of myself as a religious "insider."[20] Yet even when I aspired to "fit in" with the congregations I visited, I never felt that my "otherness"—my cultural "difference" vis-à-vis Jamaican Pentecostals—was in question. A shared belief system linked me to the saints I met, but theological common ground did not preclude cultural and ritual unease. In some churches I attended, the prevailing musical styles and holiness standards were much more stringent than what I was willing to adopt on a personal level. Indeed, the heterogeneity of Pentecostal practices in Jamaica turned out to be one of the more surprising discoveries of my field research. Jamaican Pentecostals' perceptions of me also tended to shift during fieldwork. At times, they made it clear that my "Americanness" was a defining feature of how they saw me. In other situations, I was embraced as a "brother in Christ," and my faith, along with my identity as a *black* American, seemed to afford me insider status. It is worth noting, however, that Jamaica is one of several Caribbean countries in which "blackness" tends to be defined differently from the way it is in the United States. Whereas it is not uncommon for African American Pentecostals to call attention to their blackness as a symbol of African diasporic solidarity, Jamaicans Pentecostals express a more parochial "flag nationalism" that sometimes trumps race and becomes weaponized against a host of cultural and spiritual "others."[21]

I landed in Jamaica with the rather naive expectation that a common "black" identity and African diasporic consciousness would open doors of opportunity and understanding that would otherwise have remained closed. Having a shared Pentecostal persuasion, I thought, would add another layer to this consciousness, making it easy for me to gain social access to helpful people and places. I supposed that being seen as an "insider" would allow me to enjoy a soothing resonance between my racial and religious politics and the everyday realities of field research. In my desire either to blend in with or distinguish myself from the island's musical and religious communities, I also got in the habit of code switching, subtly adjusting my patterns of movement and speech to mark myself as either local or foreign, depending on the circumstance. Most of the time, the strategy that seemed most advantageous involved playing down cultural differences between myself and the Jamaicans I encountered. With varying degrees of success and comicality, I attempted to "pass" as Jamaican.[22] I also came to realize that my self-presentation could influence how those around me were perceived as well, particularly when Jamaicans saw my African Americanness, or simply proximity to it, as a potential source of money, social power, and upward class mobility. In retrospect, I see more clearly the importance of recognizing what Gina Ulysse calls the "symbolic politics of the ethnographer's identities, especially with regard to the limits and problems of how, through appearance and embodiment, one navigates the racialized spatial orders of field sites" (2008, 124).

In any case, my initial assumptions were not completely unmet, even though I underestimated the range of factors that Jamaicans would use to size me up. Race and faith alone were not master keys to unlocking channels of communication. Rather, several intersecting parts of my identity—namely, my self-presentation as a heterosexual, cisgender, nondisabled, college-educated, married, African American, Christian man from the United States—afforded me the social privilege to gain the confidence of the Jamaican women and men who entrusted me with their stories. My ability to relate to those stories as a Pentecostal believer reduced the awkwardness of potentially intrusive fieldwork and, in the end, yielded greater access to subtle ways of knowing. As Barbara Rose Lange maintains, "Pentecostals' points of view differ considerably from those of nonbelieving ethnographers [such as herself]." Pentecostals, she claims, "attribute much to divine agency that researchers do not" (2003, 13). Lange makes a valid point, although it is one from which readers might too easily infer that "Pentecostals" and "researchers" occupy mutually exclusive positions. As a Pentecostal researcher, or perhaps better yet, a researching Pentecostal, I sometimes struggle to reconcile the analyses of "nonbelieving ethnographers" of Pentecostal practice with my knowledge and experience of the faith.[23] I nevertheless prefer, as does Tedlock (1991), to critique the notion "that a subject's way of knowing is incompatible with the scientist's way of knowing and that the domain of objectivity is the sole property of the outsider" (71).

The music of black churches in the United States is by no means this book's chief concern.[24] I devote some discussion to it, but my descriptions and analyses are clearly weighted toward the Jamaican scene. Nevertheless, I view African American churches, along with the North Atlantic academy, as the epistemological home from which my discussions of Jamaican Pentecostal practice proceed. Reflections on African American Pentecostalism are not merely a foil to bring its differences into sharp relief. Rather, my musical and religious experiences enable me to sketch a multilayered ethnographic portrait that lends this book its distinctiveness. Pentecostalism binds me to those I study, as does the experience of marginalization and partial belonging. But I have not always situated my religious practice as fieldwork, nor did I initially plan to use it as "data" on which to build a scholarly project.[25] Such a task requires an acknowledgement of the complex interpenetration of "home" and "field" and a willingness to perform "the duality of belonging and alienation, familiarity and investigation, which implicitly function as fieldwork strategies" (Knowles 2000, 54). Sociologist Caroline Knowles poses questions that are, for me, more than rhetorical: "What happens when the field is also home? . . . What happens when here and there contain both home and field?" (54). In this exploration of musical, cultural, and spiritual flow, I hope readers find an insightful response to her queries.

Synopsis of Chapters

Chapter 1 discusses commonalities and differences between Jamaican- and North American–derived styles of Pentecostal worship music as I experienced them in New York City and on the island of Jamaica. It also chronicles my arrival and adjustment to Jamaica's northern coast. My experiences in Pentecostal assemblies near Montego Bay provide insight into the aesthetics of local worship, the musical and theological overlap among churches, and the challenges of conducting fieldwork in a spiritually charged setting. Drawing comparisons between Jamaican and North American ways of making music, I explore some of the porous boundaries I encountered in both New York City and Montego Bay congregations. Chapter 2 examines social and sonic constructions of holiness as expressed by Pastor Philips and the saints at Mercy Tabernacle in Liliput. I argue that these constructions reinforce distinctions between piety and pleasure that, in turn, influence the kinds of musical behavior saints deem appropriate. Women's behaviors and bodies are a topic of concern by those who view music as one part of a broader holiness aesthetic.

Chapter 3 introduces the life and ministry of Pastor Hermine Bryan, with whom I lived for six months in Spanish Town. I use her explanations of ritual flow and spiritual anointing as critical "data" to support my analysis of Pentecostal conceptions of human and divine musical agency. Pastor Bryan's outspokenness regarding the important role of women in musical praise and worship is helpful in understanding the negotiations of spiritual and social power that occur within Pentecostal services and in the broader contexts of Christian practice. Chapter 4 focuses on modes of longing and belonging that shape modern-day Pentecostal Christian identities and musical practices. Reverence for tradition and nostalgia for the "old-time way" are critical to processes of remembering the past and making sense of the present. Church leaders sometimes consider newer gospel sounds a threat to the established sound ideal of Pentecostal worship. This heightens generational tensions that have become acute as younger and more progressive leadership has assumed control of one of Jamaica's prominent Pentecostal organizations. I include the testimonies of five Pentecostals who describe their conversion experiences and subsequent efforts to lead holy lifestyles.

Chapter 5 examines "religious ethnicity" as a layered mode of self-presentation encompassing, to varying degrees, Jamaican, Pentecostal, and "black" musical markers of identity. I explore the musical styles through which saints perform their religious ethnicity, both at home on the island and abroad. The recordings of contemporary African American gospel singers provide a means for Jamaican youth to perform a modern Pentecostal identity cast as oppositional to the "white-sounding" hymnody preferred in conservative churches. Borrowing from Marti (2012), I argue that saints perform "pan-ethnic," "ethnic-specific," and "ethnic transcendent" identities. While competing stylistic preferences are sometimes reconciled through discourses of generational difference, saints choose to live and worship in the complexity of seemingly incompatible musical repertories. The concluding chapter examines discourses of unity in relation to the cultural and theological divides affecting gospel music and Pentecostal worship. It also expands on some of the theoretical implications of this project, while revisiting some of the challenges of reflexive writing and fieldwork. Drawing on Simon Coleman's study of the global culture of charismatic Christians and what he describes as their shared "orientations to the world" (2000), I suggest that Pentecostal ritual in Jamaica provides a creative means of reconciling the global and the local, particularly as the transnational flow of musical repertories and a belief in a universal Holy Spirit facilitate the growth and survival of an extensive faith community to which both Jamaican and African American Pentecostals belong.

· · ·

Pentecostal Christianity is widespread in Jamaica and has been developing steadily there since the 1920s (Austin-Broos 1997, 21). As a branch of Christianity whose practitioners experience gifts and physical manifestations of the Holy Spirit, it thrives alongside *Kumina*, Revival, Rastafarianism, and varieties of denominational Protestantism. Wherever they reside, Pentecostals put beliefs into action through social behavior that both promotes and problematizes the construction of difference. Music and spoken testimony are creative channels through which they push narratives of affirmation and affiliation. In so doing, they make a public declaration of who they are in relation to a variety of others. Pentecostals both construct and transcend the self, performing their identities while using musical worship to access a higher spiritual plane.

This book inspects the ritual boundaries constructed and collapsed by Pentecostal Christians. These sisters and brothers in Christ use music to perform their identities while occupying spiritually charged sanctuaries that transcend the local lodgings of biological kin. I use the discursive trope of flow to evoke the experience of Spirit-influenced performance, in addition to the transmigrations that fuel a controversial sharing of musical and ritual resources between Jamaica and the United States. As a marker of social and spiritual difference, musical performance facilitates the policing of boundaries between self and other, local and foreign, holy and worldly, and sacred and secular. This book scrutinizes these dichotomies and the musical expressions that allow Pentecostals to position themselves in the interstices of an African diasporic framework and a biblically informed global imaginary. It thus delves into the strategic enactment of Christian faith through musical style. While attending to the phenomenology of the Holy Spirit, it underscores the relationships between the spaces of global theology and those of local congregational practice. These pages tell a story—or, rather, a variety of stories—about how musical and religious flow engenders a sense of belonging among Jamaican people of faith.

CHAPTER 1

Boundaries and Flows

Music in Jamaican Pentecostal Churches
at Home and Abroad

" Jamaica has more churches per square mile than any other country in the world." Or so goes a common saying.[1] It seemed to me that a church of some kind stood on every corner of the neighborhoods I visited. Newspaper articles, television programs, gospel radio broadcasts, and casual conversations were daily reminders of the discourses of Christian morality, expressed daily via repetition of song lyrics or Bible verses applied to current events. Thus, Jamaica comes across to me as a very "Christian" place. One by-product of the island's high concentration of churches is that their practices influence one another. Although official statements of belief may imply opposition between different denominations, Pentecostals appropriate music from a wide range of sources. Furthermore, flows of people and media from the United States reveal the fluidity of boundaries between local and foreign expressive cultures.

In her smartly titled ethnography *Colored Television: American Religion Gone Global* (2016), Marla Frederick examines Jamaica's "long history of religious crossover both through on-the-ground missions and especially through religious broadcasting in the latter half of the twentieth century" (22). The rise of televangelism on the island during the 1980s and 1990s, she argues, need not be understood solely as "the wholesale exportation of American religious media and its simple absorption by Jamaicans" but, rather, as part of ongoing "globalization of cultural ideas" that can be described in less reductive ways (22). Pentecostalism, with its holiness ideologies, musical boundaries, and ritual expectations, sits atop legacies of cultural hegemony, as do most modern forms of Christianism in the Americas. If its practitioners are, as an old song says, "wrapped up, tied up, and tangled up in Jesus," they are also inextricably embedded within asymmetrical relations of power that impinge on their life choices, religious and otherwise. But Pentecostalism and the media through which it is disseminated need not always be understood as something that is done *to* Jamaicans. It is done *by* them as well in the course of pursuing happiness and affirming their place in Jamaican society and the wider world.

I find that while boundaries are constructed in public discourse, they melt away in private conversation and when scrutinized at the level of musical practice. By saying that boundaries are "constructed," I do not mean to dismiss them as "fake" or the product of "false consciousness." Boundaries are, as Lamont and Molnar explain, "tools by which individuals and groups struggle over and come to agree upon definitions of reality" (2002, 168). In contexts of Pentecostal worship, styles of musical performance signify "difference" and become unstable sonic boundaries between holiness and worldliness. Perhaps the fragility of these boundaries is what prompts Pentecostals to protect them, along with an awareness that they can also "generate feelings of similarity and group membership" (168) and enable the saints to nurture a sense of unity with their spiritual brothers and sisters. Pentecostals make music to carve out distinct yet overlapping identities in an attempt to make themselves "at home" on the island and in their particular churches.

In this chapter, I examine boundaries and flows through a discussion of Jamaican church communities in New York City and in the Jamaican towns of Montego Bay and Liliput. I call attention to the musical "equipment"—musical repertories, narratives, and styles—saints use to build the walls of their religious homes. But I also strive to bring into relief the musical common ground between Pentecostal assemblies in these locales. The worship services of the three congregations explored in this chapter feature musical qualities that reflect a shared Pentecostal identity and emphasis on being "filled with the Holy Spirit." But as I will explain, these communities also set musical boundaries that index their theological differences. In each of these Pentecostal churches, musical worship gives rise to a sense of spiritual "at-homeness" that relies on the ritual reconciliation of "local" and "foreign" musical material. On the one hand, music plays a key role in shaping perceptions of cultural, theological, and moral exclusivity. These perceptions feed a home–world musical dichotomy that is pervasive and richly layered. On the other hand, it is clear to me that worship services are flavored by an assortment of religious practices and musical repertories. In particular, music blurs lines of cultural distinction between Jamaican and North American ritual practice. It also muddies theological distinctions between varieties of Pentecostalism, other forms of Christianity, and religions such as Rastafarianism and Revivalism. Musical distinctions between "home" and the "world" are thus shown to be ambiguous. I believe such distinctions are also built on fragile assumptions about the origins of, and influences on, modern-day Jamaican Pentecostalism. The ethnographic narratives and lyrical analyses in this chapter and throughout the book underscore contradictions between belief and musical practice and reveal cracks in the boundaries thought to separate "Jamaican" Pentecostal church rituals from those of the wider world.

An important aspect of my fieldwork involved a transition from New York City to the towns of Montego Bay and Liliput located on Jamaica's northern coast. I experienced Montego Bay, Liliput, and New York City's Caribbean communities as overlapping fields of social and spiritual encounter. These fields immersed me in a rich pool of musical and ritual practices that shaped my understandings of Pentecostalism in Jamaica. While certain aspects of the island scene were foreign to me, much of what I heard and saw felt quite familiar. In terms of music-making, I was sometimes struck by the commonalities, not only between my home and field experiences but also between Christianity as I know it and other religious forms. This dialectic of foreignness and familiarity would inform most of my interactions in Jamaica. I set the stage by considering the dynamic interactions that take place among Jamaican and African American believers in the New York City area. This leads into a subsequent narrative of my arrival from New York to Jamaica's northern coast, where my stay with the Massey family gave me insight into local constructions of Jamaican identity and ways of adjusting to life on the island.

Wondrous Love and Emmanuel Temple

In New York City–area churches, Jamaican Pentecostal identity takes on special significance. As is true on the island, performances of identity involve strategic uses of musical style. Wondrous Love, a seventy-member apostolic Pentecostal church in Nassau County, is a meeting ground for Jamaicans who choose to worship the way they and their relatives did back home. The church's location in the United States, where the prevailing forms of black Pentecostal music draw inspiration from African American gospel recordings, makes it unreasonable to expect that worship services remain unaffected by the broader cultural environment. Yet Wondrous Love serves as a "sanctuary of style" in which ethnic-specific identities are reinforced through what believers champion as a distinctly Jamaican mode of worship.

From 1997 until I left New York in 2004, I traveled to Wondrous Love at least twice a year with members of my Brooklyn church, Emmanuel Temple. I still chuckle when I recall my first visit. One of the ministers who knew I was a musician asked me to help out during the congregational praise and worship, and I was happy to oblige. Having arrived early, I took my place at the organ situated up front on an elevated dais near the preaching podium. During the third piece, "Highway to Heaven," a couple of electric guitarists approached and threatened to drown me out with their double-time up-beats. I was intrigued by the bouncing ska rhythm that characterized the up-tempo singing but could not figure out how to make my gospel- and jazz-influenced accompaniment gel with the less familiar sounds. Trying in vain to look unfazed, I struggled to find some stylistic middle ground that would enable me to continue contributing on the organ. But what was I supposed to play? To make matters worse, the guitarists began to crank up their volume. The organ was no longer loud enough to be heard, and no one seemed to care. The Jamaican congregants reacted with great enthusiasm to what the guitarists were doing. Their singing and clapping grew even livelier, as if to say, "Now we're *really* having church!" Hampered by my organ's pitiful speaker, and feeling increasingly unneeded and out-of-place, I contented myself to smile and clap along, pretending to feel the Spirit. I was going through the motions—using physical gestures of praise and worship while plotting my escape from a situation that grew more musically frustrating by the moment. I eventually resigned myself to an academic mode of observation. My focus turned to the ritual efficacy of this "other" kind of black church music and its capacity to facilitate spiritual transcendence for those accustomed to it.

Emmanuel Temple and Wondrous Love are "sister churches": they belong to the same global religious organization, the Pentecostal Assemblies of the World; they share membership in the New York State–Ontario District Council; and they also belong to the same subdistrict of ten local churches that gather for "unity meetings" at least three times each year. All but two of the members of Wondrous Love are Jamaican first- and second-generation migrants. This ethnic makeup has a major influence on the sound of worship services, and it distinguishes Wondrous Love from Emmanuel Temple and other black churches in the region.

"Old-time" Jamaican choruses were sung before the sermon and again at its conclusion. At this latter moment, the worship leader sang "Fire, Fall on Me," sparking the liveliest musical segment of the evening.

Fire, fire, fire! Fire fall on me.
Fire, fire, fire! Fire fall on me.

On the Day of Pentecost, the fire fall on me.
On the Day of Pentecost, the fire fall on me.

Whenever I heard this piece, either in Jamaica or New York, the congregational singing was propelled by a driving tempo, high volume, and repetitive melody. The musical accompaniment, with its ska rhythmic up-beats, gives sonic form to Jamaica as a wellspring of musical and spiritual familiarity. The effectiveness of this chorus also stems from its textual and functional aspects. Invoking the biblical narrative found in the Book of Acts, in which "tongues of fire" rested upon the Spirit-filled apostles in Jerusalem (see Introduction), the lyrics suggest a connection to modern-day Pentecostal practices. Indeed, "Fire, Fall on Me" is a "tarrying" song (see chapter 4) rendered during post-sermonic invitations to receive the baptism of the Holy Spirit. Those fluent in both Jamaican patois and standard English understand the verb "fall" in dual tense. Its ambiguity encourages the conflation of a biblical past with the ritual present, reinforcing the idea that "Pentecost can be repeated" in the lives of those who believe and choose to open their hearts.[2] The exuberance of the singing is meant, furthermore, to usher divine presence into the sanctuary by entreating God to release "fire"—that is, the Holy Spirit—from heaven, while charging the atmosphere with musical praise in order to help spiritual seekers to get into a "proper mindset." As the ritual atmosphere is filled with sound, believers hope that those who seek salvation will be filled with the Holy Spirit. "Fire, Fall on Me" thus works on several levels to reorient worshippers in ritual time and space. Musical participation takes believers "home," easing the flow of memory and Spirit to facilitate an experience of transcendence. But what about the African American believers in attendance? How did performances of religious identity at Wondrous Love influence their experience? As my experience has shown, not everyone feels free to make themselves "at home" in this kind of musical environment. For some believers, the singing of Jamaican choruses and the use of ska accompaniment may disrupt rather than facilitate flow.

The service had begun with "What a Mighty God We Serve," which everyone seemed to know. People stood and clapped while they sang, and I accompanied the congregation with my usual jazz chords and bass lines on the organ. A young drummer from Emmanuel Temple played along with a swing rhythm that matched what I was doing. Once the Jamaican guitarists joined in, I took note of how Emmanuel Temple's African American members responded to the shift in musical styles. I also spoke with them after the service to get a sense of what they thought. I received responses ranging from "It was different but nice" to "I couldn't really get into it." Most had still participated in the singing as best they could, but like me, they no longer felt at home during the service. Even if they identified with the religious message of the lyrics, the musical style with which the lyrics were delivered created a dissonance that made it hard for participants to "get into" the flow of worship. Following Kyra Gaunt (2002), I see this dissonance as a "social participatory discrepancy." It exemplifies the "difficult encounters raised by the togetherness of making music in mixed company" (127). As I will explain later, similar situations sometimes occur at Emmanuel Temple, where a feeling of musical at-homeness is not always easy to obtain.

When I returned from Jamaica in late 2002, I came to realize that members of Wondrous Love cling more tightly to Jamaican-specific worship styles than do most of the Pentecostals I had gotten to know on the island. Whereas church leaders in Jamaica are prone to incorporate African American gospel music as a way of attracting and maintaining a contingent of young people, music ministers at Wondrous Love express no desire to cater to youth desiring an African American church experience. Nor do they articulate an urgent need to promote a Jamaican-American (or "Jamerican") musical identity by featuring a blend of island- and U.S.-based styles. In this regard, laity and music ministers at Wondrous Love are in step with their church's leader, who came to the United States in the 1960s as part of an enormous wave of Caribbean migration.[3] She strives to maintain both the cultural and spiritual integrity of the congregation in the face of outside influences. During our conversations, she described Wondrous Love's Jamaican musical style as one of the church's most attractive attributes. I also spoke with the youth president, who noted that the church's teenagers and young adults enjoy maintaining a cultural connection to the island.

While Wondrous Love is the product of migratory flows between Jamaica and New York in the 1960s, the birth of Emmanuel Temple in the 1940s is tied to a series of "Great Migrations" in the United States, as black men and women relocated from the agrarian South. Christians of all stripes flowed into northern cities, bringing with them their styles of gospel music (Burnim 2015, 189–95; Boyer 1995, 57, 152; Harris 1992). Gospel music also influenced Pentecostal churches as far east as New York City, and blacks also migrated there from the South. One such migrant was Tommy L. Seals, who arrived from Mound Bayou, Mississippi, in 1957 and was shortly thereafter chosen to become the pianist at Emmanuel Temple. Playing for the worship services required more improvisation than he had been accustomed to, and the music sounded "more gospel" than that of the stricter style of his hometown church. Rather than relying on a hymnal, Seals recalls, "I had to get used to playing by ear, in whatever key they started singing in." By adapting his technique of playing to fit the Emmanuel

Pastor Tommy Seals at the piano. Photo by the author.

Temple style of the late 1950s, Seals began developing the self-described "old school" style of playing he employed until his 2012 retirement.

During the ten years I spent at Emmanuel Temple, negotiations of musical style between African Americans and Jamaicans occurred on a regular basis.[4] Unlike Wondrous Love's mostly Jamaican congregation, Emmanuel Temple's Jamaican congregants were in the minority, representing only about one-fourth of the active membership. Although African Americans outnumbered Jamaicans, most of the latter held positions of leadership such that there were relatively greater opportunities for their voices and musical styles to be heard. The frequent interactions between saints at Emmanuel Temple and Wondrous Love provided additional opportunities for Jamaican and African American Pentecostals to exchange musical ideas as women and men ministered through culturally inflected gospel musics during unity meetings. Jamaican repertories and styles of singing were remembered and kept alive by Jamaicans at Emmanuel Temple, despite their being outweighed by the African American majority.

The situation at Emmanuel Temple is not unique.[5] But neither has it always been the norm in black churches throughout the United States. In his 1983 study, William Dargan found only a trace amount of interaction between

African Americans and Jamaicans within the New England church he observed. "Although Jamaican choruses are warmly appreciated when they are sung," he noted, "they are only performed infrequently. . . . Jamaicans constitute a small and recent element in the congregation, [so] no real dynamics of borrowing or cross-influence have been observed between the two styles" (66). With its employment of both African American and Jamaican varieties of gospel music, Emmanuel Temple's congregation stands out from those in which only a single musical style takes precedence.

One of the challenges of serving as minister of music at Emmanuel Temple was learning to shift between older and newer styles of playing hymns. This ability to shift between styles proved most helpful in accompanying Jamaican singers who felt more "at home" musically if I maintained an allegiance to the straightforward rhythmic and harmonic scheme provided in the hymnal. Jamaicans I interviewed favor strophic hymns such as "Victory in Jesus" and place comparatively high value on lyrical content. African American members expressed a greater preference for "one-liners" such as "What's the Matter with Jesus," wherein feelings of spiritual fulfillment derive from repetitions of short phrases rather than through meditation on a lyrical narrative. Note the difference between these two song texts, as shown below:

"VICTORY IN JESUS"

I heard an old, old story
'Bout a Savior came from glory.
How He gave His life on Calvary
To save a wretch like me.

"What's the Matter with Jesus?"
Leader: What's the matter with Jesus?
Congregation: He's all right!
Leader: What's the matter with Jesus?
Congregation: He's all right!
Leader: He's all right!
Congregation: He's all right!
Leader: He's all right!
Congregation: He's all right!

Jamaicans at Emmanuel Temple tended to shrug at the apparent waste of time and energy expended by African American members, most of whom seemed strangely content to clap on beats two and four for several minutes while repeating lyrics that lack what Jamaican saints referred to as "substance." African Americans, on the other hand, described the hymns preferred by the

Jamaican members as "strict," "boring," and "old-fashioned," in part because the lyrical density and slower tempos of these hymns rendered them less conducive to the types of improvised vocal embellishments and "holy dancing" that the church's African American worshippers enjoy. Some of Emmanuel Temple's African American members found Jamaican-style church singing unsatisfying simply because the accompanying rhythmic "groove" was unfamiliar to them. The question of how much emphasis to place on the words of a song vis-à-vis its rhythmic pulse was among the fundamental points of tension as Emmanuel Temple's members negotiated their contrasting stylistic preferences.

It is nearly impossible to overemphasize the influence Pastor Seals had on the musical style at Emmanuel Temple. Born in the Deep South in 1930, he had lived through several stylistic shifts in gospel music and had witnessed his traditional way of piano playing become increasingly out of step with the contemporary gospel music trends to which Emmanuel's Temple's saints were drawn. Over the years, he adjusted to musical elements brought in by the influx of younger, more contemporary-minded congregants. He maintained a certain reverence, however, for older hymns, and he sought to instill in his members a respect for tradition. In so doing, he created, I believe, a musical atmosphere that welcomed both African American and Jamaican members. Pastor Seals tempered the "one-liners," which were especially appreciated by the African American youth, with a healthy dose of versed hymns preferred by "the island-ers," as they called themselves. Pastor Seals also encouraged worship leaders to use the hymnal, a practice that had become less popular among younger saints but was still embraced by the older Jamaican congregants. In this way, the distinctions between African American and Jamaican styles of musical expression intersected with the generational differences between younger and older members of Emmanuel Temple. What this also means is that African Americans and Jamaicans were able to voice their stylistic preferences in terms of how relatively older styles of gospel differ from newer ones. As the influence of newer styles was tempered by a healthy respect for more traditional repertories, a creative window of opportunity opened wherein musical differences were negotiated and coherence in the worship service was maintained.

At Wondrous Love, African American gospel music is marginalized in favor of styles that register as distinctly Jamaican. The situation is different within majority African American congregations such as Emmanuel Temple. There, Jamaican-style church music is tolerated, but most members are fondest of the African American gospel songs that resonate with their ethnic and racial self-identities. Taken together, Wondrous Love and Emmanuel Temple are emblematic of the Jamaican and African American musical relations this book illumines.

These churches also shed important light on how performances of tradition, race, and ethnicity interact.[6] The blend of musical styles adds distinctiveness to churches in the diaspora, just as it does in Jamaica.

As I emphasize throughout this book, Pentecostals use gospel music to perform their identities in complex ways. My conversations with Jamaican saints reveal contradictory perspectives on music's relation to their sense of religious and cultural distinctiveness. Some gravitate toward songs that contain sonic markers of Jamaicanness. These markers include the use of ska rhythms or lyrics that derive from the Revivalist tradition. Among Jamaican Pentecostals living in the United States, religious, cultural, and long-distance national identities become a source of personal strength and a foundation for minority group consciousness. However, others with whom I spoke enjoy several distinct church music styles and see them as a means of conveying the fluidity of a modern Jamaican Pentecostal identity. They use music to convey something meaningful about the boundlessness of their faith and the efficacy of the Spirit they believe flows through them.

Familiarity and Difference at Home-in-the-Field

By the time I was ready to visit Jamaica's northern coast in February 2002, my curiosity was stoked by the experiences I had gained at Emmanuel Temple, Wondrous Love, and throughout New York City's broader Jamaican community. I would finally be able to witness firsthand what the Jamaican saints back home raved about. "You just have to *go* there, and you'll see the difference," one sister declared. Things would be "so different" in Jamaica, she boasted, reimagining a purer church life less corrupted by the sins that sometimes accompany monetary wealth. At Emmanuel Temple, most of the Jamaican members waxed nostalgic about yesteryear, when life was supposedly simpler and people appreciated "the finer things in life," such as family gatherings, church meetings, and, of course, the music that accompanied them. "In America, everybody is always in a hurry," another sister explained, "but back home, the people just *worship*. At church, they're not so concerned with the time." Although my inner skeptic could have dismissed such rhetoric as idealistic, I found myself giddy with anticipation as my plane took off from New York's LaGuardia Airport. I wondered mostly about differences and similarities, and I felt highly invested in the task of identifying them. What was it about Jamaican churches that led the saints to romanticize them in such a way? How would it feel to be the only African American in a Jamaican church service, to be on their turf for a change? To what extent would the music and the Spirit flow for me within a less familiar cultural environment? Such concerns were for me both personal and academic.

Upon landing in Montego Bay, I discovered that my baggage had been misplaced and would have to be delivered later. How typical this would be, I thought, for an arrival narrative. This situation was exacerbated by a problem with my student visa, which led to my being stuck in an office for about an hour while my ride waited outside. Movement across national borders had gotten noticeably more restricted since George W. Bush launched the War on Terror. In no way did being a U.S. citizen grant me carte blanche in the minds of the airport's immigration officials. On the contrary, they seemed to count it as a point against me. This is payback, I joked to myself, remembering a conversation I'd overheard not long ago among Jamaicans at the Consulate Office in New York. They were upset about the difficulties of traveling back and forth from the island to the States. "The terrorists messed it up for everybody," one man sighed, referring to the World Trade Center attacks that had occurred just five months prior. As I sat waiting for a supervisor to appear, a young lady in uniform inquired, "So what type of research are you doing?" "Music in the Pentecostal churches," I replied. My answer evoked an approving nod. I regained a point or two. I imagine she reckoned that I must be a "respectable" person to be studying such a thing. But my documentation was insufficient to allow me to stay in Jamaica for the length of time indicated on my round-trip ticket. After three months, I would have to go to an office in Kingston to apply for an extension.

After sorting through some red tape and making my way out of the airport terminal, I greeted my hosts with an apology and explained the reason for the holdup. The Masseys and I had never met, but a connection had been established for me through my home church in Brooklyn. Mrs. Massey's daughter had joined Emmanuel Temple after emigrating from Jamaica in the 1970s. She and her husband eventually became associate ministers, and they were a source of wisdom and encouragement during my decade-long tenure in New York. The Masseys and I got acquainted during the twenty-five-minute drive to their home in Liliput, a town development district about twelve miles from Montego Bay. A foreign investment company had bought up a huge tract of land and sold lots to Jamaicans and Americans. Most of the families in this part of Liliput were retired residents who, like my hosts, had returned to Jamaica to buy houses in the district.

Mr. and Mrs. Massey described themselves as "strong Christians." Mrs. Massey, in particular, took pride in her moral standing, which she expressed in terms of her dislike of dancehall music. For her, maintaining a "good Christian home" meant setting clear musical boundaries. Years ago, she'd forbidden her children to attend "sinful" dancehall events, and she now found the audible sounds of nightclubs an annoying fact of life. Mrs. Massey's labeling of dancehall as "sinful" exemplifies a moralization of embodied music-making, but this way of thinking about popular music is not specific to one particular Christian (or religious) tradition. An aversion to dancehall music, in particular, is common among Christians in Jamaica. Likewise, there are Christians in the United States who gleefully "dance for Jesus" while insisting that other forms of social dancing are "not of God." Mrs. Massey's moral beliefs about music were therefore not new to me. As a Pentecostal, I had been taught that dancehall-type events were not spiritually edifying or, as pastors would say, not "becoming of a saint." Unlike Mrs. Massey, however, I was not inclined to describe musical activity in terms of sinfulness.

There were moments in which theological differences surfaced between me and the Masseys. My hosts made it a point to tell me, for example, that they were "not Pentecostal," and they adopted a defensive stance toward me, perhaps thinking that I intended to win them over to the Pentecostal faith. As far as I was concerned, this stance was unwarranted. I cringed at the thought of trying to "witness" to them within their home and felt it would have been inappropriate and presumptuous on my part. To my dismay, Mrs. Massey picked a theological fight with me a few days after my arrival in a barrage of questions for which I was unprepared: "Why you hafta speak in tongues? Do you understand what you're saying?" "Well . . . I mean . . . not *always*," I sputtered, "but tongues can be a *heavenly* language that only God underst—." Mr. Massey cut me off, "How come you don't know what you're saying? You mean you speak in tongues but you don't even know what you're saying?" He scoffed, "That sounds like foolishness, you know." In hopes of avoiding further tension, I offered no rebuttal. Besides, I got the impression that they were carrying on with me a running debate they'd started with their daughter. I was unwilling to play along, and I thought it wisest not to risk derailing whatever progress their daughter might have made with her parents up to this point. Preferring not to pollute my home-in-the-field with the smog of religious controversy, I let the matter drop.

While living in the Massey's home, I came to see our relationship as emblematic of Jamaica's Christian landscape. Churchgoers of different stripes express both the commonality of their faith and the distinctions between their brands of Christianity. They also live in accordance with the country's motto, "Out of Many, One People," recognizing the value of diversity within a nation that is unified by virtue of their shared cultural identity and geographical location. Theological debates flourish within the island "household" in which Christians agree to disagree. At least once a month, the Masseys attended services at a Baptist assembly in nearby Montego Bay. They embraced the idea of church attendance but simply didn't understand the need to be in church two or three times per week, as Pentecostals typically were. They tolerated my frequent excursions to evening services, so long as I respected the boundaries they set, such as adhering to a curfew and remembering to call when I would be returning late.

Abiding by the rules of the Massey home was no problem for me, except on one occasion when I attended a rehearsal that went long. A gospel ensemble based in a local Church of God was practicing in Montego Bay for an upcoming concert. The woman who had invited me promised to have me back home by 10 P.M., but things were running behind schedule. I also lost track of time, returning home around 1 A.M. to find the lights off and the front door locked shut. A legitimate fear of break-ins and violence had put the country on edge, and the increasing murder rate had become a point of political discussions relevant to the national elections coming later in the year. I knocked for three whole minutes before Mr. Massey finally answered the door. He looked upset, and I knew I was in trouble. "You can't *call* when you're running late? Why you don't call? You cyaan stay *here* if you're gonna do that!" Mortified, I sent myself to my room to contemplate my fate, hoping that sleep would soothe my hurt feelings and heal my psyche from the infantilizing tongue-lashing I knew I deserved. First thing in the morning, I apologized profusely, worried that my negligence had solidified their misgivings about me and all other Pentecostals. But despite that embarrassing incident, and what I perceived to be a mounting cynicism toward my faith, the Masseys were kind and gracious hosts. Mr. Massey drove me into Montego Bay a few times during my first week in Jamaica so that I could get acclimated to the area. In ways I did not expect, the Masseys taught me much about the importance of understanding and respecting boundaries in the field, not only when conducting fieldwork but also in the course of "everyday life." Moreover, the boundary between field and home became increasingly fluid for me. I would continue to gain valuable insights in a variety of social scenes, regardless of whether I viewed them as "field sites."

The towns of Liliput and Montego Bay provided me with a wealth of information about the beliefs and practices of Christian congregations on the island. The soundscapes of these two towns gave me important clues about musical, social, and religious boundaries and flows as well. As I hope to demonstrate, some church songs make the discrete layers of a home–world dichotomy more discernible than others, particularly when they are performed by groups invested in showcasing cut-and-dried features of their collective identity. "One God Apostolic," to which I now turn, is an excellent case in point. As we shall see, the song operates on several levels as signifier of theological specificity and overlap.

"One God Apostolic": Musical and Doctrinal Discourses in Liliput

From my bedroom window in Liliput, I could hear singing emanating from several churches in the area. Each Saturday afternoon, a Seventh-day Adventist church held services, and the sound of their hymns wafted through the neighborhood. By nightfall, the pounding bass rhythms of a nearby dancehall filled the air, sometimes competing with the musical worship being offered by a Baptist church holding an evening service. There were also Pentecostal churches nearby, and I would sometimes listen to early Sunday morning worship taking place a few hours before I set out to attend my own service of choice. Liliput was home to five Pentecostal churches. The area these churches served was made up of middle-class houses occupied by returning residents like Mr. and Mrs. Massey, as well as a significant number of "poorer people" who lived in one-room dwellings with corrugated iron roofs. Two of the Pentecostal assemblies were independent, while the other three were nominally affiliated with the Assemblies of God, the Church of God, or the United Pentecostal Church. The latter organization's assembly, Mercy Tabernacle Apostolic Church, would eventually become my church home during my stay with the Masseys.

The "apostolic" Pentecostal ministers I met at Mercy Tabernacle and elsewhere are quick to articulate their theological distinctiveness. They promote an apostolic doctrine mandating that water baptism be done "in the name of Jesus," following the biblical example recorded in the Acts of the Apostles. Apostolic Pentecostals generally believe that the infilling, or baptism, of the Holy Spirit, evidenced by speaking in tongues "as the Spirit gives utterance," is essential to one's eternal salvation and spiritual identity.[7] The titles Father, Son, and Holy Spirit are understood to denote three "offices" or manifestations of the indivisible God, and the term "oneness" is used to describe the "unity of the Godhead." While all of those whom I consider Pentecostals experience music as a vehicle for ecstatic, celebratory worship, specific beliefs sometimes influence musical style, repertory, and function.

Music is a mode of theological expression at Liliput's Mercy Tabernacle. One of the songs frequently rendered there is "One God Apostolic." The lyrics express unabashed confidence in the validity of demonstrative practices such as speaking in tongues and holy dancing, which some denominational Protestants have described as strange and unorthodox.[8] The lyrics are thus a means through which saints revel in a "sanctified" experience shared among Pentecostals and some other Christian denominations. They also point, however, to the specific "Jesus' name" doctrine espoused by the subgroup of Pentecostals who identify themselves as apostolic.

> I have been washed by his blood, sanctified by his faith, and suggest you do
> the same.
> I've been set free at the Pentecostal altar.
> Pardon me if I'm not ashamed to be a one God, apostolic, tongue talking, holy
> roller
> Born again, heaven bound, believer in the liberated power of Jesus' name.

It is worth noting that for believers this piece registers not only as a theological statement distinguishing those of the apostolic Pentecostal faith but also as a cultural emblem peculiar to Jamaica. It is, however, the rhythmic accompaniment, rather than the lyrics, that contributes most strongly to this sense of Jamaicanness. One keyboardist described the church's musical style to me as "old R&B." Other instrumentalists characterized it as "ska," the commercial popular music genre that developed on the island during the late 1950s and 1960s. Instrumental accompaniment and hand clapping, in particular, employ a ska-derived arrangement of up-beats, "emphasizing the 'and' in a 'one-AND-two-AND-three-AND-four' rhythmic pattern" (Kauppila 2006, 75). As I will explain later, the use of an "older" form of popular music is more than a reflection of musical "taste" or preference. In fact, Pentecostals tend to equate older with better. Whereas dancehall music is directly associated with the sins of "worldly" nightlife, saints describe "gospel ska" as a more respectable form of popular music performance. This respectability stems, in part, from the perceived temporal distance of its secular counterpoint (that is, ska without biblically based lyrics) from the present day.

A sonic reference to ska, in particular, lends "One God Apostolic" a local flavor experienced as distinct from that of songs recognized as definitively "American." Consequently, Mercy Tabernacle's members claim "One God Apostolic" as an original Jamaican product, and worship leaders will sing it in an attempt to offset a preponderance of musical material tied to the United States. But despite this perception of Jamaican cultural distinctiveness, there is ample evidence to show that the historical connections between the popular musics of Jamaica and the United States are strong.[9] The aforementioned references to ska and "old R&B" acknowledge an overlap between Jamaican popular music and African American rhythm and blues. At the level of musical style, "One God Apostolic" is thus a multivalent signifier, "read" in different ways through a series of "interpretive moves" (Feld 1984, 8). The song's meaning is contingent and unstable, and its cultural "ownership" is determined in accordance with how those experiencing the piece position themselves in relation to it. Those familiar with the deep and tangled roots of ska may see its musical style as an index of a home whose walls extend beyond Jamaica to encompass Pentecostals in the United States. Those who experience ska as a uniquely Jamaican sound may interpret the piece's musical style as a sonic icon of Jamaicanness. This interpretation becomes particularly compelling among the Jamaican diaspora in the United States, where gospel music connects Pentecostals to Jamaica, a geographical homeland tied to their past, as well as to heaven, a spiritual home they hope to inhabit in the future. As the style of Jamaican musical worship is intimately linked to both the cultural and spiritual identities of Pentecostal believers, it acts as a powerful "sonic index" that produces "deep associations and a sense of belonging," becoming the basis for what Elizabeth McAlister calls a "Christian diasporic sensibility" (2012, 27–28). In both Jamaica and the United States, "One God Apostolic" is also a means of performing membership in a "transstate cultural formation" of Jamaican apostolic Pentecostals.[10]

What also tends to go unacknowledged is the fact that "One God Apostolic" is not the product of a Jamaican composer. Only after I returned home from my fieldwork and began researching the song's origins did I discover that it was written and recorded by Lance Appleton, a Pentecostal from the United States.[11] Another interesting aspect of "One God Apostolic" is that it emerged, as does its composer, from the United Pentecostal Church (UPC), a predominantly white organization based in the United States. The song is part of a large repertory of music that is now shared between the United States and Jamaica. But why is "One God Apostolic" so prominent in Jamaican apostolic Pentecostal churches but not in African American ones in the United States? The reason must certainly involve the social forces that influence the flow of music within and between Pentecostal communities. Black Pentecostal congregations in the United States have long developed their own repertories and styles of music with varying degrees of overlap with the practices of other ethnic and racial religious groups. Moreover, recordings of gospel and contemporary Christian music are consumed by churchgoers in accordance with the specific styles they have learned to appreciate. I believe the answer to this question is also tied, however, to a legacy of racial strife among Pentecostal organizations in the United States, along with the fact that it is common for Jamaican Pentecostal churches to be linked to the UPC.[12] Indeed, despite more than two decades of involvement in apostolic Pentecostalism, I have never heard the song rendered within a predominantly black church. It was therefore easy for me to experience "One God Apostolic" as a distinctly Jamaican cultural product. It felt theologically familiar because of the lyrics but culturally foreign to me until I became acclimated to its Jamaican musical style. I mention this because it drives home the fact that while boundaries between Jamaican and North American church music are fluid and shifting, musical practice can make them feel concrete and permanent. Music gives imagined boundaries experiential reality. It lends them the appearance or, rather, the sound of stability. For Jamaican saints, the song's compositional or racial origin matters much less than the feeling it engenders in present-day ritual performance. And cultural differences, even when made known, are sometimes deemed less important than theological common ground.

Musical Transcendence and Overlap in Montego Bay

During my first few weeks on the island, I spent my afternoons strolling around Liliput and Montego Bay, popping into a church from time to time to inquire about the services and organizational affiliations. I soon became comfortable taking a taxi into Montego Bay to explore what the city had to offer. One of the first churches I encountered in Montego Bay was the New Testament Church of God. As I perused the sign outside, a young woman approached to let me know that the Sunday morning services would begin at 7:30 and 11:00 and that I was welcome to attend either or both of them. Such personal invitations are never required to attend Pentecostal churches, but they help in encouraging passersby to feel welcome. I posed a few short questions before thanking her and resolving to return tomorrow for Sunday school at 9:30 A.M., which would be followed by the second morning worship service.

The next day, inclement weather made Sunday school attendance sparse. A blessing in disguise, I thought, as I sat enjoying the social intimacy of the Bible study. Later that morning, about five hundred congregants took part in the worship service. If not for the rain showers that discouraged some from making the trek, there might have been an additional one hundred attendees, I was told. The song leader was a woman with a strong, well-tuned voice. The instrumentalists mostly played with a rock or R&B accompaniment, but occasionally the rhythm section would switch into reggae-sounding grooves, especially after dismissal, when the musicians were free to improvise or "jam."

I found the high point of the service to be the heated segments of musical worship, when congregational singing grew loudest and a mixture of hand-clapping patterns punctuated the lyrics of the Jamaican "choruses." These choruses make up a significant body of the congregational songs rendered during Pentecostal church services, and they stand in contrast to other pieces, such as hymns, which are considered more pious and "formal" in style. Choruses are typically short in length and sung as part of a medley. Unlike hymns, choruses are passed down through oral tradition rather than notated in liturgical books. That morning, choruses were interspersed throughout the service with musical selections I knew from my experiences in the United States. Opening songs included the hymn "Blessed Assurance," written by the American Methodist lyricist Fanny Crosby, and the slow rock piece, "You Are Awesome in This Place," popularized by contemporary Christian group Hillsong United. I recognized both of these pieces from my time at Emmanuel Temple, so I sang along, appreciating the shared repertory that helped me to feel at home within the congregation. Midway through the service, a children's choir rendered what is known as an "item," a special selection featuring a soloist or group. They sang "I Almost Let Go," a commercially popular song written and recorded by African American gospel artist Kurt Carr. It is one of several gospel pieces by black American singers that I would hear repeatedly in worship services and on the radio in Jamaica. These musical selections stood in contrast to island-flavored pieces, especially choruses such as "We Shall Have a Grand Time up in Heaven" and "Suppose We Don't Meet on That Judgment Day," which were sung as part of an upbeat medley just before Bishop Notice, the church's pastor, took the podium to deliver his sermon.

Bishop Notice enjoyed both singing and preaching, and as was the norm for him, he launched into another Anglo-American hymn before beginning his discourse. Hymns are, for most clergy, a musical marker of respectability and a means to connect present-day gospel music and worship to time-honored practices referred to as "the old-time way" (see chapter 4). This is another way that music becomes a vehicle for a particular kind of temporal transcendence. It is a means of bringing the past into the present for the purpose of lending worship services an air of legitimacy and spiritual authenticity. Throughout the service, I also took note of how music and words situated this congregation in a transnational sphere. The pastor's sermon highlighted the connections Jamaicans have in the United States, and these connections were reemphasized in some of the prayer requests printed in the weekly bulletin handed out to each attendee. Congregants were reminded to pray for a sister who "leaves the island on Tuesday" and another whose mother is ill and "resides in the USA." I learned quickly that such prayer requests are commonplace. Likewise, Jamaicans in the United States habitually offer prayers for Jamaicans living on the island. The mix of musical styles, along with the frequent references to the United States, exemplifies the ritual construction of a church home situated physically on the island but located conceptually in transnational and spiritual space. As music provides the impetus for reaching toward an invisible God, it also facilitates the sonic construction of a transnational Jamaican Pentecostal identity.

I later returned to the New Testament Church of God for 6:30 P.M. service. It was Harvest Sunday, and there was a full program of what Bishop Notice referred to as musical "performances." Before the actual program began, a woman serving as emcee led the congregation in musical worship, which consisted mostly of medium-tempo pieces from *Church Hymnal*, a small paperback booklet published in Jamaica for the New Testament Churches of God. A series of musical performances followed, and these were interspersed with choruses and other up-tempo songs, which were led by a group of praise singers. As I took in the service, I reflected on what the saints in Brooklyn had told me about the "difference" between Jamaican and North American musical worship. But I did not feel as though I was witnessing something foreign and inaccessible. On the contrary, the congregational songs, especially the handclaps, reminded me of the gospel music I had experienced at Emmanuel Temple and also at New York City–area Jamaican churches.

As is the case in Jamaican churches in New York, choruses at Montego Bay's New Testament Church of God were sung with a quickly moving underlying accompaniment. In particular, I took note of the rhythmic groove that characterized most of the up-tempo singing. Handclaps began on beats two and four, as is commonplace in African American churches. However, after a few moments this pattern was supplemented by the ska-derived pattern of up-beats I mentioned earlier. The composite hand-clapping rhythm produced by the merging of these two patterns provides a sonic representation of the overlapping of Jamaican and African American worship aesthetics that I have experienced in both Jamaica and the United States.[13] I was also fascinated by the instrumentalists, who were well versed in a number of accompaniment styles from both countries. For example, the keyboardist played the faster-moving up-beats with his right hand, while the left doubled a 1950s-style rhythm-and-blues line played by the bassist. In terms of musical style, this service was similar to others I attended while in Jamaica. It differed in that more songs were featured than is usually the case during normal worship services, and this was due to the fact that it was a special "Harvest Sunday" event. Worship at Montego Bay's New Testament Church of God thus exemplified a mixture of local and transnational musical styles that I would encounter in Pentecostal churches on the island.

One way to interpret the church's music is as a vehicle for constructing a cultural and spiritual "home." For example, certain Jamaican choruses and musical styles lend the services what Jamaicans refer to as an "island flavor," and several churchgoers with whom I spoke take pride in the cultural distinctiveness of their worship. Yet Pentecostals also demonstrate an understanding of how music enables them to "transcend" Jamaica from a cultural standpoint. They include in their church services hymns such as "Blessed Assurance," African American gospel pieces such as "I Almost Let Go," and a variety of contemporary Christian "worship songs" that have been disseminated to worldwide audiences. In some churches, the lyrics to hymns and other imported pieces are sung to local-sounding rhythmic grooves, maintaining a sense of "home" in worship. Nevertheless, Jamaicans make use of repertories that travel around the globe and complicate constructions of a home–world dichotomy as it applies to the sound of musical worship. I turn now to a more detailed discussion of how "homes" are constructed through the performance of song lyrics in Pentecostal churches.

Hearing "Home": Localness and Lines of Influence

As we have seen, music from the United States has a profound influence on Jamaican Pentecostal worship services and on the identities that are fashioned within them. Music gives the saints a sense of belonging and a feeling of spiritual and cultural "home." As I have argued, the walls of Jamaican church homes have ears, and North American musical genres are vital tools in their construction. For example, the hymn "Softly and Tenderly" is prevalent in Jamaican Pentecostal churches, including Mercy Tabernacle and the New Testament Church of God. However, the lyrics, which state, in part, "Come home, come home. / Ye who are weary, come home," were composed in 1880 by Will Lamartine Thompson, a storeowner and music publisher from Ohio (Bence 1997, 248). When Christians speak and sing of home, they refer to the sanctuaries of congregational worship, within which the Holy Spirit bestows power to live a life that is set apart for divine purpose. This process of sanctification requires the nurturing of dispositions and practices that are distinct from those of the outside "world." Hymns such as "Softly and Tenderly" describe the world as the tumultuous territory of the lost sinner while presenting the church as the ultimate source of salvation and rest. They invite the world-weary unbeliever to renounce sinful ways that prevent self-knowledge and to "come home" to the church where he or she can claim his or her rightful place in God's family. As I explain throughout this book, the music of Pentecostal ritual transcends the local homes that practitioners construct. Yet it also fosters feelings of group exclusivity that lend urgency to a localized politics of Christian authenticity. Musical performance is a critical means through which Jamaican Pentecostals attempt to "make themselves at home" as they negotiate religious, cultural, and generational boundaries in Jamaica and abroad.

In church parlance, "home" may also refer to heaven, a transcendent dwelling to be inhabited by the soul after bodily death. Worship services and concerts feature songs about "flying away" to this home in "glory," on the other side of a boundary between earthly and spiritual dimensions. Among Pentecostals, songs such as "I'll Fly Away" and "Fly Away Home" discuss the "catching away" of the church, an event also referred to as "the rapture." This phenomenon is understood to entail a mystical transformation of human bodies from a terrestrial to a celestial state upon Jesus Christ's return to earth.[14] What is most relevant to this present discussion is that Pentecostals seem to hold varying interpretations of the origins of these two pieces. My sense is that they "hear" them in different ways.

Written in the 1920s and since recorded by multiple artists, "I'll Fly Away" has long been a staple among Christians in the United States. Jamaican Pentecostals in Montego Bay and Liliput described it to me as a "foreign" song, even though it has been widely incorporated into local churches.

"I'LL FLY AWAY"

I'll fly away, O glory, I'll fly away.
When I die, Hallelujah, by and by,
I'll fly away.

By contrast, "Fly Away Home" registers as a distinctly Jamaican religious song.

"FLY AWAY HOME"

Fly away home to glory.
Fly away home.
One bright morning
when my life is over,
I will fly away home.

What accounts for these different hearings of the two pieces? How does music inform perceptions of "localness" and foreignness among Pentecostals and other religious practitioners? One possible answer to these questions may be found by examining the lines of historical influence between "Fly Away Home" and other musical and cultural phenomena. These lines of influence suggest that the perceived localness of "Fly Away Home" derives from its long-standing associations with other religious practices, namely Rastafarianism and Revivalism, which are powerful symbols of Jamaican cultural identity. For example, Bob Marley and the Wailers recorded an almost identical version of "Fly Away Home" in 1973. The lyrics of this reggae rendition, entitled "Rasta Man Chant," replaces "glory" with "Zion," which refers to Ethiopia, the birthplace of Haile Selassie and the earthly homeland to which Rastafari expect to return.

> Fly away home to Zion.
> Fly away home.
> One bright morning
> when my work is over,
> Man will fly away home.

In the Bible, "Zion" signifies heaven, Jerusalem, or the church, but, as I explain below, Jamaican Pentecostals avoid this term, as it indexes a Rastafarian perspective considered antithetical to Pentecostal belief and doctrine.[15] Does the Rasta repertory that inspired Marley's recording predate the Pentecostal version? Or did Rastafari adapt the lyrics from a preexisting Pentecostal repertory instead? Twentieth-century Jamaica witnessed the maturation of both Rastafarianism and Pentecostalism, and as their followers multiplied in number, they most certainly influenced one another at the level of musical practice. Positing a strict directionality of influence would be less rewarding than recognizing the historical permeability of socioreligious categories that have, nevertheless, become musically and theologically significant. In any event, Rastafari and Pentecostals likely picked up "Fly Away Home" from nineteenth-century Revivalists.[16] This in itself is not surprising. In fact, the Revivalist version of "O Let the Power Fall on Me, My Lord" is still sung in Pentecostal churches throughout Jamaica, including in Montego Bay and Liliput. Both "Fly Away Home" and "O Let the Power Fall on Me" reveal an overlap of Pentecostal, Rasta, and Revivalist repertories.

The songs I have just discussed signify social and spiritual realms that Pentecostals tend to describe as incompatible. For these saints, the boundary between "God-approved" Pentecostal worship services and the rituals of other spiritual traditions is unambiguous and impermeable. However, other saints acknowledge the fluidity of musical and religious boundaries and lament the fact that such fluidity seems unwanted. For example, a Jamaican Pentecostal organist once responded to my query about the influence of Rastafarianism by complaining that certain words have become divisive identity markers. Biblical terms such as "Zion," "Most High," and "Jah" trigger protests that he finds unreasonable. "You could never preach about 'Jah' in a Jamaican apostolic [Pentecostal] church," he noted. "They would look at you strange, very strange. If you write 'Most High' in your songs, they think that you are straying [from the faith]. They like to hear 'Jesus' all day long. I have even heard people say that if [the word] 'Jesus' is not in the song, then it is not gospel!" But the musical connections among Rasta, Revival, and Pentecostal repertories come as no surprise to those most familiar with the island's religious development. In fact, Frederic Cassidy's decades-old observation about the peripatetic nature of spiritual practices still rings true. He stated, "Many elements of Christianity . . . have overflowed the bounds of any of the Christian churches and become mingled quite inextricably with the remains of African cultist practices brought over by the slaves" (1961, 232). We can appreciate the modern-day relevance of this assertion by recognizing that some nineteenth-century ritual musics have survived in early twenty-first-century Pentecostal practice.

My discussion has thus far focused on my experiences within two communities that laid the groundwork for my subsequent research among Jamaican Pentecostals. The saints I met bring to their congregations specific conceptions of what home sounds like. Home sometimes sounds to the saints like "Jamaica," but they feel that home should also sound "Christian" as the faith is understood from within their particular Pentecostal congregation. What emerges from this chapter's consideration of stylistic and repertorial overlap is the fact that while a song may be perceived as "Jamaican" (or culturally local), this does not necessarily mean that it will be accepted as "Christian" (or theologically local). More to the point, cultural localness alone does not render a song appropriate for use in worship. Ideas concerning which sounds are "Jamaican" and "Christian" may or may not overlap in the sonic imaginations of churchgoers. For example, songs such as "Fly Away Home" are sometimes deemed theologically foreign and thus ill-suited for use in Pentecostal churches. Whether a song lies in the "safe" zone of overlap depends precisely on how the saints hear and perform it and on the degree of emphasis they place on its stylistic qualities, lyrics, and perceived origins.

In both Montego Bay and Liliput I witnessed attempts on the part of Pentecostals to worship in culturally and theologically specific ways. They did so through the use of Jamaican choruses and also other songs that, regardless of their country of origin, may register as Jamaican to church attendees. On the other hand, I observed also that church music can sound "foreign" or convey a sense of what we might call "cultural translocalness" and still be deemed appropriate for worship. It is the point of overlap between the culturally translocal and the theologically local that sometimes constitutes a sonic sweet spot for saints. This holds especially true for those wishing to enjoy gospel music in a Pentecostal church service without the "distractions" of Jamaican-sounding material. Songs such as "I'll Fly Away" or "I Almost Let Go" are sometimes chosen because they fit within a definite Christian frame and may also be experienced as having origins in the United States.

Timothy Rommen explores a similar phenomenon in his ethnomusicological study of Protestant Christianity in Trinidad. The "negotiation of proximity," as he terms it, involves the processes through which churchgoers develop a preference for musical styles that are farthest from them. Discussing similar controversies, Rommen explains that some genres are "situated far too close to home to remain unfettered and uncomplicated" (2007, 66). By contrast, North American gospel songs remain "fundamentally Other" despite their integration into local religious culture. Likewise, "Jamaican songo" may be too "implicated in the messiness of everyday life," whereas musical material from abroad maintains a distanced position that ultimately makes it easier to incorporate into worship services. However, estimations of musical distance and proximity hinge on the age, background, and religious identity of the listener, and controversies may just as easily swirl around the use of "foreign" genres that have become popular in local commercial markets. As Jean Kidula (2010) observes, "if the popular style is in vogue, dissension is greater [among] an older or more conservative congregation, or with recent converts who perceive it to be deeply embedded in their 'previous' lifestyle" (72). In her discussion of the use of reggae by gospel recording artists in Kenya, Kidula explains that although reggae had been part of that country's sonic landscape since at least the early 1980s, "it had not achieved enough distance to be embraced by the then ultra-conservative crop of gospel musicians [she] interviewed in 1995 and 1996" (72). My key analytical point here is that distinctions between local and "foreign" are most relevant at the levels of discourse and perception. While a sense of "at-homeness" depends, in part, on the construction of an exclusive religious community, Pentecostals also see "home" as an arena of cultural transcendence—that is, an area of overlap between the theologically local and the culturally translocal. A sense of at-homeness for these saints is generated precisely through the flourishing of multiple musical styles and points of sonic access to the spiritual realm.

Conclusion

This chapter has examined the sharing of musical resources among Pentecostal and Protestant communities in Jamaica and the United States. As I have shown, saints express feelings of both belonging and difference through the songs they sing. They construct and collapse boundaries with varying degrees of intensity, especially as they strive toward the ideals of Christian and cultural authenticity. The expressive contours of church homes are mapped by Pentecostals who borrow from "the world" but nevertheless invest themselves in their local congregations and make music to distinguish themselves from those operating within other national, cultural, and religious frames. It is inevitable that discrepancies between belief and practice will emerge as we look even more closely at the creative mechanisms through which boundaries are crossed within church services and their broader social spheres.

Despite the claims of some churchgoers that Jamaican Pentecostalism is "pure," my experiences in New York City and on Jamaica's northern coast reveal otherwise. As it turns out, purity is not always even a desired attribute among the saints. There is significant overlap in a variety of areas, and this overlap, especially between musics held to be local and foreign, is perhaps what lends Jamaican churches their particular relevance to those who delight in "American" styles and in the shared cultural legacies that give gospel music in Jamaica its particular sound. "Softly and Tenderly" is shared across denominations and is common to both Jamaica and the United States. "Fly Away Home" is shared across denominations but distinct to Jamaica. "One God Apostolic" is distinct to apostolic Pentecostalism and common to both countries. It is, I think, a mistake to regard stasis as the default position from which things subsequently move across borders. On the contrary, religious traditions are better understood as having borrowed from a variety of cultural pools. Worship leaders may opt to sing a traditional Jamaican chorus such as "Fly Away Home" as a way of infusing services with a local flavor. Performing localness carries, however, a certain risk, as musical pieces closest to home may wear the perfume of styles outside the boundaries of "appropriate" Christian practice. Still, if song leaders are worried about the spiritual origins of such choruses, their concerns can sometimes be outweighed by a desire to sing a sacred piece that sounds reminiscent of their island home. As I discuss later, sentiments of nostalgia and cultural nationalism influence the extent to which lines of distinction become meaningful in ritual, particularly as Pentecostals enact cultural and religious identities that stand in some tension with one another.

Strategies of differentiation become clearer if, following Turino (2008), we understand "culture" not as bound to a fixed locale or comprising a total "way of life" but, rather, as "habits of thought and practice . . . that are shared among individuals" (95). For Turino, identity "involves the *partial* selection of habits and attributes used to represent oneself to oneself and to others by oneself and by others" (95). Thus, the perception of a stable Pentecostal identity hinges on the success with which one thinks and practices like members of the Pentecostal "household of faith." This does not mean that Pentecostal, Revivalist, and Rasta identities share no common ground whatsoever. On the contrary, some Pentecostals with whom I spoke consider all of them aspects of "Jamaican culture." They maintain a sense of cultural togetherness with other Jamaicans regardless of religious affiliation. Others prefer to see "culture" as something to be held at arm's length and choose to speak in terms of their "religious" identity as Pentecostal. Still others have told me that being a "true Jamaican" means embracing the Christian faith and rejecting "cultural baggage" that hinders their closeness to God. In all three cases, "home" is bounded by a moving set of walls, the contours of which are contingent on the particular social and musical situation of its "inhabitants." In chapter 2 I will discuss the musical construction of boundaries at Mavey Tabernacle in greater detail.

I have also tried to demonstrate that the sound of Revivalist or Rasta music is sometimes experienced as a positive attribute of a belief system otherwise viewed as spiritually unhealthy. This phenomenological distinction is harder to draw, however, within Pentecostal constructions of secular dancehall culture, which many saints dislike because of its sound as well as its social setting. Chapter 2 explores shifting understandings of worldliness and holiness as they pertain to recording artists who straddle the sacred–profane fence and to the Pentecostal believers who attempt to reposition it. There are thus more controversial forms of overlap that exist between the country's sacred and "profane" practices and ways of being. I gesture here toward the classic sacred–profane dichotomy as expounded first by Émile Durkheim (1915) and later by Mircea Eliade (1959). Whereas Durkheim understood the sacred and profane as the intrinsically social, Eliade (1959) posited them as "two modes of being in the world, two existential situations assumed by man in the course of his history" (14). Eliade's writing leans on the prior work of German theologian Rudolf Otto (1923), who describes *das heilig* (that is, "the sacred" or "the holy") in terms of a transcendent experience of the "wholly Other" that is both awe inspiring and fear inducing. As I discuss throughout this book and especially in chapter 2, Jamaican Pentecostal experiences of holiness can be theorized in social constructivist as well as theological terms. There is, in other words, explanatory value in both Durkheim's and Eliade's writings on the nature of religious experience. It is "both-and," not "either-or," when it comes to applying their foundational theories.

The use of the ska rhythm in Jamaican Pentecostal churches evidences popular culture's influence on musical worship. Pentecostal Christians are also not immune from the sway of other types of religious expression, as is shown by the use of "Fly Away Home." Home and world are thus complicated domains. They are socially imagined but also experientially real, particularly as they are constructed through musical sound. For some, home sounds like Jamaican culture. For others, it transcends Jamaica to reference a Christian church built on a global and biblical foundation. I now turn to more in-depth discussion of how music problematizes moral boundaries between sacred and secular expressive forms—that is, between the practices of baptized Christian believers and those of the "unconverted."

The boundaries I came to expect between Jamaican and North American repertories and styles were at times nonexistent. However, it would be going too far to say that there is no sonic difference at all. Indeed, I found most Jamaican saints to be expert code switchers. They displayed expertise and fluency in styles of gospel music that registered to me as distinctly Jamaican, as well as those that borrowed from church styles more characteristic of the United States. Thus, my experiences on the northern coast revealed quite a bit of common ground. That common ground is characterized by a creolized musical and ritual landscape that defies facile attempts to label it in cultural or racial terms.

CHAPTER 2

Perfecting Holiness
Musical Theologies of Piety and Pleasure

Pentecostals describe holiness as an inward state attained through an ongoing process of spiritual maturation, during which they strive toward "perfection." Perfection, in this sense, does not mean without fault but, rather, suggests dedication to a consecrated Christian walk in which one cultivates a close personal relationship with God. This relationship is maintained through an ascetic lifestyle, obedience to ordained leadership, and diligence in prayer and fasting. Perfecting holiness requires saints to cleanse themselves of "all filthiness of the flesh and spirit" (2 Corinthians 7:1). They are instructed to work toward this goal by abandoning worldly pleasures, which include any non-Christian music associated with the dancehall. Saints discuss the call to holiness in terms of "coming out" from among the world. The coming out process requires adherence to a set of prohibitions that are mostly discussed in terms of the comportment of women and girls, who are required to wear skirts or dresses that extend below the knee and to abstain from cosmetics and jewelry. There are also dress restrictions that pertain to men, including a ban on the wearing of shorts, jewelry (except a wedding ring), and facial hair beyond short mustaches. Hair styles that carry the stigma of Rastafarianism are also forbidden, and new converts who have dreadlocks are required to cut them if they wish to remain a member of the church in good standing.

One way to understand the range of attitudes toward holiness is in terms of a theological continuum. At one end there are liberal Pentecostals who view the dress code as too rigid and legalistic. They claim that holiness standards reflect "man-made" attempts to limit behavior and that they rely on tradition rather than a sound biblical basis. They protest by claiming that standards have become an unnecessary hindrance to the growth of Pentecostal churches. At the other end there are conservative Pentecostals who emphasize biblical mandates to "lift up a standard" (Isaiah 59:19; 62:10) and maintain that one's entry into heaven hinges on toeing the line and avoiding even the "appearance of evil." They sometimes repeat the phrase "holiness or hell" to signal the severity of God's condemnation of sin and to remind themselves and others that perfecting holiness is serious business. The most conservative pastors see great danger in relaxing holiness standards, as the eternal salvation of their flock is believed to be at stake. In the middle of the continuum lies a variety of less extreme stances held by those who stress that holiness is a matter of one's heart and defined only to a limited extent by physical appearance or style. These "middle-of-the-road" Pentecostals agree, however, that holiness should manifest itself through one's daily comportment. Through their dress and behavior, they, too, mark themselves as a pious "cultural cohort" distinct from the world of popular culture.[1] Avoiding the dancehall and its music is one of the ways they hope to accomplish this goal.

Although Pentecostal organizations exert some influence over the way holiness is interpreted, it is the church pastor who establishes the dress code for his or her congregation. Some pastors lament that saints are eager to adopt fashionable practices from abroad. For these pastors, upholding the standard involves maintaining one's Jamaican identity and a critical distance from "foreign" things, especially those associated with the United States. Some women have told me that they dislike stringent dress codes but follow them out of obedience to their pastor. Others adopt the holiness standard wholeheartedly, particularly if their less "modest" apparel is an unwanted reminder of a preconversion lifestyle. Explanations for the dress code hinge on an expressed need to maintain the Pentecostal tradition handed down to them by their mothers and grandmothers. Tradition bearers promote the view that the standard of holiness is a sacrifice to God and a sign of virtue.

The rest of this chapter addresses the role of music in attempts to perfect holiness and construct Pentecostal identity. How is the meaning of holiness and worldliness conveyed through music? To what extent do song lyrics, in particular, reinforce the theologies of piety that are so prevalent in Pentecostal churches? What do piety and pleasure sound like? In what ways does music-making support the drawing of boundaries between these styles of expression? Although holiness is a gendered practice, it includes a gender-neutral requirement that all non-Christian musical genres be kept at arm's length. My experiences at Mercy Tabernacle taught me much about how music fits within a broad set of symbols to position saints in relation to the world. Believers associate piety and holiness with flows of sound across cultural and spiritual boundaries. The regulation of these controversial flows and categories is vital to the formation of Pentecostal identities. Drawing a distinction between the "joy of the Lord" and the "pleasures of the world" is of utmost importance to those who see music as posing a special challenge.

Pleasures of the World

Pentecostals and other Christians sing hymns and choruses supporting the belief that walking the pious path of faith requires one to sacrifice the pleasures of the world. It is worth emphasizing that the reason worldly musics are banned is not that they are felt to be unpleasant. Rather, the fact that they could induce the "wrong kind" of pleasure is what renders them spiritually threatening. Preachers describe the pleasures of the world as a dangerous enticement— nothing but a "trick of the enemy"—that can lure the weak saint down a path of destruction. Living in the path of holiness requires a firm commitment to resist worldly temptations and a willingness to draw spiritual strength from the "joy of the Lord." Choruses such as "Goodbye World," which I discussed earlier, express this idea of being convinced to forsake the world, particularly the "pleasures of sin." Lyrics such as those speak to a prevalent concern with performing and maintaining one's spiritual identity in all aspects of life. The call to "come out from among them" (2 Corinthians 6:17) rests on the notion that a spiritual Promised Land awaits those who willingly leave behind a worldly lifestyle and claim their inheritance as one of God's chosen children. A verse of the following hymn conveys this symbolic meaning.

> I fled from Egypt's bondage; I heard that help was near;
> I cast my care on Jesus, and He dispersed my fear.
> I passed between the billows, walled up on every hand.
> I trusted to my Captain, and sought the promised land.[2]

Once born again, an individual is considered a "babe in Christ" who is newly embarking on the path to holiness or sanctification, as described in the lyrics of the following verse to Leila Morris's hymn "Holiness unto the Lord." Like the previous hymn, this piece equates worldliness with spiritual bondage.

> Called unto holiness, Church of our God.
> Purchase of Jesus, redeemed by His blood;
> Called from the world and its idols to flee.
> Called from the bondage of sin to be free.[3]

A theology of holiness and pleasure was popularized throughout much of Protestant Christendom via the Holiness movement of the late nineteenth century (see Introduction), during which hymn composers used music as a means of spreading the gospel. For example, the hymn, "I Surrender All" includes the following lyrics:

All to Jesus I surrender,
Humbly at His feet I bow;
Worldly pleasures all forsaken,
Take me, Jesus, take me now.

What accounts for the twenty-first-century relevance of these theologies? Why are they able to thrive within Jamaica's contemporary social scene? To answer these questions, we must consider the historical and current representations of Jamaica that shape how the island's Christians view their place in society. I argue that these representations reinforce dichotomous ways of thinking about pleasure and morality and inform perceptions of holiness that endure both within and outside of church settings. While the hymns of yesteryear inform much of the discourse surrounding holiness and worldliness in Pentecostal churches, modern-day happenings also play a major role.

During the late winter and spring months, in particular, Pentecostals are perhaps most vigilant in their safeguarding of holiness standards, as the island's tourist sectors are gearing up for the annual return of college-aged "Spring Breakers." According to the *Gleaner*, "the spring break season usually lasts for six weeks beginning in mid-February and attracts more than 50,000 college students annually" (Clarke 2002). Each year, this contingent of party-hungry foreigners faithfully descends upon Jamaican resorts in and around Negril, Montego Bay, and Ocho Rios, where all-inclusive resorts, such as Sandals, Breezes, Club Ambiance, and Hedonism, cater to pleasure-seeking young adults who crave fun and romance in a tropical locale.

Sensationalistic media portrayals of black Caribbean culture have dramatically influenced outsiders' perceptions of Jamaican men and women, who are typecast as dreadlock-wearing Rastafarians, drug dealers, marijuana addicts, or witch doctors. Notwithstanding the pervasiveness of negative stereotypes, the island remains a hotspot for foreign tourists and "snowbirds," hundreds of thousands of whom descend upon the island's sandy beaches each year in search of a pleasurable departure from their "normal" routines.[4] In a book aptly titled *Consuming the Caribbean*, Mimi Sheller highlights a perception of exotic difference that is fueled by advertising campaigns, tourist brochures, and word of mouth. She writes, "The deep layering and reiteration of such representations of the Caribbean tends to reinforce an imaginary geography in which it becomes a carnivalesque site for hedonistic consumption of illicit substances (raunchy dancing, sex with 'black' or 'mulatto' others, smoking ganja)" (2003, 165). Jamaica is thus inscribed as a mysterious "paradise" of escape where moral or behavioral boundaries can be safely transgressed by those hoping, like the fictional Stella, to "get their groove back."[5] Such fantastical narratives also "reflect a long history of the inscription of corruption onto the [Caribbean's] landscapes and inhabitants" (Sheller 2003, 166).

While Jamaican news reports celebrated tourism as a boon to the local economy, some commentators gave voice to Christians' concerns that vacationers from the United States were having a negative moral effect on Jamaican society.[6] The previous year, an article in the *Gleaner* had commented on the history of "lewd and excessive conduct" among visiting Spring Breakers who reportedly "stripped naked and used their tongues to clean whip cream [sic] from each other's bodies, while a large crowd cheered them on at a popular establishment in Montego Bay" (Clarke 2002). Following a great deal of public complaint, the Jamaica Tourist Board and the Jamaica Hotel and Tourist Association issued a code of conduct discouraging sexually explicit acts among patrons and threatening to take severe actions against establishments that allowed them. Public discourses concerning worldly and holy expressive behavior are prevalent in print media. Another local paper, the *Western Mirror*, placed an article announcing the opening of a new adult nightclub, Pleasure Dome, adjacent to a poem titled "Christianity versus Heathenism," which called for the espousal of a holier, more biblically based lifestyle among Jamaica's citizens. The journalistic juxtaposition of these two pieces indexes for me a moral dichotomy that is particularly discernible among Jamaica's Christians and also present within the broader society. My sense of a pervasive dichotomy between the church and the world was reinforced by Pentecostals' constructions of the dancehall and its worldly music as oppositional to the mores of the holy Christian church. These boundary-making practices help Pentecostals to pinpoint a common band of enemies and to "perceive themselves as a community, articulating 'who we are not' as much as 'who we are'" (Gidal 2016, 15).

Pastor Philips and the Call to Transformation

Sharp banging sounds pierced the air as I roamed the dusty town of Liliput. The sounds grew louder as I climbed the hill to Mercy Tabernacle Apostolic Church. It was not my first trip here, but on this Saturday afternoon I felt impelled to put some pep in my step, anticipating that an actual person and not just an empty building would be there to greet me. As I approached the building, I noticed a man working off to the side, his hammer pounding out a steady rhythm. Despite the humidity, he wore a white cotton shirt, the long sleeves of which were rolled up just enough to reveal thin but muscular arms covered with sweat. A handful of others were toiling away inside. I could hear them discussing the proper alignment of pews for the next day's service. "Praise the Lord!" I offered, extending the traditional apostolic Pentecostal greeting in between hammer blows. The man glanced at me but continued his work until I drew close enough for him to ascertain that I was a stranger. Surmising that he was the pastor of Mercy Tabernacle, I rambled through an explanation of my purpose: I was from the United States, visiting Jamaica and hoping to find a Pentecostal church in the area. Establishing my credentials as a believer would become a common strategy in the field—a way of performing belonging that gave me access to the intimate and informal corners of church life. I added that I was a member of an apostolic Pentecostal church in New York. He raised an eyebrow. "Who's your pastor?" he shot back, as though needing verification of my status before granting me the privilege of a warmer tone. I understood this as a test, and I wanted to pass with flying colors by showing a willingness to walk the path of Pentecostal holiness.

For Pentecostals, acknowledging one's pastor is not merely a way of identifying a symbolic figurehead. Rather, it reflects an understanding of the importance of being accountable to a church family. It constitutes a recognition on the part of the believer that there must be a spiritual leader responsible for "watching over" one's soul. Most important, it signals a willingness to work on behalf of the church and to submit to whatever standard of holiness its leader requires. "My pastor's name is Tommy Seals," I reported, "He's a suffragan bishop in the Pentecostal Assemblies of the World." With this last tidbit of information, I hoped to account for any unfamiliarity this pastor might have expressed toward the name I had dropped. The extra detail was, I felt, necessary because Mercy Tabernacle was in a different organization, the United Pentecostal Church (UPC), which was large enough by itself to make name familiarity a rare treat. I also expected that this man, who finally introduced himself as Pastor Philips, would recognize the PAW as an organization whose members shared doctrinal beliefs and holiness standards with the UPC. At this point, Pastor Philips began to open up, asking me how I liked Jamaica so far and how long I would be staying. We conversed for a few minutes longer, and after confirming the start time for Sunday service and midweek Bible study, I headed back down the hill, listening to the hammering that had resumed and whistling a tune to its steady pulse.

Pentecostal pastors uphold standards of holiness that apply to just about every aspect of saints' lives. In particular, they require congregants to avoid the supposed trappings of "worldly" pleasure, while placing a premium on lively styles of musical worship. To embrace a holy lifestyle is to abide by biblical teachings and to reject the ways of "the world," which include drug and alcohol consumption, profanity, extramarital sex, and "immodest" apparel. This all-encompassing standard of holiness also mandates that saints eschew commercial popular musics such as dancehall and reggae, which some Jamaicans describe as sonic cultural icons of their island nation. Pentecostals also use other musics to express Jamaican pride and emphasize their cultural distinctiveness. Amid steady flows of music from the United States, they celebrate their cultural identities by infusing their church music with indigenous stylistic characteristics. However, they are instructed to maintain a healthy distance from commercial dancehall music, which is even more likely than "American" genres to be considered worldly and inappropriate.

Pentecostal pastors see it as their duty to protect their flock from wolves in sheep's clothing. They welcome visitors but also wish to avoid unnecessary disruptions to social and spiritual flow within their congregations. My brief introductory meeting with Pastor Philips is thus noteworthy for several reasons. It allowed me to verbalize an awareness of church traditions and to speak the language of belonging (for example, "Praise the Lord!"). It also enabled him to assess how I might fit in as a saint under "watch care" at Mercy Tabernacle. Watch care status is typically granted to churchgoers who seek temporary pastoral "covering" while away from their home congregation. With regard to standards of holiness, outward appearances are not everything, but they still matter. In fact, Pentecostals assert that there should be both visible and audible evidence that an individual is filled with the Holy Spirit.[7] With this in mind, I had been careful to dress for the occasion, knowing that my collared shirt, long pants, and clean-shaven face would register as markers of church membership. I also had the opportunity to affirm my membership in a broad Pentecostal "household of faith." My role as an ethnomusicologist was less relevant to establishing rapport, so I opted to wait until later to explain that aspect of my identity.

Over the course of three months, I got to know Pastor Philips and his family well. Pastor Philips carried himself with sternness, if not shyness, much of the time. Sister Philips's rosy personality was conducive to making strangers feel at home, and so she served as leader of the Sunday school. She had a special gift for working with children, but I too benefited from her buoyant demeanor, which contrasted with the stoicism Pastor Philips displayed. They had been married for seventeen years and were raising two children, Paul, age fifteen, and Pamela, age twelve. Paul played drums during most services but was itching to play for bigger audiences. Pamela was timid and usually sat near the front left side of the sanctuary, except when the Spirit touched her and she found herself weeping with outstretched arms in the center aisle. Pastor and Sister Philips were working hard to build a healthy family, and they sometimes expressed concern that their children would be lured away by worldly temptations. Mercy Tabernacle, as they saw it, was a safe haven, one Pastor Philips hoped would protect them from repeating the "mistakes" of his youth. Pastor Philips had no qualms about telling others how God had saved him from "a life of fornication." As a younger man, he'd lived with a woman to whom he was not married. He seemed to blame some of his youthful "mistakes" on his Baptist upbringing, which he claimed had not instilled in him a love for holiness. But even as a child he could feel a certain "conviction." Upon realizing his call to the pastorate, Pastor Philips vowed to emphasize the importance of pleasing God, which meant adhering to a lifestyle of separation from earthly pleasures.

On several occasions, I spoke with Pastor Philips about the holy–worldly dichotomy as it related to his commitment to evangelism. He used the word "commitment" when speaking of his responsibility to please God and surrender to divine will rather than pursue career goals that might yield greater financial reward or personal pleasure. "I never wanted to pastor," he once admitted. "The most important thing is for people outside the church to get saved. We spend too much time sitting down *inside* the church." Noticing that there were no Pentecostal churches in Liliput, he originally came to the area with the hope simply to reach lost souls by teaching and preaching the Word of God. During one early prayer meeting in 1998, when a lady was filled with the Holy Spirit, Pastor Philips became inspired to continue his work. A man who lived nearby in a small, one-room house, donated the church land. "I feel God sent you here," the man had declared, "so I'm gonna give you this land." Pastor Philips concluded that it was God's will for Mercy Tabernacle to be established in its current locale. The biggest source of frustration for Pastor Philips is that he lacks the money to "go out" and preach like he wants to. He prays for the means to purchase a truck so that he can carry the Christian message to the people, "because there are a lot of areas that need to hear the gospel."

Pastor Philips also expresses discontent with his own church members, whose level of commitment is not always what he expects. During one service, Pastor Philips interrupted the praise and worship to scold the saints for displaying a lack of enthusiasm in their singing. "I know you might be tired, but the Lord deserves our worship. Come on, everybody, let's worship!" His voice became gravelly as he felt the leading of the Holy Spirit. He launched into a song about "dry bones," drawing from an Old Testament parable in Ezekiel, chapter 37. "These dry bones must live!" he yelled and sang simultaneously. The instrumentalists—a bassist, keyboardist, and drummer—started an up-tempo groove, and the congregants stood and joined in, feeding off Pastor Philips's excitement. I normally would have sung along, but this piece was unfamiliar to me. I read the lips of those near me, straining to piece together the lyrics, which consisted of only two short phrases: "Ye dry bones, hear the words of the Lord. Rise, stand up on your feet, and move."

As this musical worship grew more intense, the vocalizations were transformed from words into unintelligible utterances and ecstatic cries as saints fell under the influence of the Spirit. Next came a moment of ritual uncertainty that Pentecostals have learned to anticipate. Will this chapter of the service uneventfully draw to a close? Or will the Holy Spirit "step in" and enliven the atmosphere in such a way that the saints are compelled to keep worshipping? While the organist and drummer decrescendo in an effort to bring the song to its final note, the saints lift their hands and release shouts of praise, suggesting that they are unaware, perhaps blissfully so, of the instrumentalists' sonic clues. Pastor Philips did not help matters. He egged on the saints, segueing into another lively piece, the lyrics of which resemble the traditional African American gospel song, "You Got to Move."

> You got to move. You got to move.
> When God gets ready, you got to move.
> You may be rich; you may be poor.
> You may be high; you may be low.
> When God gets ready, you got to move.

Judging from the heightened emotional atmosphere, God had indeed gotten ready, as what had started as a ho-hum affair quickly became a collective dance of deliverance. Some rushed toward the altar at the front of the sanctuary, while others did a celebratory dance in the pews where they sat.

Pastor and Sister Philips planned services to be this way. "We want transformation, not simply information," Sister Philips rhymed. She and her husband understood the power of music and took advantage of its role in facilitating transcendent experiences. The goal was always to experience the power and presence of the Holy Spirit, a process the saints refer to as "getting anointed." As the dancing subsided, Pastor Philips offered some explanatory remarks on what had taken place: "When I worship God, that's when I get anointed. I get the Holy Ghost connection." And for the unsaved skeptics presumably in attendance, he added, "It's not the music; it's the Holy Ghost! It's not the keyboards; it's the Holy Ghost! It's not the drums; it's the Holy Ghost!" The Spirit's manifestation is not limited to ritual settings, he assured the congregants. "Some only can sing and dance on Sunday, but let me tell you something, I dance in my bedroom!" The task of the saint, he taught, is to be in the proper spiritual mindset to worship God when he "gets ready," as the song suggests. By participating in dozens of services at Mercy Tabernacle, I gained insight into how the saints express themselves when under the influence of the Holy Spirit. I also learned a great deal by talking to church members outside of service.

Brother and Sister Crooks answered a series of questions about how they "came out of the world" and into the church and about how their lifestyle was transformed thereafter. "Me used to be a bad man," Brother Crooks noted, "stealing, beating up people—spending time in jail." He had been invited to church on several occasions but had always scoffed that he wanted nothing to do with church and church people. During one four-year stint in jail, he felt a touch from God while singing "Satan don't hold me back," a song he had heard some church folks render during a street meeting. While singing, his Rasta cellmate began "makin' a lotta fuss," but Brother Crooks sang on until he found himself outstretched on his bed in a crucified position with arms out and legs straight unable to move for several minutes. Still, upon getting released from jail, he did not convert. His girlfriend, Giselle, got pregnant and they moved from MoBay to Liliput. A friend of Giselle's invited them both to church. Giselle consented, however. She had already been hearing the services from her back porch. "I could hear them, but only the singing. Then they would start screaming and making a lot of noise. So one day, I decided to go see what goes on up there, to see why there's all that screaming and noise. So I went one Sunday. The next Thursday, a visiting minister preached during a revival, and I got the Holy Ghost." Giselle wanted desperately for her boyfriend to be saved. He had taken one positive step by agreeing to marry so that they would not be "living in sin," but he adamantly refused to come to church. One day she pleaded, "Do it for my sake!" It took one year, but he finally relented and agreed to attend Mercy Tabernacle in February 2000. He sat in the back, planning to remain uninvolved in the service; but the Holy Spirit got hold of him and had him pounding the pew, confessing his sins, and jumping in the aisle. A couple of months later, he was filled with the Spirit, and he has been at Mercy Tabernacle ever since. Such testimonies of transformation are commonplace among the saints.

Gendered Discourses of Sin and Pleasure

"Praise the Lord, Brother!" I smiled and nodded to return the greeting, but I could not disguise the puzzled look in my eyes as I searched the woman's face and my memory trying to recall how and where we'd met. Sympathetic to my uncertainty, she reintroduced herself as Sister Wright from Mercy Tabernacle Apostolic Church. This was a pleasant surprise. Having just arrived at the Montego Bay hospital, due to an unfortunate stumble by one of my hosts' elderly guests, I had not expected to encounter anyone from the Liliput congregation. Sister Wright sang in Mercy Tabernacle's choir and was hoping to minister with the group at one of the sister churches in MoBay later that evening. Her plans were now in jeopardy, she explained, because her doctor's appointment had been rescheduled for a later hour. As we waited, I took advantage of the opportunity to ask Sister Wright about her views concerning holiness. We discussed standards for men and women, the role of marriage, the challenges she faced raising teenagers, the factors that led to her conversion to Pentecostalism, the worship services at Mercy Tabernacle, and her favorite kinds of music.

Born into a Pentecostal household, Sister Wright works hard to instill biblical values in her two teenaged children. She feels that sexual temptation is a tremendous obstacle for young people, and she finds raising her children and keeping them committed to a holy lifestyle to be an arduous task. Sister Wright values the institution of marriage and sees it as a desirable alternative to promiscuity for youth who lack the self-control necessary to "contain." She explained to me that young folk tend to covet the attention and gifts others receive from boyfriends or girlfriends and are enticed by the contemporary hairstyles and jewelry of their peers. It is fitting that our conversation took place in a hospital. Just as doctors urge the sick to come to hospitals for treatment, Sister Wright described Mercy Tabernacle and other Pentecostal churches as healing stations where the "sin-sick soul" may find relief and be placed on a path to holy living. She explained that she used to attend the large "mother church" in Montego Bay where Pastor Philips had served as an associate minister. In 1997, when Pastor Philips was sent to Liliput to start up a new church, Sister Wright and her husband relocated to the area and decided to take up membership at Mercy Tabernacle.

Sister Wright also spoke to me at length about the temptations of "worldly music," which she defined as "the reggae beat." She explained, "Sometimes you hear it [on a sound system] and you want to start moving. [*Imitates secular dance moves.*] And the children have it hard because the bus driver and the car driver could play music loud, and you can't ask them to turn it down!" When I asked her about the kinds of *gospel* music she dislikes, she responded, "Calypso . . . I don't like the calypso." By this, she referred to the genre known as "gospel reggae," which is enormously popular among young Pentecostals but critiqued by elders because of its dancehall-influenced characteristics. Given the fact that dress codes seem more prohibitive for women than for men, I asked Sister Wright whether she felt holiness standards make it harder for girls than boys to stay committed to the church. "No, it's the same," she insisted, "because boys have more peer pressure to get sexually involved." The disproportionately large number of men in church leadership roles no doubt reflects a long-standing gender bias in the broader society. However, as Austin-Broos suggests, the "assertion of a patriarchal status [through a leadership role] mitigates the inevitable denial of [other] signs of masculinity" (1997, 123). I would add that musical participation, particularly instrumental performance, is also a highly significant way through which Pentecostal men derive a sense of empowerment, a vehicle for self-expression, and a vital means of male bonding within these social and religious circles.

Sunday morning congregations at Mercy Tabernacle average about seventy-five women and twelve men. The "shortage of men" is one of Pastor Philips's most pressing concerns, and he expressed plans to ask the saints to pray more fervently for an increase in their numbers. "We're gonna pray for thirty men," he declared, "and when we get thirty men, we'll pray and ask God for another thirty men." I asked him to tell me why women are the strong majority in most Pentecostal churches. His response echoed what I had heard from countless Pentecostals: "Men have a lot of power," he answered, "and if they take charge and become the leaders God want[s] them to be, the devil knows he has no chance. That's why he fights men very strongly." Pastor Philips also believes that worldly temptations are one of the spiritual weapons used against men to keep them away from the church. "So the church really need[s] to pray," he added. "A lot of men you see are really timid and they just let the women rule them. And you see the men in the football field or around the TV and in the sound system and smoking ganja, so you can see that they need deliverance. And this is what the church need[s] to realize, that the devil is really fighting men." Some months later, after leaving Liliput and reflecting on my interview with Pastor Philips, I regretted not having asked him to elaborate on how timid men "let the women rule them." I assume he was critiquing men's refusal to stand up and take responsibility for their families' economic and spiritual well-being. Both women and men made similar comments to me during my fieldwork. The general consensus was that women are more likely to have a "heart toward God," accounting for their preponderance in churches. Such remarks corroborate those of a man Austin-Broos interviewed: "Woman is more firm to the gospel. She is a more humble spirit. Men want to get material thing. The Spirit cyan work wid dem so well" [The Spirit can't work with them so well] (1997, 127).

Pastor Philips's explanation of gender imbalance relies on an essentialist notion of gender identity that is problematic. There are, however, sociological assessments of the situation that, while imperfect, offer further insight. For example, Austin-Broos (1997) argues that women outnumber men in Jamaican Pentecostal churches largely because the secular symbols of womanhood in the broader society do not clash as harshly with Pentecostal holiness standards as do symbols of masculinity, such as drinking alcohol, gambling, and engaging in sex outside of marriage. These activities are considered off limits for Pentecostal saints but presumably pose little temptation for women, who, unlike men, are socialized not to partake in them. As Austin Broos explains, "The moral signs indicative of being a clean vessel ... bear on why [Pentecostal] practitioners are more often women than men. While childbearing more than sexuality itself is central to definitions of femininity, it is the persona of sexual practitioner that is far more central to Jamaican men" (123). Notwithstanding the logic of Austin-Broos's analysis, it seems to map a feminine–masculine gender binary onto the holiness–worldliness dichotomy in a way that strikes me as too facile. Moreover, Jamaican Pentecostal churches are not immune from heteronormative patterns of thought and behavior, which privilege "manly" ways of moving and sounding and rely heavily on what Alisha Jones (2015a, 216) refers to as "an unstated but assumed masculine ideal." Pentecostals rejoice when men who join their fold are unashamed to worship freely and without inhibition. But a man whose movements become too "flamboyant" risks arousing suspicions of "unnatural" sexual behavior, especially if the man seems just a bit *too* holy to be bothered by the (hetero)sexual temptations that entice "normal" men, even those who are Spirit-filled. In Jamaican churches, as in the African American churches Jones discusses, perceptions of an ideal masculinity fuel "forms of misogyny in which congregants and gospel music patrons police femininity that is performed in male bodies" (234).

What I find equally remarkable about gender boundaries in Jamaican Pentecostal churches is the fact that gospel music-making plays such an influential role in how these boundaries are not only maintained but also transcended, as I discuss in chapter 3, during acts of worship. Pentecostals cite examples of music-making to validate their perceptions of gender difference, as though the ways women and men sing and dance confirm that they "just are" a certain way. As we have seen, such notions are by no means unique to nonmusical context. As Martin Stokes points out, these "naturalized" boundary-making discourses and practices pervade all aspects of a social and political order, including musical performance. It is through music, he argues, that "men learn to be gentlemen and women to be gentlewomen." Speaking to the taken-for-granted quality of gender boundaries, Stokes thus emphasizes the role of music in solidifying perceptions of male and female difference. He writes, "The boundaries which separate male and female and assign to each proper social practices are as 'natural' as the boundaries which separate one community from another. Musical practices are no exception—it is as 'natural' that men will make better trumpeters as it is 'natural' that women will make better harpists. Musical performance is often the principle means by which appropriate gender behaviour is taught and socialized" (1994, 22).

Dancing around Dancehall

Commercial popular genres influence the musical worship of Jamaica's Pentecostal churches in profound ways. This is, in part, because music is such an efficient conveyor of theological meaning, as well as a sonic marker of the shifting boundaries between holiness and worldliness. The commercial musical genres of the dance club are not generally believed to possess the same levels of inherent spiritual potency as the ritual musics of *Kumina* and Rastafarianism. Dancehall music is, however, seen as highly problematic, largely because of its lyrical associations with violence, immodest dress, and sexual wantonness. Dancehall lyrics are delivered with a driving syncopated rhythmic accompaniment that Pentecostals tend to interpret as an audible symbol of worldliness or, in some cases, a scourge on Jamaica's national soundscape. Frustrated by the apparent ubiquity of dancehall sounds, church leaders set strict guidelines on the kinds of music they permit their members to enjoy. Most Pentecostals learn these guidelines concerning the kinds of music acceptable for worship services and home listening, and they strive to adhere to the holy, consecrated standard of living advocated by church leaders.[8]

It is not uncommon for Pastor Philips to attribute the sparse attendance at an evening prayer meeting to secular distractions. "If there was some dancehall going on tonight, you could not find room," he declares. "So we have to know Satan is busy." Remarks such as these portray the dancehall as the devil's playground and speak to church leaders' deep concerns about the allure of nightclubs and the activities taking place within them. People would flock to see a dancehall artist, he explains, but only a few come to church and follow the Bible's mandate to "delight yourself in the Lord" (Psalm 37:4). Whereas Pastor Philips views church music as a sacred activity that both God and humans enjoy, he casts dancehall music as a harmful temptation that stokes the wrong *kind* of pleasure. He thus situates the "worldly" pleasure of dancehall music in opposition to the "holy" pleasure of God. This rhetorical move also calls to mind Martin Stokes's observation on music's social meaningfulness. Music, he argues, "provides means by which people recognize identities and places, and the boundaries which separate them" (1994, 5). During evening services at Mercy Tabernacle, I could often discern the pounding of a bass drum emanating from some distant sound system, a ubiquitous reminder of the expressive power and influence of secular dancehall culture.

Anthropologist Norman Stolzoff (2000) recognizes dancehall as a phenomenon that is both global and also deeply historical, having been a major force in Jamaica's musico-social landscape for decades.[9] As Stolzoff points out, dancehall music is a cultural product that is central to Jamaican society and relevant to the lives of all classes and races of people, in large part because people "define themselves in relation to it" (6). Middle- and upper-class Jamaicans (commonly referred to as "uptown" people) generally oppose dancehall and view it as a sign of cultural and moral depravity, which they associate with the "downtown" members of the black lower class. According to Stolzoff, downtown people see dancehall as an important means of cultural expression and a source of potential resistance. He states that it "is a symbol of pride in the ghetto, in black identity, and of African culture." For youth in particular, dancehall is a means of "ideologically challeng[ing] the hegemony of the ruling classes and state apparatuses," marking a "charged cultural border between people of different races and class levels" (6). Although this conceptual distinction between uptown and downtown is helpful in understanding how expressive culture indexes race and class, it also seems to reify "the black lower class," all of whom presumably embrace secular dancehall culture and oppose "middle and upper class" conceptions of morality and respectability. Like uptown people, Pentecostals who hail from "the black lower class" describe dancehall as "boom-boom music" or "obnoxious noise" and see it as a threat to their quality of life. Stolzoff deserves credit for emphasizing that the support for dancehall among lower class blacks is neither unanimous nor without contradiction. "Culture and ideology," he argues,

> are not congruent with the divisions of a particular social structure. For example, not all members of the middle class feel the same way about dancehall or other controversial cultural practices. And particular people are not necessarily consistent in the viewpoints they espouse or in the practices they perform. In this sense, their interpretations and actions depend on the context in which they find themselves. (231–32)

Moreover, just as dancehalls provide the means to create "cultural counterworlds," Pentecostal churches serve as platforms for the musical and bodily articulation of Christian(ized) values that both contest and overlap with a dancehall aesthetic. This dual role prompts Robert Beckford to point out that while dancehalls and Pentecostal churches may appear to be antithetical, "both reworked African and African American materials (music and religion) to produce distinctive Jamaican inflections in music and worship respectively" (2006, 45). These "Jamaican inflections" become particularly powerful for Jamaicans who have emigrated and seek to reassert their cultural identities in a foreign land. Thus, Beckford notes that the dancehall and the church hall "may appear diametrically opposed. . . . However, in reality . . . both were drawn together by the common cultural and social milieu of their patrons. Moreover, when transported to Britain, both became important countercultural spaces and healing communities seeking ways to heal minds and bodies, far away from home and in a hostile environment" (44). Still, it is important to note that island-based church leaders such as Pastor Philips complain that the proximity of dancehall sounds produces a dangerous temptation for teens and young adults, who are challenged to adhere to acceptable forms of musical expression in the midst of what is described to them as a "hostile" sonic and social environment. "We're fasting for revival in Jamaica," Pastor Philips once announced. "Every dancehall must be shut down!" Despite the anti-dancehall rhetoric, Pentecostal worship is never immune from the influence of Jamaica's soundscape, and this includes the sound of dancehall reggae played in nearby clubs.

The gospel music rendered at Mercy Tabernacle provided me with invaluable insight into embodied negotiations of holy and worldly styles. These negotiations frequently involve the church's youth. Near the conclusion of one service, a group of teen congregants began singing the traditional Jamaican chorus "Jesus Name So Sweet" as others stood at the altar seeking the infilling of the Holy Spirit. The teens began with a traditional rendition of the lyrics but then, feeling less inhibited since the service was nearly over, they switched into a patois version repopularized in Jamaica through a reggae-styled recording of the piece by African American gospel singer Donnie McClurkin. McClurkin includes a well-known patois refrain: "Every rock me rock upon Jesus, Jesus name so sweet!" Although this phrase does not translate easily into "standard" English, churchgoers explained to me that the repetition of the word "rock" and the idea of rocking "upon Jesus" suggest the idea of "movement" with Jesus—literally through holy dancing, metaphorically through life's ups and downs. The chorus thus celebrates the "sweetness" of Jesus, who serves not only as a spiritual dancing partner during collective praise but also as a guide and comforter amid the "rocky" road of everyday life. This idea of movement is underscored by the chorus's additional patois refrains, which, although not performed by McClur-kin, are sometimes sung in Jamaican "country churches."

Me slip and me slide and me rock upon Jesus.
Jesus name so sweet.
Me dilly and me dally and me rock upon Jesus.
Jesus name so sweet.

In some cases, Pentecostals take issue with both the musical style and the use of Jamaican patois in traditional choruses such as this. Although preachers do occasionally switch into patois during sermons, hymns and choruses are nearly always sung in standard English, which is viewed as the more respectable lan-guage within Jamaican society. The tendency to steer clear of Jamaican patois in sung expression may indicate a desire to avoid the social stigma historically attached to Pentecostal musical and bodily expressions.

"Jesus Name So Sweet" is normally performed with a rhythmic feel less identified with 1970s-style reggae or with the contemporary dancehall. How-ever, in this case the instrumentalists at Mercy Tabernacle picked up on the teens' linguistic shift and adjusted their rhythmic groove to resemble McClur-kin's dancehall reggae accompaniment, which I discuss further in chapter 5. Pastor Philips, who already had been trying for the past ten minutes to calm things down and stop the musicians from playing so he could dismiss service with prayer, gestured more urgently for the musicians to stop. "Okay, okay," he admonished, "We're getting carried away. Let's stick to the original. We want the Holy Ghost to always be in control." By this time, several Spirit infillings or refillings had already taken place, and most congregants were enjoying the celebratory aspects of Pentecostal praise. Nevertheless, Pastor Philips felt that the musical style of the chorus had begun to get too worldly. The boundary of appropriate church music needed to be monitored all the more vigilantly as saints "rejoiced in the Lord." For Pastor Philips and those who share his out-look, a shift into worldly sounds accompanies entry into a realm of sexual sug-gestiveness embodied within the dancehall but consciously avoided within Pentecostal churches. A disdain for dancehall events is commonly expressed by those who had frequented them before getting saved. For some men, the dancehall represents an ever-present threat capable of wooing them back into a lifestyle they have renounced. This perceived threat no doubt contributes to the stricter dress guidelines pertaining to women's dress. Women's bodies are masked to reinforce the aesthetic boundary between the church, where tight clothing, makeup, and jewelry are seldom permitted, and dancehalls, where such items are the norm and an assertive femininity is accentuated.

Policing the boundary between worldliness and holiness is one of the most difficult challenges Pentecostal leaders face in trying to keep young people from falling away from the church, a process known as "backsliding." Mercy Tabernacle's minister of music also expressed to me concerns about the youth. At age forty-one, Eric has learned much from what he calls his "mistakes of the past," and he now works with the church's teens, giving them music lessons and encouraging them to stay faithful to God. Eric feels that he and other leaders have a crucial responsibility to help prevent the youth from yielding to worldly temptations and becoming enmeshed in dancehall culture.[10] After one church service, I heard a young bassist start to play a line from a popular dancehall piece, after which Eric rebuked him: "Never play that in the church!" Like other church musicians, the bassist viewed the moments after service dismissal as a time for musical play. But Eric was concerned to maintain the sanctity of the church's ritual setting, regardless of whether a service was taking place there at that moment.

Eric spoke to me about the significance of generational differences within Pentecostal churches as they relate to the need for young people to find an appropriate means of musical self-expression.

M: Do you think music helps to keep young people in the church?

E: That's one of the things the church needs to do. Young people—even in the young people's choir, 'cause we have two choirs here—they want to sing music they can't sing, because, you know, they not ready for it.

M: You mean the young people's choir isn't ready? Or the congregation?

E: The congregation—it's the leadership. You know, the young people waan [want to] sing the Donnie McClurkin, the—

M: Kirk Franklin?

E: Yes! And the church people they not ready for that kind of thing. So what we need to do is try to meet the young people halfway. Not to give up too much, but you know, come halfway. A lot of kids come to church and the music help[s] them express themselves. You know, the beat is fast and they can dance and move. But sometimes they say, well, "In the church me cyaan express myself, so me nah stayin' in de church. Me goin' to the dancehall where I can express myself." ["In the church, I can't express myself, so I'm not staying in the church. I'm going to the dancehall where I can express myself."]

M: So right now do you think the church is succeeding? Is music helping to stop young people from backsliding?

E: Sometimes. But we still have to do some more work to meet them halfway. It's goin' take time, because they like to sing—like the choir, they wanna sing this song, "Shake Your Booty for Jesus" by Beenie Man.

I later discovered that Eric was referring to "Gospel Time," the opening song on Beenie Man's 1999 recording, *The Doctor*. Among Beenie Man's recordings, "Gospel Time" is unique in that it juxtaposes traditional church choruses against a hip-hop groove and a dancehall vocal style, creating a stylistic dissonance between the sacred and the profane, the church and the dance club. The introduction to "Gospel Time" is a slow gospel rendition of "Praise Him" in triadic harmony, after which the rhythmicized chorus is sung.

> Move to the left in the name of Jesus.
> Move to the left in the name of the Lord.
> Shake that booty that Jesus gave you.
> Shake that booty in the name of the Lord.

These lyrics are interpolated between classic gospel choruses, such as "Everybody Has to Know," "He's So Real to Me," and "Down by the Riverside." But what is the real problem with Beenie Man's lyrics? Given that the saints place a premium on bodily praise, which inevitably involves a fair amount of "booty" shaking, what's the problem with enjoining listeners to do so? Pentecostal churchgoers to whom I spoke find Beenie Man's use of the word "booty" jarring. Some are offended by what registers as a deliberately irreverent attempt to make money and get a laugh at the expense of true Christians. In the words of one saint, Beenie Man "was trying to create some fuss" by releasing the song. Although Beenie Man's lyrics are gender neutral, I believe the "booty" to which Beenie Man refers registers as that of a woman; and the performer exploits notions of the irresistible, seductive, and dangerous female body. In reference to women who frequent dance clubs, men sometimes steal a bit of wordplay from gospel artist Lester Lewis, who once quipped, "People call dem Kentucky." Punning on the famous fried chicken franchise, Kentucky Fried Chicken, he added, "All you see is breasts, hips and legs" (Jebbinson 2006).

Eric's struggle to keep Mercy Tabernacle's youth engaged in the church through music is reminiscent of a generational tension discussed by anthropologist John L. Jackson (1998), who recounts a humorous argument that broke out between three women in his "rather conservative congregation" in Brooklyn, New York. Sister Daley, Sister Rosalind, and Sister Madeline have been tasked with drawing more youth into the church, but they disagree about where to draw the boundaries of appropriate music.

> "Young folk need to be in the church," says Sister Daley, a twenty-seven-year-old Jamaican-born nurse.... "They aren't here, and we got to bring them in.... Give them good music and a welcoming spirit, and they will come."
>
> "The church has good music," responds Sister Rosalind, who has been a deaconess in the church for over twenty-five years. "You are talkin' bout that drum-

ming, drumming and all that worldly sounding music. Them things promote a certain kind of feeling in the church that doesn't lead to understanding the serenity of God."

"I'm not trying to say that we got to have only an organ in the sanctuary," Sister Madeline, a newly baptized member from Trinidad, chimes in. "We just can't be bringin' all that bup, bup, bup, into God's house. Once you start wit de tump, tump, tump, your mind move from God and your head start moving to the beat—then your backside sure to follow. Save all dat fa' Saturday night. Dis here ain't no nightclub to be wiggling, wigglin' ya bamsy."

"You can move your backside to the lord, though," is Sister Daley's quick response. "King David's Psalms tells us to play all our instruments to the glory of the lord. And summa y'all should be tankful you still got bamsies ta wiggle." (175)

The concerns raised by Sister Rosalind and Sister Madeline mirror those expressed by Eric at Mercy Tabernacle. He recognizes that music can be an effective tool, particularly for youth who enjoy lively songs in which "the beat is fast and they can dance and move." But Beenie Man's "Gospel Time" is, for Eric, a bridge too far. It connects with young people but crosses the line by compromising the standard of musical holiness church elders demanded. But what really jumps out at me from Jackson's ethnographic script is the fact that at least two of the three women, Sister Daley and Sister Madeline, are from the Caribbean. Jackson does not mention Sister Rosalind's ethnicity, but we nevertheless get a sense that this is a Brooklyn church not unlike Emmanuel Temple, where, as I discuss in chapter 1, African American and Anglophone Caribbean stylistic preferences are negotiated on a regular basis. Without additional information, we can only speculate about whether Sister Daley's Jamaican background shapes her more liberal stance toward musical beats and dancing bodies in church. Perhaps of greater relevance is the generation gap between her and Sister Rosalind, who has served in a position of church leadership for almost as long as Sister Daley has been alive. The women's conversation helps to further illustrate how anxieties concerning the boundaries of musical propriety are expressed among churchgoers not only in the Caribbean but also throughout its diaspora. Moreover, it shows that debates about the usefulness of "worldly sounding music" have to do with much more than sound. They reflect an apprehensiveness toward "a certain kind of feeling," as discourses of gendered embodiment shape the religious identities Christians negotiate in relation to experiences of musical and sexual pleasure.

Pentecostal critiques of Beenie Man's "Gospel Time" are also constructed with awareness of religious sentiments deemed representative of a "truer" and more authentic divine experience. Eric noted, "If you look at the lyrics, they don't really say anything of substance. A lot of the new songs [are] like that. Young people like to sing them, but they don't really speak of a true experience, like as in 'How Great Thou Art'—where you just look outside at the trees and the grass and say how great God is. The older songs tell of a true experience." However, the lyrics are perhaps less flawed than the messenger, whose oeuvre is notoriously tinged with a "slackness" viewed as anathema within Christian circles. In this context, "slackness" refers to a sexually explicit subgenre of dancehall music. As Norman Stolzoff explains, slackness performers "are fully committed to the hedonistic path of individualism, sexual desire, and material consumption. In turn, the audience sees these artists as the very embodiment of these qualities" (2000, 163).

Stolzoff also details the rise of "conscious" lyrics in the early 1990s by dancehall artists reacting to an abundance of slackness. In some cases, artists' conversion experiences result in a commitment to "cleaner" lyrics that focus on critical social commentary rather than the pleasures of promiscuity or the dangers of gun warfare. By the middle of the decade, talk of a "Rasta renaissance" had spread such that "DJ after DJ began growing dreadlocks and writing lyrics about King Selassie and the virtues of Rasta philosophy" (113). For most Pentecostals, these conscious dancehall artists fall outside the realm of acceptable musical practice insofar as they are allied with an incompatible belief system. However, saints also tend to recognize that these artists occupy a middle ground, of sorts, by virtue of their rejection of slackness and gun violence. The dancehall remains, in any case, characterized by "pragmatic neutrality" (113). As Stolzoff explains, "even after Buju Banton's turn to Rasta, he continued to occasionally perform slack lyrics in order to retain his popularity with that portion of the dancehall audience" (113). Given Pentecostal concerns about social and musical eclecticism, it is not surprising that Rasta-oriented dancehall is something the saints tend to eschew. Most Pentecostals have little tolerance for the lyrical shifts that DJs make to broaden and maintain their marketability. They are, publicly at least, unamused by singers such as Beenie Man, who feigns naïveté by asking, "What's the big deal?" Such individuals are regarded as the devil's advocates, and they are believed to act in a literal sense on behalf of a worldly paradigm that opposes the will of God. But given Jackson's reminder that "the movement of bamsies, backsides, and behinds for the Lord has been going on for centuries now" (1998, 176), perhaps Beenie Man unwittingly makes a good point.

The practice of secular artists performing gospel music elicits strong reactions from Pentecostal listeners, even when the artist's lyrics are less obviously satirical. This type of boundary crossing has raised eyebrows in African American religious contexts since at least the 1920s, when, as Teresa Reed explains, black Christians in the United States were "particularly offended by bluesmen and women who sang both racy material and traditional hymns." It was a simple matter to rebuke and perhaps reclaim those who reveled in a life of worldly music and saw themselves as "lost sinners." But churchgoers were more greatly affronted by what they saw as the "shameless oscillation between God and the Devil," a transgression committed by a number of prominent blues singers of the day (2003, 91). According to Portia Maultsby (1999), crossing secular–sacred boundaries has also involved the recycling of a range of gospel music's aesthetic principles and qualities, including vocal delivery styles, timbres, and improvisatory techniques, in addition to the selective appropriation of Christian lyrics. Criticisms of Beenie Man bear some resemblance to those launched against African American rapper Kanye West. This artist's Grammy Award–winning single, "Jesus Walks," stands in sharp contrast to his broader body of work, including most of the other songs on his 2004 recording, *The College Dropout*. A major controversy erupted among gospel music enthusiasts in the United States when "Jesus Walks" was included on the Stellar Awards ballot as a nominee for Rap/Hip-Hop Gospel CD of the Year. Some feared that West's inclusion would taint the image of the Stellar Awards as geared toward authentically Christian artists. The title of the article, "Kayne West Sings Gospel . . . or Does He?" could apply to a number of secular dancehall artists who have recorded religiously themed songs. "It just seems that it shouldn't have gotten through," one gospel industry spokesperson complained. "For this to be the Stellar Awards they should have known Kanye West, Roc-A-Fella records, that's not [a] gospel album."[11] The Stellar Awards senior management and nominating committee subsequently decided that West's CD did not meet the award criteria and removed his song from the ballot. In September 2004 they issued a press release explaining their rationale:

> The Stellar Awards certainly encourage the many facets of gospel music; however, after being made aware of the explicit lyrics in the other songs from the CD, the Stellar Awards nominating committee felt the CD lyrical selections were not in the best interest and spirit of gospel music. Therefore, the Kanye West CD was immediately removed from the Hip Hop CD of the Year category and the entire ballot.[12]

The committee's statement included an apology for their "glaring oversight," along with a reassurance to gospel fans that they had "implemented corrective actions to make sure that such an error never happens in the future."

Just as gospel artists experience criticism when they perform secular material, dancehall musicians are viewed with scorn for their forays into gospel.

Beenie Man and other dancehall artists who employ Christian themes are always held in suspicion as potential wolves in sheep's clothing, performers who at any given moment may hop back to the other side of an us–them dichotomy. Notwithstanding these criticisms, some churchgoers do not take offense at secular artists who dabble in Christian thematic material. Rather, they are delighted by what they perceive to be the church's influence in a secular realm. From the perspective of secular dancehall artists, such as Ninjaman and Shaggy, the influence of the church is not always seen as positive. These artists use musical performance to critique hypocrisy and lambaste what they perceive to be self-righteousness among those who insist on separating themselves from those who do not appear to be authentic Christians. While Pentecostals attack the dancehall as immoral and ungodly, secular dancehall artists thus find creative ways to speak back by injecting humor-laden critiques into their recordings and engaging Christianity on its own moral-ethical terms.

Eric had experienced the tension between sacred and secular genres on a personal level. He believes that the church's unwillingness to understand that music is a ministry worthy of monetary compensation contributed to his spiritual instability. "The problem," he explained, "is that the church leadership doesn't see music as a ministry. And that [is] one of the reasons I backslide. I had a wife and a child and needed to make money. But they told me you can't play for money in the world and then come and play for God. And that's a problem for a lot of people; they need to have a job and the church tells them you can't do it." In this case, Eric's backsliding was signaled, in part, by his participation in worldly musical performances for which he received compensation. The stigma attached to deriving income for musical performance is related to the belief that music is a gift from God that should be freely shared within the church. Pentecostal pastors sometimes preach that other uses of musical gifts are akin to selling oneself out to the world. Hence, they refuse to compensate musicians who play for church services, and this strengthens the temptation that talented instrumentalists feel to explore other venues of performance, where they can exercise their gifts and receive a financial boost in return. Church leaders are thus faced with a dilemma. They strive to maintain the perceived integrity of their local music ministries by raising up instrumentalists who will give of their talents. But they are finding it difficult to withstand the outsourcing of their musicians by dancehall club owners, whose influence is thought to have an even more deleterious effect on the spiritual health of the church ministry.

Conclusion

In this chapter, I have examined the roles of sound and style in constructing religious identity. As we have seen, Pentecostal church leaders at Mercy Tabernacle face many challenges as they enjoin saints to uphold a standard of holiness. The church's pastor and minister of music serve as "border agents" who bear primary responsibility for safeguarding the congregation from worldly influences they perceive to be morally and spiritually threatening. Styles of music-making are intimately tied to a cultural politics of pleasure that governs ways of sounding, dressing, and behaving in society. I contend that sounding holy and looking holy go together. Moreover, perceptions of musical holiness influence the types of flow that are operative in Pentecostal services. My experiences at Mercy Tabernacle thus reveal that music never stands alone in constructions of holiness. Rather, music is part of a broad constellation of variables that Pentecostals choose to negotiate as they position themselves before God and country as exemplars of authentic Christianity in the Jamaican cultural sphere. However, we have also seen that the line between worldliness and holiness is blurred. I find it particularly significant that the theme of movement crops up so frequently in sung and spoken performance. Lively music-making signifies deliverance from sin or from earthly hindrances that block access to God. Saints are urged to move away from the world and toward divine presence and power. I think it not coincidental that a premium is also placed on physical movement—in some cases from back pews to altars—to seeking God and being filled with the Holy Spirit, and on movement across national boundaries to gain access to the United States. Pastor Philips, for example, expressed a desire for God to "enlarge his territory" by granting the pastor the opportunity to travel to the United States. This desire to step into a transnational realm is perhaps demonstrated through the merging of musical repertories, as I experienced at Mercy Tabernacle in Liliput and also in various Pentecostal churches in nearby Montego Bay.

I believe notions of dancehall "corruption" stem as much from a fear of sexual temptation as from the musical sound itself. Moreover, certain musical traits, such as the rough vocal timbre employed by dancehall artists like Beenie Man and Buju Banton, and perhaps the syncopated bass rhythm of dancehall tracks, have become iconic representations of sexuality. I would argue that to conservative Pentecostals, dancehall music *sounds* like sex. This is due to the layering of meanings the music has acquired over time and its associations with nightlife and the taboo pleasures of bodily encounter.

CHAPTER 3

The Anointing Makes the Difference

Power, Presence, and Gendered Worship

I was apprehensive en route to the home of Pastor Hermine Bryan. Somewhat shy by nature, I rarely found the first encounters of field research easy. While making the trip down from Liliput, I reminded myself that the insights gained through person-to-person dialogue are well worth pressing through the nervousness I felt. Still, I did not enjoy having to rely on others for my well-being; nor was I comfortable imposing on someone else's time and territory. Such dependency was to me one of the more unpleasant aspects of fieldwork experience. It was reassuring to know that my new host was a Pentecostal, but the fact that she also was a pastor created for me another set of small anxieties: What were her expectations? Would she think positively of me? How closely would I be scrutinized? I would have to be on my best behavior. Or so I had convinced myself. Things will be much different with Pastor Bryan from the way they were at my previous locale, I thought. In the northern parish of St. James, where I had spent my first three months, my hosts were content to be outsiders to Pentecostalism. As I explained in chapter 1, they saw my frequent trips to church services, even in the role of researcher, as excessive, and they dismissed the baptism of the Holy Spirit, evidenced by speaking in tongues, as odd and unnecessary. By contrast, Pastor Bryan had been a committed Pentecostal for forty-five years, and I knew she was an expert on biblical doctrine and at peace with the challenges of living a sanctified lifestyle. Among African American Pentecostals at my church in New York, Jamaicans were known for being rigid in their adherence to traditional standards of holiness. So I braced myself for some serious boundary setting. Strict house guidelines, inflexible curfews, and a Spartan-like fasting regimen were parts of an imaginary scenario I anticipated a Jamaican pastor of her generation might perform. Despite the seriousness with which Pastor Bryan clung to her faith, I soon realized that my initial apprehensions about staying in her home were unwarranted. Her down-to-earth demeanor and sense of humor put me at ease, and I found her remarkably easy to talk to. I became especially appreciative of the wisdom contained in the stories she told. Throughout my six-month stay in St. Catherine, Pastor Bryan provided me not only with room and board but also with a wealth of insight on the intricacies of her faith and on what she saw as the distinguishing characteristics of Pentecostal Christianity in Jamaica.

In this chapter I examine narratives of power, presence, and gender to consider the effect they have on Pentecostal music and worship, and vice versa. I call special attention to Pastor Bryan and other Pentecostal women and men who regard music-making as an opportunity to receive and channel spiritual "anointing." As they seek access to spiritual flow, Pentecostals acquire a sense of piety and divine empowerment that they rely on to distinguish themselves from those who do not share their beliefs. Through song and speech, they also describe themselves as spiritual warriors who fight battles for deliverance from perceived sources of social and spiritual despair. Music and spiritual warfare are thus vital tools in efforts to attain religious transcendence and construct boundaries between the saints and their "worldly" adversaries. But this chapter also demonstrates that worldly adversaries include not only those powers explicitly labeled sinful or "demonic." Rather, they may also comprise "carnal" propensities of those who profess Christianity. Through self-discipline, prayer, and "true worship," saints strive to shun worldly carnality while honing a sense of collective moral distinctiveness that is both challenged and reinforced by the sharing of musical resources across the boundaries of cultural and ritual practice. The gendered processes of experiencing transcendence and "being anointed" by God are of paramount importance to those seeking divine approval and power. Reaching these goals requires saints to engage their bodies and minds in the act of worship, and music is critical to the success of this endeavor.[1]

Pastor Bryan and the Touch of Transcendence

Hermine Elaine Bryan was born and raised in the rural settlement of Croft's Hill in the parish of Clarendon. "We didn't really think of it as poverty," she explains. "It was more like underprivileged. You know, we were aware that some had more, but we never went to bed hungry." Her father had a few acres of land on which he planted sugar cane and bananas. Times were tough in the 1940s, so Ernest Bryan also looked abroad to find sources of income. "My father worked in Cuba during those years," she recalls. "I remember when I was little he wasn't around." Pastor Bryan nevertheless has fond memories of her youth. It was a time during which she developed the sparkling sense of humor she still possesses. Pastor Bryan enjoys recounting some of the playful events of her childhood, including the times she used to play "duppy" (ghost) pranks on some of the younger kids in her area. She admits having a little fun at the expense of those who feared the power of popular religions such as obeah. "I never believed in it," she insists. "I never believed anyone could 'obeah' me." In any event, Pastor Bryan had by then acquired a sense that her life was protected by a greater spiritual power. Her entry into Pentecostalism was still a few years away, but she was absorbing Christian principles through her mother's Anglican faith, which also provided a measure of social and religious respectability. Her confidence in the protective power of Jesus Christ became solidified with her conversion to Pentecostalism in 1958. Much of the religious respectability associated with Anglicanism was replaced, however, by derision, particularly from elite quarters of society. "Pentecostals were looked down upon," she remarks, recalling the stigma that was attached to them during those days.

Hermine Bryan was appointed pastor of Riversdale Pentecostal Church in 1977 after the church's previous leader, a man, migrated to the United States. Although some of the saints balked at the idea of having a woman as their leader, those who remained at Riversdale came to value the wisdom of her teachings. Women have been influential within the Pentecostal Assemblies of the World in Jamaica, having founded a handful of churches in nearby Spanish Town and Kingston. Riversdale Church is what Pastor Bryan calls "a country church." The town of Riversdale is poorer than Spanish Town in terms of jobs; therefore, some of the saints commute into Spanish Town during the week to seek or maintain employment. A few of the saints actually live in Spanish Town and get a ride out to Riversdale from Pastor Bryan, who picks them up for midweek and Sunday services. In country churches, few, if any, of the members earn a regular salary. This is particularly true of farmers, who depend solely on their produce. Although most Pentecostals are from what Jamaicans call the "poorer class of people," an increasing number hail from the middle class, particularly in Montego Bay, Spanish Town, and Kingston. Two of Riversdale's members are schoolteachers, several are domestic helpers, others sell produce, and one prepares and sells bammy (made from cassava root) for a living.

It was a bright, sunny morning in mid-May when Brother Green and I first pulled up in front of Pastor Bryan's garden-flanked home. Her roses were most precious. The St. Catherine Horticultural Society had twice awarded them top prize in its annual competition. Pastor Bryan cultivated her flowers with great care, much like she nurtured the saints under her spiritual watch at Riversdale Pentecostal Church. Brother Green was one of the young preachers at the church that I had frequented while in St. James. He drove a taxi for a living, and I had hired him to shuttle me down to Spanish Town in the southern part of the St. Catherine Parish. As we climbed out of his sedan, Pastor Bryan unlocked her carport gate and came outside to greet us with a cheery "Praise the Lord!" We exchanged pleasantries for a few minutes before Brother Green waved goodbye and Pastor Bryan and I made our way inside. After setting down my things, we sat and talked for the next couple of hours. That preliminary conversation paved the way for others throughout the subsequent months, during which I gleaned important details about Pastor Bryan's life, especially her musical preferences, spiritual development, and commitment to serving God. On multiple occasions we spoke about Pentecostalism as both a universal gospel and a local Jamaican practice.

Mondays after breakfast were special. Pastor Bryan and I would linger at the table, engaging in a relaxing conversation about Pentecostal praise and worship. During one such occasion, we spoke as usual about the operation of the Holy Spirit and casually reflected on the previous day's services at Riversdale. This morning, Pastor Bryan's reflections were mostly silent. I grinned as she sat across the table with her eyes closed and her hand cupped at the side of her head as though meditating on the goodness of the Lord. Even outside of a church service, she occasionally felt the touch of the Holy Spirit. Pentecostals describe the transcendent touch of the Holy Spirit in various ways. Some report an overwhelming sense of inner peace and joy that causes them to weep. Others compare it to a sudden spark or hot electrical charge that compels them to move, cry out, or speak in tongues. Human responses to the touch of the Spirit thus differ from person to person. However, it is understood that the initial infilling of the Holy Spirit constitutes a more transformative phenomenon and is always accompanied by "the evidence" of speaking in tongues.

The fact that the Holy Spirit's touch may be felt outside of a worship service reveals something significant about the character of Pentecostal experiences. Commenting on the "holy touch" experienced by one of his interlocutors during an interview, Hinson (2000) writes, "No 'ritual context' induced its occurrence; no ceremonial surround of sound, motion, and sensory saturation invoked frames of expectation and enactment; no relentless rhythms drove consciousness down an alternate path" (2). While music is used to facilitate transcendence, the Spirit's touch is sometimes felt during moments of silent meditation, prayer, or conversation. I had come to expect a manifestation of this Unseen Party during my talks with Pastor Bryan, particularly when we dwelled on spiritual topics for which she had a passion. I gently broke the silence with an audible observation: "You know, during last night's service, there seemed to be some people there who were really seeking the Lord. I was thinking maybe somebody might get filled." Pastor Bryan nodded, "Yes, I felt the presence of the Lord there last night. But not everybody that comes to church truly has a hunger for God. We must have a hunger, a strong desire for more of Him." Over the past few weeks, Pastor Bryan had been emphasizing the importance of sincere fellowship with God. She felt a special burden for the teenagers at Riversdale, most of whom had yet to be filled with the Holy Spirit. "Sometimes I feel like the Lord is just waiting," she continued, "and he's seeking somebody who is willing to praise him and offer him true worship. God sees the heart. But not everybody has a strong desire for the Lord." Pastor Bryan used the phrase "true worship" in reference to what she believed to be an authentic form of Pentecostal Christian adoration of God. This brand of authenticity is characterized by a self-sacrificial attitude toward singing, praying, and testifying during church services, such that physical and emotional discomforts do not hinder one from engaging wholeheartedly in the activities of ritual worship. According to Pastor Bryan, true worshippers set aside the "cares of the world" in order to direct their energies to a higher power.

A seasoned woman of the cloth with thirty years of experience at Riversdale, Pastor Bryan always spoke to me with the clarity and passion of one accustomed to the task of touching hearts through the spoken Word. At age sixty-five, she now drew upon biblical wisdom and her deeply held convictions regarding the value of seeking God's presence. Pastor Bryan was also an expert on effective praise and worship, having directed song services countless times since first receiving the infilling of the Holy Spirit in 1958. I reflected on her statement that not all congregants are spiritually hungry for more of God. Discerning from my facial expression that I wanted to pose another question, she paused, giving me a moment to collect my thoughts. "Do you think that's the reason," I ventured, "why it seems as though some people get filled with the Holy Ghost very easily but others tarry for years and years and still don't get filled?" "Yes. I think that is *one* of the reasons," she offered. "But we must also learn to get into the presence of God so that we can worship him." Her eyes lit up, betraying the profundity of what she was about to say. "Brother Melvin," she sighed, "The Lord is seeking true worshippers. So often we stop short of reaching the point where we are in his presence. We are living beneath our privilege, you know!" I nodded in agreement, even as my mind raced, searching for the wording of my next question. I was enjoying the flow of our conversation and found myself fascinated on both spiritual and academic analytic levels. These two analytic levels seemed to merge during my talks with Pastor Bryan. It was as a Pentecostal that I found myself most engaged in our topic, and I found her words spiritually edifying. As much as I realized that our discussions would contribute greatly to my research project, it was mostly my desire to grow spiritually that kept me riveted. Since I had been helping out as a keyboardist and choir instructor at Riversdale, Pastor Bryan's insights helped me to be in tune with her musical and spiritual goals for each worship service. Thus, our discussions regarding praise and worship were highly relevant to my musical role in the church as well.

During sermons, Pastor Bryan enjoyed repeating one of her favorite truisms: "You praise the Lord in order to reach his presence; worship is what you do when you get there." Her thoughts on the efficacy of praise resonated with those I would hear in Pentecostal churches throughout my time in Jamaica. During sacrificial acts of praise, one shows appreciation to God by standing, clapping, singing, dancing, and shouting. In effect, the body becomes a primary mechanism for enlivening or heating up the atmosphere and evoking a response from God. It is through bodily praise that saints invite "the blessing" of God's Spirit to flow among them, to heal, to deliver, to refresh, and to empower. The notion that musical praise can "make something happen" or bring about potent divine manifestations is supported by a familiar New Testament passage.

> But at midnight Paul and Silas were praying and singing hymns to God, and the prisoners were listening to them. Suddenly there was a great earthquake, so that the foundations of the prison were shaken; and immediately all the doors were opened and everyone's chains were loosed. (Acts 16:25–26, New International Version)

This passage is cited in sermons and exhortations to emphasize the importance of praising God even in the midst of difficult circumstances. Just as the apostles Paul and Silas were freed from prison through their singing hymns of praise, Pentecostal believers are taught to gain freedom from spiritual and natural oppression by offering God sincere praise. Sincere praise serves as a catalyst for what believers refer to as "receiving the anointing" or "getting anointed" during a service. As I will explain, the concept of anointing is complex and contested. It is also gendered and performed in a variety of ways.

Oil, Blood, and the Role of Women

As I have shown, Pastor Bryan enjoys what she refers to as "basking in presence of the Holy Spirit." Rather than "going through the motions" of praise and worship, she prefers to "let the Lord to have his way" in and out of the worship service. She sometimes reminisced about services at Riversdale in which the Spirit "really moved." During one Sunday night service she had announced, "We're just going to spend the whole evening in worship. Just worship him! If you want to lift your hands, then lift your hands. If you want to cry out to the Lord, cry out to him! If you want to go prostrate before him, go ahead—however God moves you." Praise, she told the saints, "is an occupation of the heart." It involves a willingness and a determination to focus one's mind on God. It is the failure to offer sacrificial praise that keeps some churchgoers from experiencing the presence of God and truly worshipping. "But when the Holy Spirit is really manifesting and the service is anointed," she explained, "it's like time just stop[s]. You don't care about the time!"

The concept of "the anointing" is a global feature in the effective transition from praise to worship. Pentecostal preachers compare it to oil, which is a biblical trope symbolizing the presence and power of the Holy Spirit. As one minister related, "The anointing is like oil. It lubricates and makes things flow. That's what make[s] it easier to preach."[2] The notion that the anointing "makes things flow" calls to mind what Csikszentmihalyi (1990) describes as "one of the most universal and distinctive features of optimal experience." As is true for some who achieve flow through sports or the performing arts, anointed preachers may "become so involved in what they are doing that the activity becomes spontaneous, almost automatic; they stop being aware of themselves as separate from the actions they are performing" (53).

Preachers frequently use the analogy between the anointing and oil in their sermons. During a Wednesday night service in Kingston, I heard a visiting minister elaborate on how the anointing of oil and blood relates to the Holy Spirit.

In the Old Testament, the word "anointing" simply meant to smear or to put something on somebody. And so it was considered an anointing when they sanctified the house in Egypt by sprinkling the blood on the doorpost and on the lintel. But then when God brought his children into the wilderness, he taught them of anointing persons with oil as a sign of separation and a sign of selecting an individual for God. It was also considered a sign or an act of consecration, which simply means that God was setting apart lives to be used in his service. And so anointing referred to the pouring on of oil over the heads of individuals that were consecrated for the service of God. But then when Jesus came, John the

Baptist said, "Yes, I baptize you with *water*"; but he declared of Jesus, "He shall baptize you with the Holy *Ghost* and with fire." And so in the Old Testament, they poured oil *onto*, but in the New Testament when Jesus came, he poured himself *into*. And so when that Holy Spirit of God gets into the life of a man or woman, it was that anointing of God himself.[3]

One evening, Pastor Bryan and I spoke in detail about what it means to be anointed by God. About halfway through our conversation, she leaned forward as though relaying to me a carefully guarded secret. "Brother Melvin," she declared in a hushed but ready tone, "it's deeper than what people say, you know!" She continued,

> I think we have lost the meaning of true anointing and true worship. They go together. If you worship, your spirit is going to be involved. It's a reciprocity between human and divine. The human is elevated to the divine realm. This is the atmosphere in which God works. What people call the anointing now is just bodily exercise. The anointing is when your spirit is connected with God's Spirit. It is spirit and Spirit meeting. Something in *your* spirit is connected with God.[4]

Pastor Bryan and I agreed that churchgoers sometimes mistake a musician's virtuosity or skill at exciting an audience with a manifestation of the Holy Spirit. I asked her to say more about the anointing as it applies to Pentecostal preachers and singers. She continued,

> The anointed preacher is going to preach an anointed message, one that is edifying to the people. . . . Gifted is not the same as anointed. The anointing is something spiritual. We can be blessed by someone's singing when a song or singing speaks to your need. Songs can help people, but not necessarily be anointed. . . . I cannot *turn on* the anointing. Singing under the anointing means that God places his approval on the singing.

Singing, preaching, and praying "under the anointing," she added, require an attitude of submissiveness to God and a lifestyle pleasing to him. The voice of a talented singer may "tickle the ear," but only *anointed* enactment will reach the heart and bring forth fruit. Pastor Bryan disapproves of the hoopla that follows some church presentations, particularly "over-the-top" reactions to singing that include yelling and whistling only when a singer exhibits virtuosic technical ability. "I listen for tongues and I hear nothing," she complained. "Some people that carry on like that aren't even saved. So where are they being blessed from? What we have mostly is a lot of display, a lot of show." Pastor Bryan emphasized that the true anointing comes by way of a consecrated life. "I preached a sermon once," she recalled. "It was called 'There is a confederate in me!' because the flesh fights against the Spirit of God." When flesh is brought under subjection to the Spirit, the anointing may be manifested; and with the anointing, Pastor Bryan explains, "all things are possible."

A foundational tenet of the faith is that God's anointing is made available to human beings because of the blood sacrifice of Jesus Christ. It is perhaps for this reason that references to both oil and blood abound in Pentecostal services. In fact, the two substances are understood to be mystically linked. Like the anointing, the blood also symbolizes the effective power of God to protect, heal, deliver, and save from the hand of "the enemy," whether that enemy is human or spiritual in character. Pastor Bryan told me several stories of the healing power of the anointing. One narrative involving her former pastor and mentor, Bishop Norman Walters, demonstrates the effectiveness of the anointing as it is signaled by speaking in tongues.

> One day I went to see Sister Walters, who was sick. She was very weak. Bishop Walters had to carry her from room to room. Bishop Walters told me I could see her but not to talk to her because she was so weak. I went in and she motioned with her hand like this [fanning gesture], so I started fanning her. Bishop Walters's brother, named George—he is dead now—came in and prayed for her. Then he left and as he was walking away outside, Bishop Walters felt a very strange anointing and began to speak in tongues. And when he spoke in tongues, it was just so—the language was so marvelous. So, anyway, then Sister Walters was quickened and started speaking in tongues. I remember her face was toward the wall. Then she got up and put her shawl around her and began walking around the house speaking in tongues. Bishop Walters walked behind her with his arms braced to catch her in case she fell. But from that time on, she began to get healing; she began her turnaround.

Sister Walters's healing via "a very strange anointing" provides an excellent example of how the Holy Spirit is understood to act in ways beyond human comprehension. Sometimes it is, in fact, the unpredictability of the anointing that lends it an aura of authenticity. While human rituals and "performances" generally have a planned, rehearsed quality, the Holy Spirit's actions are not subject to human forethought. The "marvelous" tongues that precipitated Sister Walters's healing are thus attributed to the spontaneous manifestation of the Spirit-as-agent, rather than the abilities of the man through whom the utterances came forth. This exercise of divine healing required only genuine submission to God's will and an acceptance of faith as a preeminent guiding principle. Although the healing was, in this case, precipitated by Bishop Walters's moment of transcendence, what I wish to underscore here is that it also involved a yielding of "manly" control. To submit is to behave in ways that are, in Jamaica and elsewhere, socially and theologically gendered as feminine. Thus, while most pastors are men, the women who grant them pastoral authority may do so on the basis of their ability to worship in ways that are "against type." Dancing in the spirit, for example, is much more commonplace among women. Men who are somehow unashamed to use their bodies in demonstrative ways earn the assumption that they are sincere and devout in the faith. Put more provocatively, men are ascribed spiritual authority and authenticity when they embrace Jesus as their loving Savior, submit to him as Lord of their lives, and allow themselves to be penetrated by the Holy Spirit. It is believed that in this way, men can be "used by God" as leaders in the church.

Highlighting the embodied nature of Pentecostal worship is one way to reveal the irony of church discourses that privilege demonstrative forms of expression while also demarcating the boundaries of how the body is adorned, presented, and pleasured in public and private spaces. Dancing, in particular, could create something of a dilemma for those men who understand it to be most characteristic of an "open" body—a vulnerable body that is penetrable by a Holy Spirit typically referred to as a "he," albeit one without flesh and bones (Gordon 2000, 118–19; Jones 2015b, 318–19). Stephen Finley (2007) elaborates on this point, going so far as to argue that "the impervious, fully armored, Black male body is an impediment to finding meaning in the Black Church in that worship of God is a homoerotic entry into the body" (18). Men's refusal to dance in church can be read as way of asserting a heteronormative style of praise and worship, recouping a musical "posture of masculinity," and grappling with the existential crisis, posited Lewis Gordon (2000), who rhetorically asks, "Can one worship God and remain masculine too?" (119).

Having a willingness to submit to God does not mean, however, that Pentecostal women and men lack the capacity to exercise power or make individual choices. Following Marla Frederick (2003), I adopt an orientation to black Christianity that views spirituality as "the intersection of individual transformation and social protest—one that acknowledges the profound agency of individuals, as well as the limits of that agency, in deconstructing, creating, and recreating social realities" (29). In a sense, Bishop Walters's commitment to a holy lifestyle allows him and other saints to take ownership of power. They may take proactive steps to stymie Satan's plans, overcome obstacles, and bring about deliverance by "pleading the blood" and calling on the name of Jesus. I will return to this concept of blood pleading below. But let me first elaborate a bit on gendered discourses of worship and intimacy as they pertain to the role of women at Riversdale.

Discussions of worship often reveal gendered notions of physical and spiritual intimacy. Marla Frederick (2003) suggests that women's sexual experiences, in particular, may inform how women understand their roles as spiritual practitioners in male-dominated spaces. By redefining their sexual experiences, they gain "the potential for empowerment in ways that give them more authority over their bodies" (186–87). Women's narratives of spiritual intimacy call to mind the figure of Jesus in the flesh, as the incarnate Son of God who is able to touch, and be touched by, the human condition. A woman at Riversdale Pentecostal Church often described Jesus as the "lover" of her soul. Another woman testified that while praying, she pictures herself wiping the feet of Jesus with her hair, washing his feet with her tears, and drying them with her hair.[5] This was, for her, the epitome of worship. "Sometimes," she added, "I see myself resting on his bosom." Although the Bible attributes this latter act to a man—the disciple John—it exemplifies the embodiment of an imagined intimacy that differs from the worship experiences that men describe.

I learned about women's experiences of spiritual intimacy also by hearing them discuss the types of worship songs they enjoy. Pastor Bryan was enraptured by Cece Winans's 1999 gospel recording, *Alabaster Box*, the title track of which recounts the New Testament story of a woman who worshipped Jesus by pouring expensive perfume onto his head. During a Sunday evening sermon, Pastor Bryan once posed a rhetorical question, "Why didn't a man think of breaking the alabaster box of oil?" The next day, she shared with me her goal of prompting the congregation to think about the value of women in the church and to see them as exemplifying the kind of sacrificial worship that God desires. Women, in this instance at least, are presented as model saints whom the men in the church should strive to emulate.

Women make up the overwhelming majority of Jamaican Pentecostal congregations, and women play the most active roles in heating up services with demonstrative praise and worship. But while women are the majority holders of expressive and spiritual power, their influence is tempered by the fact that relatively few women pastor their own churches or play musical instruments. Except for the fact that its pastor is a woman, Riversdale resembles most of the churches I have visited. Pastor Bryan agreed with the sentiments of most clergy with whom I spoke regarding the importance of women and the "underrepresentation" of men's voices in praise and worship.

I know that without the women, praise and worship would be almost nil. Because the men have the women in the majority, they seem to relax. They don't put as much into it. In my opinion, there are things the men depend on women to do, even to carry the weight of the singing in the congregation. Not only that but also in the home upkeep and decision-making.

She attributes gendered worship tendencies to nature rather than nurture or a "social reason."

> It is considered a display of weakness for men if they cry. Men have different ways of expressing their emotions. I don't think men's hearts are engaged in the singing the way women's hearts are. That level of fervency is not there. Women express their emotions more. I don't think there is a social reason for it. I think that it is that they are basically made that way.

Pastor Bryan resists the notion that women are trying subdue men in the church. At Riversdale, she explained, "I tell the men that they are the head. I need them. I need the men. For certain issues I'll bring somebody else in to discuss it with the men. Riversdale is not a woman-dominated church." But she also opposes granting men authority to keep women under subjection, as has traditionally been the case. "You're wrong, and I'm right, and I'm to do what you say? Forget it! If I'm right, I'm going to hold my ground. Man is the head, that's right. But sometimes I think we take the hard line, you know, when it's not necessary." Pastor Bryan's cautionary remarks reflect her awareness that saints too often cherry-pick Bible verses to promote sexist and misogynistic views of male–female relationships.[6] I suspect her insistence that men are "the head" is partly a strategy of male appeasement. This strategy, along with her reassurance that Riversdale is not "woman-dominated," stands in tension with her assertions that men depend on women and that women are indispensable to the success of church worship. Calls for gender equity often feel muted and constrained within intractable structures of patriarchy. Pastor Bryan's pro-woman stance is thus undermined by a social pressure to reaffirm the dominant position of men in a gender hierarchy. However, younger Pentecostal women with whom I speak push back against the rhetoric of "male headship," particularly when they sense that men are using this rhetoric to keep women "in their place"—that is, subservient to men. Theologian Rosemary Ruether (2014) critiques the notion of male headship from a "prophetic-liberating" perspective, arguing that legacies of gendered and racialized oppression "do not come from specific doctrines, but from a patriarchal and hierarchical reading of the system of Christian symbols as a whole" (83).

Almost every summer, Pastor Bryan traveled to the United States to attend the annual convention of the Pentecostal Assemblies of the World. This summer was no exception, and I was tickled by the fact that we traded places, so to

Pastor Tommy Seals, First Lady Delores Seals, and Pastor Hermine Bryan at the 2002 Convention of the Pentecostal Assemblies of the World Inc. Photo by Lori A. Butler.

speak. While I stayed "home" in Spanish Town, Pastor Bryan was in Washington, D.C., making connections with North American clergy such as Pastor and Lady Seals, to whom she gave my regards. The theme of the 2002 Convention was "Power to Become."

When she returned to Jamaica, she gave me a summary of events, recalling a debate that had taken place during the business meeting. "Release your daughters!" one woman had demanded, "We have been in chains too long!" Much of the debate centered on whether women should be given designations traditionally reserved for men, such as "District Elder" and "Bishop." From time to time, Pastor Bryan surprised me with her outspokenness on gender issues. Her remarks on the differences between women in the United States and the Caribbean, along with her travel abroad, defy stereotypical depictions of the traditional, domesticated "third world" woman:

Women in Jamaica are more empowered than women in America! In the U.S., if a woman doesn't get married, it's like she's failed. But here, women take more initiative and are less afraid to go out on their own. Just the other day while you were here inside, a boy came up and said, "Hello Pastor Bryan! Where's your husband?" I said, "I'm not married." He said, "How come you have all this and you're not married?" It's like people think if you have all this, there must be a man behind it!

In response to the exploitation of biblical passages used to support the silencing of women, she huffed, "I don't think women should just fold their hands in church and do nothing! I think there are men who like to feel that women are dependent on them." Pastor Bryan's concerns about the subjugation of women point to debates unfolding in Pentecostal churches in both Jamaica and the United States. Her perception of Jamaican women's distinctiveness is shaped by her travels to the United States, where she has had the opportunity to witness how gender identities are performed within and beyond church settings. I have noticed that both Jamaican and African American Pentecostals are more inclined to express cultural and racial pride than to speak out against the marginalization of women or articulate a need for gender equity. If there is any truth to Pastor Bryan's cheeky observation that "women in Jamaica are more empowered than women in America," the social and historical differences between the two countries are certainly a major factor.[7]

When my wife visited Riversdale for a couple of weeks, Pastor Bryan asked her to lead praise and worship during a Sunday morning service. Lori taught the congregation a simple song based on the words of Psalms 30, verse 5.

Weeping may endure for a night.
Joy cometh in the morning.
Hallelujah for the joy!
Thank you, Jesus, for the joy!

Pastor Bryan used the song as an entrée into her sermon titled "The Joy of the Lord." "The joy of the Lord is my strength!" she proclaimed. "Even though I am sad sometimes, the devil cannot take away my joy. And because I have joy, I am strong in the Lord! You may look at me and think I am not strong, but my God is strong and powerful, so I am powerful too!" As I hope to make clear, women and men express a sense of empowerment by invoking the strength and authority of what lies beyond the human realm. They strive to gain God's approval by leading consecrated lives, and as they allow themselves to be anointed by God, they claim the authority to deploy Jesus's blood as an indispensable weapon of spiritual warfare.

Empowerment, Blood, and Divine Protection

Although Pastor Bryan owns her own home, she does not own a television set. In fact, she has never owned one. This example of consecration is not unusual among Pentecostal pastors of her generation. Televisions have long carried the stigma of worldliness, and Pastor Bryan felt no desire to "waste time staring at a screen." It was one of the ways she sought to avoid "the lust of the eyes." This eschewal of television was passed down to her from her late pastor. Only in the 1990s did some apostolic Pentecostals in Jamaica begin to modify traditional practices taught by Bishop Norman Walters, a staunch advocate of a lifestyle that is holy and separated from the world. Pastor Bryan identifies herself as "one of Bishop Walters's daughters." "He stood for holiness," she affirms, "and he lived an exemplary life." Pastor Bryan is proud of her spiritual heritage and is determined, in her pastoral role, to maintain the best of the Pentecostal tradition and to set an example to the world and to younger generations of Pentecostals, as well as to her church congregation.

Newspaper and radio are what keeps Pastor Bryan abreast of current events. During one October evening, she felt under the weather and made a rare decision to forgo the scheduled prayer meeting at Riversdale. There were other ministers who assisted her, and they would take charge. So Pastor Bryan and I spent the evening chatting and listening to the swearing-in ceremony of newly re-elected Prime Minister P. J. Patterson. Just a week prior, the People's National Party had won its third consecutive election, and Patterson was now giving his highly anticipated speech to the nation. Citing the Old Testament prophet Ezekiel, Patterson predicted that God would rain down "showers of blessing" on Jamaica in the years ahead. Pastor Bryan applauded, pleased with this biblical reference. She liked Patterson and had chosen to vote for him, in part because "he's always talking about values and attitudes." She emphasized that ultimately, however, we must all rely "not upon man, but upon God, because only he has the true answer for our problems." Those problems included criminal violence, gang warfare, and a climbing murder rate, which were striking fear in the hearts of citizens. During my time on the island, Spanish Town police were trying to capture a serial thief who had been breaking into local homes. There were several padlocks on the doors and outer gates of Pastor Bryan's home. She was, nevertheless, considering investing in an electronic security system. I assumed that her willingness to grant me room and board was, at least to some degree, motivated by an awareness that living alone meant she could be potentially vulnerable to a violent intruder. Since my stay in her home was only temporary, she wanted to consider a nontransient means of defense. But her trust lay ultimately in the promise of divine protection.

As an example of God's power and dependability, Pastor Bryan recounted a frightening incident that occurred during my wife's visit to Jamaica. Lori and I had left Spanish Town to spend a weekend in Ocho Rios on the north coast. Sister Jeannie, Pastor Bryan's helper, had agreed to spend the night at her house for a few days until we returned. During our absence, a burglar broke in by fishing the key from Pastor Bryan's bedroom window and using it to unlock one of the front entrances that I'd neglected to padlock before leaving. It was Sister Jeannie who first suspected that something was amiss. She awoke Pastor Bryan after hearing unusual sounds coming from the front of the house; and as they moved toward the noise, they noticed a darkly clothed man standing in the hallway adjacent to their bedrooms. Startled by the man's presence, Sister Jeannie began screaming, "The blood of Jesus! The blood of Jesus!" The intruder then bolted past them toward the front door, as the women ran behind him until he exited the house. The event was harrowing for the two women, and I was dismayed that they were exposed to potential danger while I was away. We all were thankful that neither Pastor Bryan nor Sister Jeannie was harmed. Both women resolved to draw confidence from the incident. Pastor Bryan would later speculate that it was perhaps "a test" of her faith in the protective power of Jesus. She was most confident that God allowed the incident for his glory and so that others might learn to stay "under the blood" or in the will of God in order to escape Satan's plans.

It was not the first time Pastor Bryan had been subjected to potential danger. I once asked her about other such instances, and she described some cases of demonic influence or possession. On both occasions, she noted that her safety was a result of her staying under the blood.

Once, a man who was passing by the church in Riversdale came inside and asked for prayer. He said, "Please pray for me. I was on my way to murder somebody tonight, but I heard that song and so I just decided to come in." We were singing something like, "Holy Spirit, You Are Welcome in this Place," or one of those songs. Another time a man came into the church with a knife. I prayed when the man came up to the altar and the knife just flew out away from him.

Throughout my stay at Pastor Bryan's home, we spoke about the blood every week. She and other preachers liked to make Jesus's blood the focus of their sermons, and song leaders chose "blood songs" for congregational participation just before and after the message. Some of the most interesting sermons depict the blood as a weapon that works in conjunction with prayer and Bible study. Pastor Bryan used the break-in as fodder for discussion with the saints about the power of God to deliver from any circumstance. She also cited the incident in her subsequent sermon.

Police have M16 poised and ready to be used. Use the weapon of the blood! We don't have M16 or M38, unless it's Acts 2:38.[8] Sister Jeannie used the weapon of the blood! Death is afraid of the blood. The devil is afraid of the blood.

I also heard a visiting preacher, Elder Noel Facey, use the blood as the center-piece of a sermon titled "I Am Armed and Extremely Dangerous," an expression of spiritual bravado intended as much to encourage the saints as to put Satan and his agents on notice. His sermon also admonished the youth to resist peer pressures to indulge in sin and encouraged them to fight back by deploying the "weapons" at their disposal.[9]

What do they call it? The ballistic missile? When the Americans were fighting Iraq, and Iraq sent a ballistic missile, and the Americans sent a scud missile to counteract it? Yes! Holy Ghost! Saints, pull out your scud missile! Whenever they fire, you fire! You fire back! Pull out your scud missile! Don't be quiet when they try to put you under pressure. Fire back! Sister Nelson teach[es] us to shoot them with the blood. You need to start bring[ing] your gun to school, your blood gun!

Only a few days prior, I had heard Evangelist Grace Nelson, whom Elder Facey mentioned, render her narrative, "Shoot Them with the Blood." Her sermon had recounted a trip to England during which she was visited by a witch who mocked her Pentecostal rhetoric. "The blood of Jesus! The blood of Jesus!" the witch yelled at her, laughing irreverently as she finished. To provide an aural approximation of the witch's vocal manner, Evangelist Nelson intoned the words on a higher-than-usual pitch and stretched out the final word, "The blood of Jeeeee-sus!" Nelson then described her own response to the witch's mimicking. Rather than repeat a more commonly used "blood phrase," such as "The blood of Jesus is against you!" she opted to exercise more creativity, declaring "I shoot you with the blood!" While preaching, she encouraged her listeners to do likewise whenever they encountered spiritual resistance or oppression. "Just tell them, 'I shoot you with the blood!' and they must back down!" Elder Facey referenced Nelson's sermon to add color and humor to his own discourse. He continued his advocacy of the "blood gun," using the electric keyboardist's sound effects as an added dimension to his discourse.

It's time for us to fire back! [Keyboardist plays bomb explosion sound.] And drop the bomb! Give me another bomb there! [Keyboardist plays two explosion sounds.] It's time! The enemy is under fire, and they start retreating because we're dropping the bomb!

As Elder Facey concluded, he highlighted the idea that saints should be on offense rather than waiting in a defensive posture.

The Bible says the gates of hell shall not prevail. The gates is a defensive mecha-nism. So the gates cannot withstand our attack. That's what it means. We are the ones who are supposed to be attacking. Touch yourself and say, "I'm taking the battle to the devil!" It is time to kick down hell's gate! Break down hell's wall! And let the devil know we are here! It is time!

While these words were intended to encourage the saints, Elder Facey also included a warning to those who would attempt to deploy spiritual weapons without the requisite anointing. Battling the enemy is a task reserved for those who have been sanctified by the Holy Spirit for God's singular use; and sanctification, he insisted, requires a willingness to be clothed in holiness (Ephesians 6:11–17), thereby remaining "covered by the blood."

> It's time to put on your war clothes! You can't attack unless you're living holy, though. If you're slipping and sliding, having a girlfriend on the side, you better stay in here and stay at the altar.

From this perspective, to "stay" means to remain in position to receive God's anointing, with which comes the power both to lead a sinless life and also to wage effective warfare against Satan.

Through belief, sincere repentance, baptism, and Spirit infilling, believers are understood to gain access to the blood of Jesus, which can then be "pleaded" in times of distress or spiritual confrontation. "What happens when we plead the blood?" I once asked Pastor Bryan. Her eyes lit up. "The blood is *activated!*" was her ready response. It is with the understanding that the blood of Jesus is a spiritually efficacious agent that Pastor Bryan and the saints render blood songs and shout blood phrases during services. Blood songs are typically opportunities for ritual deliverance and healing. Some hymns, such as "Hide Me in the Blood," convey the blood as a source of shelter and protection. "I See a Crimson Stream of Blood" refers to blood's redemptive power as exercised through Jesus's death on the cross.

> On Calvary's hill of sorrow where sin's demands were paid
> And rays of hope for tomorrow across our path were laid
> I see a crimson stream of blood. It flows from Calvary.
> Its waves that reach the throne of God are sweeping over me.

"When I See the Blood" differs from most other blood songs in that its short refrain is sung from the perspective of God. The lyrics state, "When I see the blood, I will pass over you," reflecting God's promise to the Israelites that his death angel would "pass over" those who followed a divine commandment to place the blood of a sacrificed animal on their doorposts. The saints place a great deal of emphasis on pleading the blood, an act that can be glossed as exercising "the power to intercede" (Walker 1999, 202). This form of spoken or sung intercession involves a direct invocation of "the blood of Jesus" when an individual confronts a challenge whose origin is believed to be spiritual in nature. Pastor Bryan encourages her congregants to utter, "Satan, the blood is against you!" She also enjoys singing blood songs during praise and worship. These songs are experienced as more serious and more powerful than most of the "contemporary gospel" pieces to which youth tend to gravitate.[10]

Describing the relationship between praise and power, Pastor Bryan once noted, "Think of somebody going to war and the praises were before the warriors. One would think the warriors would be first! David was into singing, David was a praiser, and praisers went before the army." Pastor Bryan insists that praise and worship should be done both in private and in corporate settings. Regarding the former, she noted,

> We should rejoice in the Lord. Be glad in the Lord and rejoice. Not only when you come to church, you know. Right by my bed there, I've made my altar. I just raise my hands and say, "Lord, I worship you. You are *my* God. You are my provider. Hallelujah, you are my friend." Hallelujah! I must *praise* Him! I *must* praise Him! Glory to God. The Psalmist says sing aloud upon your bed. Let them think you're crazy. Amen! Wake up the neighborhood sometime and sing! That's right. Go on; get them [to] wonder, "What happened to Sister Sue this morning?" When they call out, "Sister Sue, you alright?" You tell them, "Yes, I'm all right! I'm just praising my God!" Then, begin to testify to them.

The power of private worship thus lies in its ability to touch the throne of God and also to spill over such that others notice a transformation and are drawn in. She urges the saints not to wait on others or require an emcee to beg them to praise God. The resulting corporate worship then becomes "a stronger force." However, one danger is that Satan imitates what God has created, substituting humans or himself as the object of worship as he tries "to circumvent the majestic order." Part of Pastor Bryan's mission is to inform the saints of Satan's strategies, which also include promoting a spirit of apathy and non-involvement with respect to praise and worship. "We want to improve on our praise and our worship to our mighty God. Some of us are too crisp to lift our hands," she explained, referring to the "stiffness" of Riversdale's men in particular. She prods each congregant to take an assertive role in worship rather than relying on someone else to "start a fire."

> Don't sit and look at others singing. Open your mouth and sing! You know those old Leyland trucks that you have to crank? Some of you don't know them. When I was a child, they'd put something in the front. You know, Brother Barnett? Amen. And you have to pump and crank it up for it to start. I don't want nobody to crank me to praise God! My God has been too good to me! Hallelujah!

It ought to come spontaneously from a heart that has been affected by the goodness of God!

She continued with comments that reveal her sentiments regarding God's worthiness to receive praise that stems from a grateful heart. Such praise, she asserts, ought not depend on others for its initiation.

I don't have to wait until Kurt Carr tells me to lift my hands in the sanctuary. Amen, hallelujah. I don't have to wait on sister beside me to praise God. My duty is to praise Him! When I praise Him, it will catch on. She will get jealous and start praising God too. And sometime the praise is not real, you know. It start[s] off not real, but after a while it catches on. It is our duty to praise God. He's worthy. He's worthy to be praised. And we ought to praise Him for He's worthy.

The notion that praise is contagious is regularly articulated in Pentecostal assemblies. A personal relationship with God is the catalyst for transformative worship that "catches on" and spreads from saint to saint.

Individually, one has to know God for oneself and worship [individually] before we can worship corporately. Then one in the mass might feel left out and she starts to praise and worship God and gets blessed. Even songs, perhaps because I've personalized them, they bless me. If, individually, we would praise God, then the entire congregation would be praising God.

Her earlier reference to Kurt Carr was directed primarily to Riversdale's youth, most of whom were familiar with this African American gospel singer's hit song, "In the Sanctuary," along with its lyrics celebrating the lifting of hands as an act of worship and praise.[11] While Pastor Bryan was not directly critiquing the spread of African American gospel in Jamaica, it is reasonable to infer from her remark an affinity for styles of musical worship that rely less on "outside" influences, whether those influences are musical or spiritual in nature. It is by directing one's thoughts inwardly, through personal reflection and recollection, that genuine praise and worship are generated. Pastor Bryan emphasized the importance of recognizing the goodness of God in "this place," referring, on one level, to the present ritual situation and, on another, to each individual saint who has experienced the grace of God.

God has been very good to us in this place. I say God has been very good to us in this place, and we ought to praise Him. Glory to God. Let us close our eyes and find one thing, just one thing to thank Him for. Amen.

Pastor Bryan chastised those would try to manufacture the anointing or engaging in overly "ritualistic" practices designed to lure the spiritually gullible.

Her critique extended to followers of a popular American televangelist, Benny Hinn, who is well known for his prayer and healing services, during which supplicants fall to the ground after Hinn blows on them or touches them on the forehead. Pastor Bryan lamented, "Some people need Benny to push them down. But Benny Hinn himself needs to be empowered!" Pastor Bryan sometimes injected humorous discourse such as this into her sermons as a way of keeping her listener's attention. She was particularly effective in reaching the youth of Riversdale, for whom she felt a burden.

Ministering to Youth

As I have mentioned, Pastor Bryan works hard to keep congregants of all ages focused on the Lord. But during my time in Riversdale, she paid special attention to the youth and encouraged them to stay committed to God despite worldly temptations. Before converting to Pentecostalism, Pastor Bryan remembers listening to the dance records featured on guitarist Les Paul's radio program. When reflecting on her pre-Pentecostal days, she states, "I used to like to go to the dances, and I particularly liked the quadrilles." The dancehall is a "field of active cultural production" (Stolzoff 2000, 1) that has long been considered "worldly" and unbefitting of a Pentecostal saint because of its associations with alcohol consumption, immodest dress, sexual promiscuity, and non-Christian music. For church leaders the dancehall represents a serious temptation that threatens to lure Pentecostals, especially youth, away from the church and into a pleasure-seeking lifestyle displeasing to God. The temptation of the dancehall is part of Pastor Bryan's earliest memories of being saved. Her early experiences with the dancehall and her deliverance from worldly attractions provide her with a wellspring of testimonial material, which she uses to compel Pentecostal youth to stay strong and secure in the church. However, despite the fondness she had for the dancehall prior to becoming Pentecostal, she was relieved to be rid of such a lifestyle in exchange for the blessings of safety and peace of mind resulting from her status as a child of God. Moreover, her new relationship with Jesus Christ gave her a joy and contentment that she had never experienced before. She testifies, "I was glad to be rescued from the world."

The term "testifying" applies to narrative accounts and musical renditions in which a saint recalls and gives praise to God for a divine healing, financial blessing, or deliverance from a trying circumstance. A moderator may ask those with a testimony to stand, after which each congregant is recognized in succession. Moderators encourage the saints to testify, but they also must be watchful of the time so that the duration of an individual's testimony does not preclude others from participating or disrupt the flow of the service. They are usually skilled at interspersing songs that relate thematically to the testimonies that are rendered. Through one person's testimony, others are uplifted, not simply because they are "cheered up" by the testifier's successes but, rather, because this type of voiced remembering is contagious. On numerous occasions, I have heard a saint testify about a financial blessing, only to be followed by a dozen or so individuals who, in turn, related similar accounts of God providing money in times of need. Social theorists such as Maurice Halbwachs (1976; 1992) and Paul Connerton (1989) have dealt extensively with the social construction of memory, claiming that religious affiliations provide social groups with the means to acquire and recall memories.[12] Halbwachs's and Connerton's theories concerning the relation between individual and collective memory are relevant to Pentecostal practice insofar as they point to the inherently social aspect of saints' testimonies. Although spoken testimonies are personal and unique to the testifier, it is the congregation that provides the social framework within which each recollection becomes meaningful. A congregation of saints serves as "a community of interests and thoughts" (Connerton 1989, 37) encouraging its members to reconstruct and rearticulate memories for individual and collective benefit. These memories are, as Connerton remarks, "located within the mental and material spaces of the group" (37).[13]

Through testimony, Pastor Bryan uses her past to relate to present-day youth. Worldly lusts, she preaches, fail to satisfy the hunger and thirst that people have for the Spirit of God. "If you are hungry for the Lord," she exhorted one Sunday evening, "the Lord will satisfy your hunger. I don't want to be entangled with the things of the world anymore, all of the fashions and the dance. The world is full of sin and death!" She then launched into "Goodbye World," the old Jamaican chorus repopularized by Donnie McClurkin, a contemporary African American gospel singer.

The chorus lasted about seven minutes and was repeated several times as saints, young and old, were "touched" by the Holy Spirit while singing. To be "touched" or, as Pastor Bryan expresses it, to "get anointed" is one of the primary goals of musical participation in apostolic churches. The touch occurs when the Holy Spirit "gets into a song," sometimes resulting in outbursts of joy, cries of "Hallelujah" or "Thank you, Jesus," ecstatic and glossolalic utterances, holy dancing, and other energetic bodily movements. At other times, however, the Spirit's touch can manifest in less demonstrative fashion. As the chorus concluded, cries of joy and glossolalia continued as Pastor Bryan sat with one hand uplifted, giving God praise. I and the other instrumentalists gradually faded out the musical accompaniment, allowing only the voices of the congregation to punctuate the still-charged atmosphere. Like a shepherd watching over her young flock, Pastor Bryan kept an eye on the saints as the Spirit continued to move among them. After a few minutes, the mood calmed and she stood once more behind the lectern to address the congregation. "We thank the Lord," she started, "for blessing us with a manifestation of His Spirit." She then resumed her earlier testimony, allowing it to flow into a brief sermon urging those who had unsaved friends and relatives to stay strong. "My mother had seven of us, and I'm the only one saved. Pastor Bryan's willingness to share personal stories seemed to have a positive effect on those who listened to her speak. Her message was designed to resonate with those who, like her, did not fit in with their natural families. The testimony she offered was about remaining steadfast and committed to a "superior," spiritual family, regardless of life's ups and downs, and she sought to encourage the saints by example. She exhorted the youth not to allow sexual temptations or the desire to get married to cause them to abandon their relationship with God. "Marriage has teeth; it will bite!" she chided, borrowing a familiar Jamaican proverb. "I could have been married several times over. I have nothing against marriage, but how could I just leave the flock to get married?" Early in her Christian walk, Pastor Bryan had made the decision to remain single for some years, choosing to devote herself to the Lord rather than accept any of the several marriage proposals she received. Her life thus stands as a testament to "the keeping power of Jesus" that allows saints to be adopted into the spiritual family.

Pastor Bryan's impeccable reputation—the saints know that she practices what she preaches—lends her words gravitas, not only at Riversdale but at all the churches in which she is asked to speak. Her life has been one of self-sacrifice and commitment, in exchange for which, she feels, her ministry has been blessed and she experiences the anointing of God. "It pays to serve Jesus!" she declared, concluding her sermon. "I said it *pays* to serve Jesus!" She liked to repeat statements for emphasis, and this time the congregation responded with a hearty "Amen!" "Young people, it is a privilege to serve God. You have some young girls just giving their bodies. But stay with the Lord. We sang that song 'Goodbye World'? Oh yes! I've made up mind to go God's way the rest of my life." Pastor Bryan's testimony and the lyrics of that chorus were mutually supporting. The current popularity of the song among the youth made it a fitting vehicle for the exhortation Pastor Bryan had offered on this evening.

Special services dedicated to young people are common in churches throughout the country. Youth services I attended employed themes of empowerment, such as "Watching, Armed, and Ready." During day one of the annual Youth

Week services I attended at Refuge Temple Apostolic Church in Kingston, the emcee commented on the theme, "Empowered for Service."

> We are empowered for service tonight! We have to tell ourselves that we are empowered for service! We are not lukewarm people. We are supposed to be hot! Hallelujah! Burning up! Hallelujah! If somebody touch us, they supposed to feel a scorch. You know when you just touch the stove? Hallelujah. You know, when you cookin' on the stove and you touch even the steam outta the pot? You supposed to feel a shock. But tonight it seems as though we are not empowered enough. Hallelujah.

Empowerment is, in this case, linked to liveliness and enthusiasm, which are understood to index one's level of spiritual engagement and anointing. However, youth are also encouraged to apply the notion of empowerment to their purpose in life. On the back of the printed program for the Monday night service, the youth president had provided an "Exposition of Theme," which emphasized the importance of youth in spreading the gospel.

> Part of the mandate of God's children is to help in the extension of His Kingdom. We are saved to ensure that God's rule in the heart of people continues unabated. To this end, God has equipped His people with his precious anointing to carry out this rather important task. He has empowered us for service. This task of offering service in God's Kingdom is by no means small, and that's why who- ever undertakes this task has to be filled up with the power of the Holy Ghost. As young, God has called us because we are strong. He understands our frailties yet he has confidence that in Him we can conquer.

Getting children, teens, and young adults to participate wholeheartedly was the immediate goal of Youth Week events, and a different evangelist was sched- uled to preach at Refuge on each night of the week. A young brother stood up after the emcee, offering the following remarks:

> Praise the Lord Jesus! Tonight, I don't need anybody with two sticks and two stones [to] come and light any fire for me. 'Cause if it's even one stick and one stone, I know that my fire's already lit! And it will never go out as Jesus Christ is living in my soul!

Musical praise and worship has a harder edge at this Kingston church than in rural and Spanish Town churches such as Riversdale. A few slow songs were quickly followed by ska-influenced faster pieces that dealt with themes of power and victory. The effectiveness of Pentecostal ritual hinges on the ability of saints to set aside the differences among them and make music "with one accord." Gender, class, race, nationality, and other identity markers are deemed subordinate to the unifying Spirit of God, which enables corporate worship to succeed. Some Christians distinguish Pentecostals according to musical or participatory style. One young man noted singing style and function as a significant distinguishing characteristic, stating that unlike his own church, apostolic churches "use more of that gospel, Shirley Caesar kind of singing to bring down the Spirit!" His reference to Shirley Caesar piqued my curiosity about the different ways African American gospel styles are experienced within Jamaican Pentecostal ritual.

On another night at Refuge Temple, Clarinda, the youth leader, rendered the following exhortation. On this occasion, Clarinda seemed frustrated. The worship service had started, but she could tell that the church's teens seemed distracted. After fifteen minutes of trying to get the congregation to participate in the musical praise, she took the podium and began a brief exhortation in hopes of getting the youth emotionally involved in the musical praise.

> Praise the Lord! He's worthy! Hallelujah in the highest! If those without the Holy Ghost would just believe and shout tonight with a voice of triumph and know that something will happen inside here. Hallelujah, because he will make the darkness light before you tonight. All these people coming here every night and you have not come through [received the baptism of the Holy Spirit], but listen, last night we hear the word about the widow with the little oil. We heard that we don't have to give money to Jesus, but the blessing will flow tonight if we just offer up our sacrifices of praise, because that's what the Lord is asking of us tonight. And when we praise the Lord Jesus, we are the one who is going to be benefited from it. He's just asking us just to praise him so we can enter into his rest.[14]

Such exhortations are commonplace in Jamaican Pentecostal churches. What Clarinda referred to as the "sacrifice of praise" involves the congregants' willingness to put personal feelings or fatigue aside to exert the energy required to praise God as he desires. Clarinda also noted that the goal of the service was for the "blessing" to "flow," thereby linking the Holy Spirit to the human spirits of those in attendance. As Pastor Bryan explained earlier, this connection between Spirit and spirit signifies divine approval of a congregation worshipping "on one accord," and it is in this environment that saints expect the anointing to occur. One of the fascinating challenges that Pentecostal leaders face involves teaching saints, particularly young people, the difference between human and divine agency. Pastor Bryan and others like her continually ask themselves, Is the Spirit truly operative here? Or is this simply "a display of self"? While these questions are not always easily answered in Pentecostal services, the distinction is even more difficult to discern during gospel concerts, which feature a greater representation of men as soloists and emcees.

"Having Church" in a Concert Frame

Gospel concerts usually take place at times and places outside of the Sunday morning Pentecostal service. They generally feature a variety of styles, including traditional hymns and gospel reggae, as well as music recorded by contemporary African American gospel artists such as Yolanda Adams, Kirk Franklin, Donnie McClurkin, and Fred Hammond. For young people, concerts provide an acceptable form of entertainment and an opportunity to socialize with youth outside of their regular congregations. The conceptual distinctions between "concert" and "church service," "entertainment" and "ministry," "performance" and "praise" are difficult to pinpoint. In fact, gospel artists "have church" even while working within a concert setting by attempting to infuse their performances with authentic evocations of divine power. God's anointing is not believed to be contingent upon a particular frame of action. In fact, when manifestations of the Holy Spirit occur during a gospel concert, they reinforce the notion that divine actions can occur spontaneously through musical expression wherever it takes place. It is common to hear gospel artists express their desire to invoke God's presence by announcing, "We're not here to entertain you." While entertainment is understood to appeal to one's emotions, it is deemed far less important than ministry, which addresses one's *spiritual* needs by using music and speech to transmit the word of God. This is one reason gospel artists inject spoken testimonies or "sermonettes" into their concert performances, which sometimes conclude with an altar call inviting audience members to come forward, receive prayer, and commit their lives to Jesus Christ.

Concerts take place either inside a church or outside in open air, and they feature an all-star lineup of local and international artists, whose performances are interspersed with raffles, announcements, and testimonies. During a concert I attended in Kingston, one of the emcees, Kenneth, felt so moved by Sandra Brooks's performance of her hit song "The Answer" that he attempted to reframe the event as a church service. It is important to recognize that such reframings are commonplace among gospel artists who generally strive not merely to entertain or "perform" but to "minister" and bring about spiritual transcendence in their listeners by evoking divine power (see Allen 1991). Although Kenneth encountered difficulties caused by the exigencies of the concert program, he persisted in trying to "have church," moving beyond the expectations of those who had come merely to be entertained, while perhaps fulfilling the expectations of those familiar with the conventions of Pentecostal performance.[15]

> Can we just have a little church out here tonight? Hallelujah to God. When I think about Jesus and what he has done for me tonight, I just want to praise him and give him glory! Can we just have a little worship? Is there anybody here that wants to *worship*? Is there anybody here that just wanna stretch their hands up and say, "Lord, I love you! Lord, I give you praise! I give you honor!" Oh, I know *you* came to a concert, but I came to touch the hem of Jesus's garment. Can somebody just blow him a kiss tonight? Holy Ghost! I feel the presence of the Lord here! I feel God here! Oh, come on somebody, just wave your hands. Clap your hands and give the Lord a praise.

After another emcee attempts to reestablish control by "moving the program along" and continuing with some free giveaways, Kenneth interjects again. Sensing the anointing, he is compelled to interrupt the concert program and acknowledge the Spirit's presence, thus fulfilling what believers refer to as the "higher obligation" of Pentecostal worship.

> Hallelujah. I really feel a shout coming on. Oh, God! Hallelujah to God. I wish somebody would just forget that we're in a concert and just jump to their feet! I wish we never had so many things to give away at this time, so we could just go on crazy. Am I in the presence of Pentecostal people tonight? Am I in the presence of Holy Ghost people tonight?

Kenneth's comments are not at all uncommon in gospel concerts that take place among groups consisting mostly of Pentecostals. While his remarks invite attendees to participate in Pentecostal praise and worship, Kenneth also establishes his identity as a legitimate Pentecostal. He also performs his identity as a believer who experiences the touch of the Holy Spirit without allowing the concert frame to hinder his praise. His admonition to the audience to "blow [Jesus] a kiss" is also noteworthy in that it signals a willingness to worship God in ways that have been socially constructed as feminine, as I have mentioned above. Moreover, he uses a technique, employed by Pentecostal preachers, of drawing on the audience's knowledge of proper Pentecostal responses to the Spirit. His statement, "Oh, I know *you* came to a concert," gently accuses the professed Pentecostals in the audience of having come for entertainment purposes rather than to praise God. The distinction created by Kenneth's remarks between himself as a true worshipper and the audience as entertainment seekers resonates with the call and response of a Pentecostal chorus: "I don't know what *you* come to do. [*call*] I come to praise the Lord. [*response*]" Unlike this popular church chorus, however, Kenneth's remarks take place in a concert setting in which the "sincerity" of the listeners is more open to question. The distinction drawn between the emcee and the audience is meant to produce a tension that serves as an impetus for action. Kenneth makes this tension more palpable by posing the questions, "Am I in the presence of Pentecostal people tonight? Am I in the presence of Holy Ghost people tonight?" His questions require Pentecostal listeners to make a choice between either "sitting down on the Lord" by refusing to acknowledge God's presence, or submitting to the Holy Spirit by offering him the "sacrifice of praise." The concert attendees, perhaps wishing not only to join in collective praise but also to prove Kenneth's accusation false, begin to stand up, lifting their arms and shouting words of praise to God. These activities enable Pentecostals to identify themselves before God and one another as fellow saints who, like Kenneth, came to "touch the hem of Jesus's garment."

Most Pentecostals I know would admit that the Spirit is not automatically operative in every gospel concert setting. Indeed, it would be naïve to posit that all concert attendees who join in collective praise and worship are responding to manifestations of the Holy Spirit. Among Pentecostals, however, complete unresponsiveness may be viewed as a sign that one is spiritually cold, backslidden, or unsaved. During gospel concerts, as well as church services, there remains a considerable amount of social pressure to behave in ways that conform to an established worship ideal. Some concertgoers, Pentecostal and otherwise, may simply react to a gospel singer or emcee who is extremely skilled at captivating listeners through performance. Moreover, attendees are also aware of the potential for emotional manipulation through music, and may choose, therefore, to restrain themselves during gospel concerts to which they have admittedly come not to seek worship but to enjoy being entertained. Since their desire for collective communion with God is satisfied in church services, they see gospel concerts primarily as opportunities to socialize and take pleasure in an artist's musical talents within an acceptable public arena. I would point out further that some Pentecostals choose not to join in collective praise because they doubt the singer's or speaker's authenticity. When singers or emcees are felt to lack the anointing, a Pentecostal concertgoer may make a conscious decision not to respond to their hollow displays of "showmanship." To do so in this case would be to engage in hypocrisy, sanctimoniously going through the motions of praise in order to demonstrate one's legitimacy as a Pentecostal.

These observations are not meant to deny validity to acts of praise and worship. Validity, per se, is simply not the point. I hope, rather, to shed light on the complex social interactions that characterize Pentecostal musical events. We can see that gifts of the Spirit "are manifest in the form of particular norms of performance" and that the occurrence of these gifts is, as Matthew Guest (2002) maintains, "subject to social pressures that persist in communal contexts" where "expressions of power may effectively be contested or embraced in relation to group dynamics" (45). Kenneth's mild accusation produces the results he desires because of its subtlety along with the shared assumptions concerning gospel music and entertainment held by Pentecostals. On the one hand, the event is ostensibly framed as a gospel concert for which Christians may derive an acceptable form of entertainment. On the other hand, it is understood that while entertainment in this situation is certainly not a sinful activity, it is a much less noble endeavor than praise and worship, particularly during genuine manifestations of the Holy Spirit. Church leaders such as Pastor Bryan seldom attend gospel concerts, preferring to seek the face of God in environments where showmanship and the display of self are more strictly regulated. As Pastor Bryan declares, "we must allow self to decrease and God to increase" in order to experience the power of God in our lives.

Conclusion

This chapter has examined the concepts of power and anointing as they apply to speech and embodied worship in church and concert settings. "Anointing" is a disputed term, and discussions about when and where musical genres and performers merit that designation can be awkward and uncomfortable. Scholars of music tend not to get embroiled in such theological debates. Rather, our discussions revolve around the aspects of music-making that are observable, analyzable, and able to be subjected, if you will, to the rigors of empirical study. Nevertheless, my conversations with Pastor Hermine Bryan, along with my myriad experiences among saints elsewhere, lead me to make some assertions about the role of music in "anointed" rituals, be they sacred or secular.

Church leaders urge all members to engage their minds and bodies in worship services with the goal of receiving the anointing of the Holy Spirit. Musical activities are understood to be a catalyst for transcendent experiences that will empower women, men, and children to lead a life that is untainted by the world. In this way, the boundaries between holiness and worldliness are reaffirmed and Pentecostal Christian identities are cast as morally distinct. Even when delivered by men, these Pentecostal messages can be interpreted as calls for women's spiritual empowerment and youth participation. Given that most congregants are women, sermons about God's anointing can perhaps be read as messages of women's empowerment in the face of spiritual threats but also in response to perceived male domination. Even "the devil" is cast as a male figure. And Elder Facey's warning to those who have a "girlfriend on the side" is aimed at "carnal" men in the congregation who are unfaithful to their wives. As I have tried to convey, men gain a degree of "street cred" by ironic virtue of their sexual promiscuity, drinking, and gambling. These behaviors conform to social stereotypes concerning "manly" characteristics, but they are taboo within the realm of Pentecostal practice. Once a man converts to Christianity, and especially if he joins a Pentecostal church, he finds that expressive behaviors socially constructed as feminine are revaluated as symbols of a Spirit-filled man. Of course, not all men outside of the church fit the social stereotype. But for those who do, becoming a Pentecostal requires being open to an exchange of "street cred" for "church cred," along with a willingness to put one's singing, dancing body on ritual display as evidence of intimacy with God. Musical performance is a way of reasserting gender norms and solidifying the lines that separate men's and women's social behavior. This is, however, only part of the story. As Stokes (1994) reminds us, music "does more than underscore, or express differences already there. Music and more particularly dance provides an arena for pushing back boundaries, exploring the border zones that separate male from female" (22).

Discourses of gender and spiritual flow provide insights into the phenomenology of music, ritual, and worship in Jamaican Pentecostal practice. In this chapter, I have highlighted the words and actions of Pastor Bryan, whose decades of experience in the church have afforded her a keen understanding of how spiritual power flows among people of faith. As Elizabeth Pritchard (2019) affirms, "Pentecostals imagine 'spirit' not as a safely contained, distant, or transcendent divinity, but as a power pulsing through and linking individuals" (5). Yet I must also acknowledge that much of what is attributed to Pentecostal worship in Jamaica also occurs in other cultural and theological domains. Notions of spiritual approval and flow derive from biblical passages that are read by religious practitioners throughout the Christian world. Christians are not unanimous in their manner of interpreting the present-day role of the Holy Spirit, and it would be a mistake to declare Pentecostals the sole beneficiaries of "the anointing" or to suggest that they enjoy a monopoly on transcendent experiences. Moreover, I have heard Christians across denominations speak of "pleading the blood." Pentecostals claim solidarity with other Christians in their war against spiritual adversaries, and songs about the redemptive power of Jesus's blood form part of a shared repertory of music that cuts across denominational and cultural boundaries.

What, then, are we to make of Pentecostals' claims to moral, theological, and cultural difference? What is at stake for saints who embrace these discourses

and practices as "their own"? One troublesome tactic would be to label Pentecostals who make claims of exclusivity as unfortunate victims of spiritual brain-
washing or as the human by-products of a hegemonic religious denomination
that has led them into delusions of distinctiveness. I avoid this wholesale rejection of Pentecostal perspectives in order to give primacy of place to the role of
ritual in allowing believers to "appropriate" musical and religious styles as their
own. Helpful here is Paul Ricoeur's notion of appropriation as "understanding
at and through distance, to make one's own" that which was initially "alien"
(Ricoeur 1981; cited in Rice 1994, 6). It is also worth calling attention to the
strategies of "appropriation" through which scholars situate themselves within
spaces designated as "field" and "home." I appropriated Jamaican Pentecostal
songs as a way to grasp their rhythmic feel and to gain a thorough understanding of how they are sung and experienced. I also "made them my own" for the
purpose of gaining spiritual encouragement and sustenance while away from
my church in Brooklyn. This appropriation, on my part, was necessary because
of the stylistic and social differences between Pentecostalism as I have come
to know it in the United States and the way this faith is exercised in Jamaica.
Since Jamaican-style church music was initially less familiar to me, I needed
to acquire a more or less mundane understanding of it before it could serve as
a vehicle for spiritual transcendence.

Pentecostals throughout Jamaica find a variety of music to be an effective
means of experiencing empowerment and transcendence. Even musical and
ritual styles from opposite sides of the globe are appropriated by believers to
assert identities as Jamaicans who are most fundamentally Pentecostal believers. Moreover, it is crucial that we understand identity not as an ontologically
fixed set of facts about an individual or group. Rather, identity is "about collective self-understanding as represented by various characteristics, activities, and
customs, including music" (Rice 2007, 23). Jamaican Pentecostals' discourses of
distinctiveness are based on their experiences of spiritual flow, anointing, and
power. These experiences engender deeply entrenched understandings of what
makes musical worship special. As I have emphasized, Pentecostals believe
that to effectively touch God, praise must be done wholeheartedly, and this is
understood to mean that both body and mind are involved. A lack of energy
in a worship service is taken as a sign of disunity, which is, in turn, believed to
indicate that God is not pleased. These concerns are also a major aspect of the
Pentecostal tradition as it is imagined and reconstructed in Jamaica. I take up
this issue in chapter 4.

CHAPTER 4

The Old-Time Way

Nostalgia, Tradition, and Testimony

I found time to visit more than a dozen churches in Spanish Town and nearby Kingston while staying at Pastor Bryan's home. But most of my Sundays were spent with her at Riversdale Pentecostal Church. After morning worship, for which I played keyboards and directed a small choir, the saints went home for an afternoon meal and rest before returning for the evening service. I ate dinner at the home of Sister Sewell, who spoke at length about music and the Pentecostal tradition of which she was proud to belong. A schoolteacher and mother to three teenagers, Sister Sewell dislikes the changes that have occurred since her arrival at Riversdale in the early 1970s. She recalls that they used to sing mostly hymns and Jamaican choruses, rather than gospel songs by African American recording artists who were now popular among the youth. She yearns for "that old-time way" and expresses nostalgia for the way things "used to be."[1] Music is not the only aspect of Pentecostal practice that Sister Sewell feels has changed for the worse. She recollects that they used to wear simple head wraps rather than spend money on expensive hats. Modern-day Pentecostals, she feels, allow the latest fashions to woo them, such that "posh dressing" has become a status marker within and among certain congregations. Dress nevertheless continues to serve a social leveling function in some churches. For example, women in Pentecostal organizations such as Shiloh Apostolic have traditionally dressed entirely in white to mask socioeconomic differences and to promote modesty. Music is thus one element in a kaleidoscope of values and aesthetics that saints use to nurture a sense of collective moral distinctiveness. Through traditional song and testimonial speech, Pentecostals inhabit modes of longing and belonging, which, in turn, prompt a reimagining of pasts that are alive and "usable" in the present.[2]

The evening service got underway around dusk and lasted until around 9:30, after which Pastor Bryan and I, along with whomever needed a ride back to Spanish Town, began the forty-five-minute journey home. Pastor Bryan has been driving back and forth between Spanish Town and Riversdale since the early 1970s, when she was first asked to help out as a Sunday School teacher. Once we arrived home, Pastor Bryan would sometimes relate a few of her past experiences as we snacked on roasted breadfruit and sorrel juice before turning in. Her accounts were relaxing and full of nostalgia. They felt to me like bedtime stories meant to calm a hectic mind at day's end. One evening, she reminisced, "I remember before I started pastoring when we used to walk to church or take public transportation. And a brother had a banjo and he'd play and we'd sing songs sometimes as we walked home. Those were good old times. I enjoyed those days. People were so much more caring. Jamaica was such a paradise."

This chapter discusses Pentecostal music-making as a collective call for a return to the ways of yesteryear. While church youth are typically content with the here and now, my Pentecostal consultants old enough to remember the 1960s allege that Jamaican society used to reflect a greater degree of "respect." They express concern that the modernization of Pentecostal practice, fueled by the migratory flow of people, images, and sounds to and from the United States, amounts to "letting down the standard" of holiness that differentiates Pentecostals from "the world." Heightened expressions of nostalgia began to surface during a transitional moment within the Pentecostal Assemblies of the World in Jamaica, as younger leadership moved the organization closer to a North American model of practice. My concern is thus with the degree to which "nostalgia triumphs when the continuities with the past (especially collective identity) are disrupted or threatened" (Averill 2003, 15).

Sister Sewell and Pastor Bryan convey a nostalgia that parallels the fondness with which they recall the events of their natural and spiritual childhoods. The love that saints express for the church of the past extends to Jamaica's social landscape in those years surrounding independence, and also to a spiritual childhood to which Pentecostals attach a more intense connection with God. Moreover, I propose that the "old-time way" to which Pentecostals lay claim as a distinctively Jamaican social and musical "paradise" is part of an invented tradition and a usable past shared by Christian practitioners across ritual and cultural boundaries. Reminiscing about shared traditions and personal battles won are strategies that serve to uplift the saints, whether they are on the giving or receiving end of a testimony. Maintaining hope for the future in the face of a troubled past and present requires sung and spoken corroboration of God's ability to heal and deliver his children. "Be encouraged!" I often hear, "If he did it for me, he can do it for you!" Hearing saints' testimonies is, as Frederick (2016) explains, "a way of identifying eventual triumph" (127). When Pentecostals make music and offer spoken testimonies, they re-member past traditions, imbuing the "old-time way" with new significance as a contemporary marker of local authenticity and divine favor.

Hymns, Song Lyrics, and Meaningfulness

In 1962, when Jamaica's gold, green, and black flag replaced the Union Jack, Pastor Bryan was a newcomer to Pentecostalism. Her personal experiences with God, along with the songs and sermons she heard, were fresh and exciting. While Jamaica celebrated its political independence from Great Britain, Pastor Bryan and other new converts were enjoying a new spiritual freedom from their previous lifestyles. The music they learned during this pivotal historical moment would accrue layers of signification over the subsequent decades, and it is now part of a cherished tradition experienced as distinctly Jamaican and Pentecostal in character.

On several occasions, I have heard Jamaican saints celebrate what they perceive to be the distinctiveness of their Pentecostal tradition. They sometimes do so while knowing full well that their hymns and choruses are also sung by worshippers in the United States and elsewhere. As I explain later, it matters a great deal that songs are rendered in a "Jamaican style," a phrase that my consultants used to connote the accompaniment rhythms derived from older forms of popular dance music, as well as the "island flavor" of church songs influenced by American country-and-western music. In other words, one of the major concerns is *how* church songs are performed; their manner of performance is what makes them special and distinct. What is even more important to church leaders, however, is that their music remains thematically distinct from those performed "out in the world" of unbelievers and serves as a vehicle for religious transcendence.

Pastor Bryan and other Pentecostals draw from a many-splendored repertory of hymns and choruses. Two hymnals, *Pentecostal Hymnal* and *Redemption Songs*, were most commonly used during the time of my fieldwork, although lyrics may be "lined out" or sung from memory.[3] Instrumentation varied greatly according to locale. "Country churches"—those located outside of Kingston and Montego

Bay—usually feature a cappella singing or use only a single instrumentalist, such as a guitarist, for accompaniment. In Kingston, by contrast, there are several much larger assemblies whose membership exceeds five hundred. Such churches are generally equipped with a Hammond organ, drum set, electric keyboards, and guitars to accompany the singing of the congregation and one or more mass choirs. Even as a spiritual newborn, Pastor Bryan loved singing hymns and choruses that convey a respect for the apostolic Pentecostal tradition. As a young woman, she learned the art of ministering through song and word under the fatherly guidance of her pastor, Bishop Norman Walters, whose teachings had a major influence on her spiritual development and approach to Christian ministry. Bishop Walters soon noticed the musical abilities and spiritual dedication of "Sister Bryan," as she was then known, and would ask her to lead the congregation in song during portions of the worship service known as devotion (or song service) and testimony service.

When addressing her congregation at Riversdale Pentecostal Church, Pastor Bryan often discusses her past experiences leading congregational singing. "I used to love leading song service," she recalled. "I would pick out songs in advance, so my songs were prepared. Then I prayed over those songs and asked God, 'Lord, bless these songs!' And my songs were a blessing! Songs like 'Standing on Promise Ground.' Those words consoled me." Pastor Bryan's remarks provide a lesson for Riversdale's song leaders, some of whom are still being trained under her watchful eyes. During her earlier years in the ministry, she would draw from two hymnals, both of which continue to provide a wide repertory of songs for Jamaican Pentecostal churches. The hymnal, *The Best of All* (Carradine, Fowler, and Kirkpatrick, n.d.), published in the United States by a church affiliated with the Pentecostal Assemblies of the World, was used in Jamaica when Pastor Bryan first started leading song services. The copyright dates of hymns in *The Best of All* range from 1874 to 1908. A number of hymns such as "Old Time Power," "'Tis the Old Time Religion," "The Old Fountain," "Back to Pentecost," and "The Old Account Was Settled Long Ago," deal with themes of the past. *The Best of All* was soon replaced by *Redemption Songs*, which is still widely used and has become emblematic of Jamaican Pentecostal practice. In her copy of *The Best of All*, Pastor Bryan wrote in numbers corresponding to pages in *Redemption Songs*. As Pastor Bryan explains, "*Redemption Songs* was new at the time, so I'd give you the number in *The Best of All* and then in *Redemption Songs*. They stopped making *The Best of All*, so I think that's why we had to stop using them."

"We used to sing that one when we were tarrying," recalled Pastor Bryan, as I perused the lyrics of "Old Time Power." Pentecostals speak of "tarrying" as a ritual practice derived from the instructions Jesus gave to his disciples to tarry in Jerusalem for the gift of the Holy Spirit. Although the word "tarry" means "to wait," this is understood to mean a kind of *active* waiting, during which those seeking to be filled or "baptized" with the Holy Spirit are urged to pray sincerely while offering God audible praise. In describing the rites of "spirit possession" she experienced while attending the African American Pentecostal church of her youth, musicologist Teresa Reed (2012) provides a vivid description of tarrying that applies remarkably well to the Jamaican Pentecostal context.

> In my church, a particular rite that relied heavily upon rhythmic worship and sung invitations to the Holy Spirit was the *tarrying service* [italics in the original]. In this rite, candidates who were ready to be filled with the Holy Ghost . . . would gather at the Saturday-night prayer meeting designated specifically for this purpose. Typically, the tarrying service would begin when a song leader initiated a repetitive, call-and-response, congregational song, usually to the accompaniment of hand-claps, foot-stomps, tambourines, drums, and keyboard instruments. To the sound of this music, the "seekers" would be encircled and encouraged by helpers who assisted with prayer and praise until the achievement of infilling became evident. Often, the text of the opening song would give way to the rhythmic, continual repetition of the phrase "Thank you Jesus." After continuous repetition of the phrase, the evidence of the candidate's infilling (or possession) by the Holy Ghost was in whether or not he or she spoke in tongues. At the conclusion of tarrying service (which usually lasted for hours), candidates were asked to give their testimonies, and the leader judged at that point which cases of infilling were genuine and which were not. Those who had failed to become filled with the Spirit were admonished to return for the next week's tarrying service. (15)

Reed adds that African American tarrying services and other forms of "ritual singing" are "strikingly parallel to [those] found in Afro-Caribbean Pentecostal traditions" (16). As is the case in African American Pentecostal churches, some Jamaican "seekers" tarry for years without experiencing the baptism of the Holy Spirit, while others receive it on their first try. Pastors caution, however, that a prolonged period of waiting should not be necessary if an individual's heart is properly geared toward God. Lengthy tarrying services have, consequently, become controversial. Nevertheless, they continue to constitute a major component of Pentecostal ritual in Jamaica and throughout the African diaspora.[4] At Riversdale and elsewhere, music is understood to play a critically important role in whether tarrying will have the desired outcome. Pastor Bryan explains that while the Holy Spirit is not constrained by human actions, the ritual and social atmosphere that music creates can either help or hinder an individual who seeks a spiritual blessing. It is for this reason that so much emphasis is placed on traditional hymns that are "tried and true."

Over the years, Pastor Bryan has maintained a collection of old songbooks. "These are all really old songs!" I mused, flipping through her tattered copy of *The Best of All*. "That's right," Pastor Bryan agreed. "Those are songs with *meaning!*" I noticed that several hymns, such as "Old Time Power" by Charlie Tillman, were copyrighted around 1895. In fact, as products of the Holiness movement in the United States, most songs in *The Best of All* were composed well before the 1906 Azusa Street revival (see Introduction). Some of these songs, such as "Baptized with the Holy Ghost," composed in 1896, refer to Pentecost or Holy Spirit baptism, despite the fact that most Holiness adherents had not yet accepted or received the doctrine of tongues at the time these songs were written. What this demonstrates, of course, is that the Pentecostal revival did not begin overnight. Rather, it represented a gradual shift from the Holiness movement, as various individuals and groups of people began to experience Holy Spirit baptism over time. Moreover, when Pentecostals speak of "old-time" ways, they conflate a number of "pasts" to re-member not only the days of their spiritual youth but also an era of religious practice that precedes their physical birth.

A fondness for the Jamaica of old times is also expressed in songs such as "Give Me that Old Time Religion" and "Lord, Take Me Back to the Old Landmark." I asked Pastor Bryan to explain the biblical concept of "the Old Landmark" (Proverbs 23:10–11).[5] "We must not take away the old landmark," Pastor Bryan began. "If you do, it's like you're stealing something. That song, 'Lord, Take Me Back to the Old Landmark'? It's like you're drifting and you want to go back to the spiritual place where you used to be." Another preacher noted that "the Old Landmark means getting back to the root of the Word." He spoke of the importance of passing on the Word of God to subsequent generations. Pastor Bryan also remembers how some church leaders used to enjoy having her as moderator for testimony services because she sang "the old-time songs." Although Pastor Bryan now seeks to train younger saints to lead congregational singing, she still enjoys leading songs from time to time, selecting pieces such as "I Love the Old Time Way," "We Preach Like the Apostles," and "John Saw Them Coming." Another of the older hymns Pastor Bryan appreciates is "The Good Old-fashioned Way." Pastor Bryan learns the newer songs mostly through the radio and cassettes. However, she finds that the lyrics of contemporary gospel songs tend to lack a certain spiritual richness. They fail to communicate biblical truths in a way that touches hearts and transforms lives as the Word of God should. While Pastor Bryan hopes to instill in younger generations of churchgoers the value of the old-time way, youth tend to be enamored with contemporary gospel music that is more "secular-sounding." As musicologist Tammy Kernodle explains, although "fears that the church has 'lost' gospel [music] to the world are nurtured in many traditional circles, the influence of the music—and its accompanying images of dancing choirs, glamorized and highly coiffed purveyors in the newest and hippest fashions—on younger and secular audiences has not lessened" (2006, 90). Kernodle's observations apply well to youth in both Jamaican and African American cultural contexts. Pentecostal pastors on the island and in the United States balance their need to salvage an "old-time" appreciation for slower songs and "sober" or thoughtful lyrics with a grudging attempt to sustain the interest of youth drawn primarily to a danceable beat.

As Pastor Bryan elaborates, "With some new songs, it's just the rhythm. But these old songs, [like] 'I'm Anchored on the Solid Ground'—you sing four song[s] and you can go home!" Pastor Bryan works to instill a respect for the best of the Pentecostal musical tradition in the saints at Riversdale. She worries that youth are too eager to settle for "superficial" songs and tepid spiritual experiences rather than seeking the best that God has provided for us. She laments, "Some people, you know, can't appreciate the finer things in life." Nevertheless, Pastor Bryan is aware of the need to maintain the attention of the youth and makes conscious efforts to keep them engaged in the services. She allows members of the youth choir to sing their favorite pieces, provided the lyrics are scripturally based and edifying to the church. She also continues to introduce traditional hymns and choruses to inexperienced congregants. "But you can't go too far back," she noted, "because then the young people can't sing. You have to strike a medium. The young people like—what's that song by Kurt Carr? 'I Almost Let Go'! America cough and Jamaica sneeze! Jamaica has so many ties in America."

Lyrics are meaningful texts that help us understand how hymns and choruses shape and reflect Pentecostals' historical consciousness. But there is a significant difference between *lyrical* meaning and its relation to historical consciousness, on the one hand, and the meaningfulness of a song as a unit, independent of its lyrics, on the other. During one service, Pastor Bryan commented on my interest in her ability to recall such a wide repertory of songs. She mused, "Brother Butler marvels that I know all of these songs by heart. I sing them until the words sink into my soul!" Song lyrics carry tremendous emotional and spiritual meaning for Pentecostals such as Pastor Bryan. Like other saints, she meditates on them and derives from them a feeling of encouragement. However, just as Hinson (2000, 345) finds in his study of African American Pentecostals, not all Jamaican Pentecostals who enjoy singing older hymns do so because of an attachment to the song's lyrics. Meaning, as Hinson elaborates, "tends to get vested in the whole rather than in its parts. Hence, while the song as a unit might carry significance, the words themselves lose their meaningful particularity" (95). Hinson also points out that this absence of lyrically derived meaning need not suggest a lack of spiritual sincerity or devotional engagement on the part of the singer. He adds that

> meanings that attach themselves to a song as a whole, wholly apart from its lyrics, might themselves prompt reflection and engagement. All songs, after all, exist in a world of memory and association. The acts of retrieval and performance might well spark memories that link particular songs with people, places, and/ or events that hold special significance for the singer. These memories might then trigger praises every bit as deep as those prompted in another singer by the lyrics. Hence, though the singing might be rote, devotional engagement might nonetheless be intense. (345n9)

Jamaican Pentecostals use music not only to reference their personal histories but also to retell a historical narrative of the biblical Day of Pentecost as it occurred in Jerusalem centuries ago. Musical expression is a means through which various pasts are creatively articulated in order to underscore present-day religious identifications that define Pentecostals vis-à-vis the secular world.

Change and Continuity in a Pentecostal Convention

All Saints Apostolic Church in Spanish Town is a crucial site for the development of Pentecostalism in Jamaica, especially in Spanish Town. From 1945 until 1999, All Saints was the site of the annual summer Convention of the Jamaican district of the Pentecostal Assemblies of the World. For some saints, the Jamaican Convention supplements the much larger International PAW Convention held in the United States. For those who cannot secure a visa for travel abroad, the local Convention is a prized alternative to the one held in the United States. For Jamaican saints residing in the United States, the Jamaican Convention provides an occasion for which to return home to the island for a spiritual family reunion.

Since the turn of the twenty-first century, there has been a major shift in the way the Jamaican Convention takes place. A watershed moment occurred as the deaths of Bishops Norman Walters and Allan Peart in 1991 and 1999, respectively, coincided with the rapid influx of global media.[6] Both Walters and Peart

All Saints Apostolic Church, Spanish Town. Photo by the author.

had served as presiding bishop of the Jamaican diocese of the PAW and exerted a great deal of control over Pentecostal churches in Jamaica. Bishop Peart became pastor of All Saints when Walters died in 1991. Peart also succeeded Walters as diocesan bishop and strove to continue in the tradition embraced by his predecessor. With the passing of Bishop Peart came a number of changes. The 1999 Convention at All Saints would be the last to be held at this locale, and the following year it took place in a newly acquired venue to accommodate the growing membership in the Jamaican branch of the organization. Jamaica's new presiding diocesan bishop, Noel Jones, was born and raised in Jamaica, but most Pentecostals on the island consider him to be "Americanized" because he has lived in the United States since the 1960s and is pastor of a church in California. With Jones came a new, contemporary orientation. Several churches that had left the organization over disputes with the old guard rejoined the Jamaican district. In its new, much larger locale, the Convention took on more of the characteristics of the International Convention held in the United States. Drum sets and electric keyboards were allowed for the first time, and a new generation of singers joined the choir, led by more contemporary-minded directors. One of the music leaders in 2002 explained to me that a committee was formed to

New Site of the Jamaican Convention of the Pentecostal Assemblies of the World Inc. in Spanish Town. Photo by the author.

choose the musical selections to be sung by the Convention choir. The choir's repertory began to expand, including songs by African American recording artists such as Byron Cage, Richard Smallwood, Kurt Carr, and the multiracial Brooklyn Tabernacle Choir.

Convention services featured a mixed repertory of contemporary African American gospel and traditional Jamaican choruses. Congregations would sing something like "I'll Say Yes" in an African American style before moving into a ska version of the same song. This might then segue into a medley of Jamaican choruses, such as "One More Time" or "Born, Born, Born Again." These choruses employ the hand-clapping patterns characteristic of an older, traditional style of Jamaican Pentecostal practice (see Hopkin 1978). Although the modernization of Jamaican Pentecostal practice brought the PAW more in line with some of the more progressive Pentecostal organizations on the island, there was still a traditional flavor to the services. Much caution was exercised in an attempt to satisfy both older and younger generations. As choir repertories incorporated newer gospel styles, music directors sought to strike a balance so as to continue to draw and maintain youth in the church and avoid offending the older saints. If songs were arranged in a contemporary style, they would feature traditional, hymn-based lyrics conspicuously drawn from biblical texts. The song "There Is a Fountain" was selected precisely because one of its verses is lyrically identical to an eighteenth-century hymn with which older choristers were familiar.

> There is a fountain filled with blood
> Drawn from Emmanuel's veins
> And sinners plunged beneath that flood
> Lose all their guilty stains.

During the Convention I attended in 2002 there were frequent references to the past, and church leaders advocated a respect for the tradition. While choral performances featured songs by contemporary African American gospel groups, congregational songs leaders were also careful to include a significant portion of traditional hymns and Jamaican choruses. It is interesting that some of the most popular Jamaican choruses were relatively new ones, composed only within the previous five or ten years. These choruses are particularly popular among youth who learn and compose new choruses in a traditional Jamaican style, containing musical traits, such as a ska-like rhythmic accompaniment, and using Jamaican patois. These characteristics mark the chorus as a local piece whose composition is assumed to predate the more "modern sounding" gospel music imported from abroad. Thus, it seems "the Jamaican tradition" is continually redefined and reappropriated to fit the needs of contemporary Pentecostal youth. Nevertheless, since the 1990s, Convention participants have gradually moved toward greater incorporation of African American gospel music.

In talking to saints about how they experience the changes taking place in the Jamaican Convention, I found that some of them were uncomfortable with the push toward contemporary styles. Members of Wondrous Love, a Jamaican Pentecostal church in New York (see chapter 1), spoke to me about the uniformity and "oneness" of mind and spirit that characterized the Convention when it was held at All Saints, particularly in terms of dress, standards, and music. Sister Andrea is a thirty-three-year-old mother of three who currently serves as youth president at Wondrous Love. She has been going to Wondrous Love since 1979, when she relocated with her parents from Jamaica to the United States. Despite attending Wondrous Love for nearly twenty-five years, Andrea was not saved until 1999. She has fond memories of her first visit to Convention that year and enjoys reflecting on the "oneness" that characterized the services she attended.

> I went because everyone was saying how rich it was and that it was a place of blessings, and that the anointing was there. And when I went, I saw how they

were so much on one accord. Here, there are like sects, but there, it was like everyone was together, even the look, the dress. There was still that oneness. Here, in the U.S., it's so diverse. There are different standards. But in Jamaica everyone has similar dress and pretty much the same standards, even the way the services are held. If you go to church there, you know you're going to see the same things.[7]

Reflecting on the traditional standards established by past leaders, she states, "The choir was a hymnal choir, selected by the bishop. Sleeves had to be down to here [past the elbow], and you couldn't wear open-toe or open-back shoes!" Although she admits that during her teenage years she felt that those traditional standards were too strict for her, she now embraces them and has an unfavorable opinion of the changes that have begun to occur since 1999. In 2000, when Andrea returned to Convention, she noticed significant changes stemming from the appointment of a new presiding bishop and the acquisition of a new Convention site. She returned to Convention in 2001 and 2002, mainly to witness how the plans of the new bishop were being implemented and to get a feel for where the Jamaican PAW was heading. Discouraged by the continuing liberalization of traditional standards in Jamaica, she insists, "I just don't really have a desire to go back." What she has seen since 1999 lacks the "unity" of previous years; and, for her, that unity was what made the Jamaican Convention worth attending.

Sentiments of nostalgia for Jamaica's past are expressed most strongly by older saints who grew up attending services and conventions at All Saints since the 1950s. Sister Shields, age seventy, beams while reminiscing about the days shortly after Jamaica's independence in 1962 when she was a young woman still living on the island. Like Andrea, she attends Wondrous Love. Since Convention time was approaching, she had made her annual trip to Jamaica, where she would spend the next two weeks at the home of Pastor Bryan. During the 2001 Convention commemorating the seventieth anniversary of the PAW in Jamaica, both Sister Shields and Pastor Bryan were among the "Heritage Singers," a choral group made up of former members of the Convention choir. Sister Hall, age fifty, also spoke much about the way things were back in the old days. A member of All Saints since the time of Bishop Norman Walters, she recalled how much different and better things were in those days. Referring to the musical practices of saints in the PAW, she noted that Walters would not tolerate all of the "racket and carrying on" that now occurs. He did not allow drums to be played, for example. This established a tradition of not having drum sets in PAW churches. During my fieldwork in 2002, this tradition was still being maintained at All Saints, Wondrous Love, and other apostolic Pentecostal churches in Jamaica and the United States. Sister Hall believes that this uneasiness regarding the drums stems from a perceived proximity to Revival churches, which I discussed in chapter 1.

While some of the Pentecostal churches I visited in Jamaica, especially those affiliated with the Pentecostal Assemblies of the World, did not allow drums, this is no longer the norm. Indeed, the 2000 Convention set in motion changes in musical style, repertory, and instrumentation that have had undeniable staying power. I should add that the absence of drum use during worship was certainly less typical of U.S.-based Pentecostal churches I attended. Given the prominent role that drums play in black churches in the United States, the relative *infrequency* of drums to which my Jamaican consultants referred is one of the more remarkable elements of the particular historical moment during which I conducted my fieldwork on the island. My conversations with Jamaican saints, such as Sister Andrea, Sister Shields, and Sister Hall, reflect the tenor of that particular time and capture a shifting phenomenon in which the churches I studied were undergoing a transition from a "stricter" type of musical worship to one that leans more heavily on North American gospel music influences. These influences include the use of drums during worship.

A former keyboardist at All Saints explained how he tried to compensate for the absence of a drum kit: "I used to play drum sounds on the keyboard, first just a cymbal sound, then I added other parts." Another young man suggested that the pastor had no problem with drums himself but simply wanted to avoid vexing long-standing members who would disapprove of the departure from tradition. "With the change that is taking place in the PAW," he noted, "we believe we can have drums soon." Not all young people favor drums, however, as evidenced by the remarks of a sister who gave the following response to my query about whether she would like to have drum accompaniment in the worship service: "No, because sometimes people just clap for the drums. But you must know I'm probably a bit more old-fashioned. I heard that this drummer once started playing and people started quarreling and arguing. The drum beat brought in a spirit of discord." Although Pastor Bryan is a keeper of the tradition, her worship services feature drums, along with guitars and an electric keyboard. She sometimes expresses concerns about the "undesirable" influence of drumming on praise and worship, remarking that some people can be entranced not by the Holy Spirit but by a "drum madness" that she likens to "African" rituals. "Drums are acceptable," she once explained, "but we have to be careful to keep the focus in the Lord." Pastor Bryan suspects that drum madness sometimes occurs when organists accompany a preacher by interjecting chords between lines of a "chanted sermon."[8] In her humorous critique of this practice, which is more common in African American–influenced services, she recalled with laughter a time when a preacher "got himself all worked up" during his message and started skipping through the main aisle crying "J-J-J-J-Jesus!!!"

Despite the objections raised by their parents and conservative peers, most of the teens and young adults I spoke to hold a positive view of how Convention has evolved since 1999. Under Bishop Jones, the dress standards have begun to move in a more liberal direction as jewelry, makeup, and straightened hair are infiltrating some of the churches. Televisions, which were previously forbidden, have become much more prominent in Pentecostals' homes, giving them access to sounds and styles from abroad. Some Pentecostals feel that church leaders who forbid saints to own televisions have failed to confront an obvious contradiction between preaching and practice. For example, some pastors continued to frown upon television sets even though the new presiding bishop appeared weekly on his own television broadcast. Youth especially welcome the opportunity to express themselves musically by drawing on what some refer to as "black"-sounding music stemming from the United States. They draw heavily on African American gospel sounds and more contemporary recordings that have come into Jamaica via LOVE 101 FM since the inception of this popular radio station in the early 1990s. National Christian television networks Love Television and Mercy and Truth Network emerged in 1998 and have also become vital outlets for the transmission of newer gospel styles. These radio and television media have played a tremendous role in shaping the evolving tastes of Jamaican Pentecostals, both young and old. Thus, the shift that took place in Convention was fueled by religious broadcasting that had begun to spread throughout Jamaica in the decade just prior to my arrival. Local radio and television programs worked in conjunction with U.S.-based televangelism, paving the way for new leadership and pushing the Jamaican PAW closer to a North American sound and worship ideal.[9] While younger musicians and choristers tend to express a positive view on the changes, there continues to be skepticism among older generations of Pentecostals, who want to hold on to "the old-time way."

The theme of the 2002 Convention, "Committed to Kingdom Building: Keeping the Unity of the Spirit in the Bond of Peace," reinforces efforts to experience a oneness that transcends local churches and binds Jamaicans living on the island with those visiting from abroad. There is a fascinating relation between African American gospel musics and Jamaican Pentecostal practice. Hymns deemed "traditional" in African American churches are experienced similarly in Jamaica. Indeed, when Jamaican Pentecostals speak of "the Pentecostal tradition," they seem to refer to practices that, on the one hand, transcend any national boundaries yet, on the other, have historical linkages to the black church in the United States. Congregational song leaders at the 2002 Convention in Spanish Town selected hymns and choruses of which both Jamaicans and African Americans might claim ownership. One evening, a song leader led the congregation in singing the chorus to the traditional gospel hymn "Oh Happy Day" in the style popularized by African American gospel artist Edwin Hawkins in 1969. This was followed by a slower hymn, "Jesus, the Son of God," composed by G. T. Haywood, one of the founders of the Pentecostal Assemblies of the World. At the conclusion of this piece, the moderator announced, "I want to mention, that particular song we were singing was written by Bishop G. T. Haywood many years ago. He was one of our first presiding bishops." In this way, Convention can be seen as a commemorative occasion during which preachers and song leaders make frequent references to the past, evoking a Pentecostal legacy that helps to generate a feeling of oneness among the saints.

Retellings and Rememberings

"Every now and again we have to roll back the curtains of memory. We must never forget where the Lord has brought us from!" The impassioned words of this grandmother's testimony resonated with the congregation, eliciting a chorus of amens. Her remarks were also an allusion to "Remind Me, Dear Lord," a song frequently rendered in Pentecostal churches I attended. The song highlights the crucial role of memory in Pentecostal worship. I first heard it during a service at Mercy Tabernacle Apostolic Church, located in the parish of St. James on Jamaica's northern coast. Of the songs I heard during testimony services in Jamaica, most are locally composed and have been handed down for decades through aural transmission. None of the saints I spoke with knew the name of the composer of "Remind Me, Dear Lord," but I later learned that it was written by Dottie Rambo, a white "Christian country" singer-songwriter from Kentucky. The song is thus an example of how the style of country-and-western music from the United States has become "localized" in Jamaican churches.[10] Coming from the United States where saints in a "black" church expected to hear "black-sounding" music, I had to adjust to the sonic difference of churches such as Mercy Tabernacle, where both "black" and "white" Christian-themed music from the United States was influencing the sound and style of musical worship.

Songs and musical styles acquire racial associations, particularly among the youth in Kingston and Montego Bay. I was surprised, however, that the island's Pentecostal congregations were willing to absorb a such a wide range of songs and styles, including country-and-western-influenced "southern gospel" music. The reasons for this are complex. I should at least note that the binary system of racial classification in the United States cannot be unproblematically mapped on to the Jamaican social landscape. The infamous "one-drop" rule, which historically has labeled individuals "black" as long as they have any amount of African ancestry does not apply in African Caribbean societies where persons of color may be considered "red" or "brown." Without the strict black–white racial dichotomy that exists in the United States, most Jamaican Pentecostals with whom I spoke are much less concerned to racialize musical styles or discriminate against imported musics, even if they sound "white" to them.[11]

What I find most compelling about "Remind Me, Dear Lord" is that the lyrics effectively and affectively convey the significance of one of the most crucial activities in Pentecostal worship: remembering. It is through the acts of remembering from whence they came and meditating on the goodness of God that believers acquire the compulsion to testify, thereby encouraging one another through their personal narratives of victory over, through, and in spite of life's obstacles. The relation between personal and collective remembering can be elucidated by attending to the special role of musical participation in the process of retrieving and articulating memories of the past. A spoken testimony is "a solitary act, one that calls the speaker to *individually* address the full congregation" (Hinson 2000, 92; italics in the original). Consequently, saints experience varying degrees of personal engagement during a spoken testimony, ranging from wholly passive, in the case of an apathetic hearer, to fully active and creative, in the case of the one testifying. However, congregational singing "demands a kind of engagement that few other acts of worship require." Lively choruses are usually interspersed between spoken testimonies precisely "to foster a spirit of devotional collectivity by engaging churchgoers in collective action" (91). Hinson provides a vivid portrayal of the interplay between memory and song in African American Pentecostal worship. His description applies equally well to the testimony services I experienced in Jamaica, which derive their particular efficacy from an intertwining of memory, song, speech, and Spirit.

As the mouth sings, so do the ears hear, taking in the words chorused by the assembly. These too pique the mind, leading to a layering of thought that listens to both self and singing other. The lyrics, borne on waves of passion, press themselves into consciousness, seeking relevance in memory, finding resonance in experience. Fueled by emotion and faith, the words strain for connection, struggling to ground the sung message in personal experience. With each connection, with each moment of resonance, the mind focuses a bit more, turning away errant thoughts while turning toward the contemplative fullness of worship. Saints say that only when this focus begins does one stop *hearing* the lyrics and start *feeling* them. No longer mere words, they now present themselves as piercing fragments of understanding. As they penetrate ever deeper into consciousness, the singer finds ever more reasons to praise. (92; italics in the original)

The role of music and memory in helping saints find "reasons to praise" is supremely important in Pentecostal worship because, as I discussed in chapter 3, corporate praise opens the door to a tangible manifestation of the Holy Spirit, resulting in true worship and communion with God. Hinson expands the meaning of testimony to include any "telling" of a lived experience:

In the community of saints, a "testimony" is any expression whose focused referent is lived experience. Unlike the academic designations "personal experience narrative" and "memorate" (with the latter's specific reference to belief accounts), "testimony" knows no restriction of form. In its most common usage, it refers to a personal account of experience and thanksgiving presented before a gathering of saints. This recounting often assumes a highly elaborated form.... Whatever the form, testimony's core feature is the telling of experience. Hence personal stories related in conversation are also called testimonies, as are songs whose words resonate with personal history. Linking all these expressions is a focus on testified truth. This quality, in turn, echoes with undertones of passion and heartfelt witness. A testimony thus stands as much more than a simple telling; it is a telling imbued with the authority of truth. (328–29)

During a testimony service I attended at a Pentecostal church in Montego Bay, songs referencing the past were interspersed with spoken testimonies that detailed victories won, hardships overcome, and sicknesses cured. Some testifiers sang choruses in lieu of a spoken narrative. One woman offered the following song:

When I look back over my life
And I think things over
I can truly say that I've been blessed
I've got a testimony.

After the last testimony, the moderator remarked on the importance of song and dance as a form of praise, contrasting secular and sacred musical practice. Her comments also served to summarize the previous testimonies, and she exhorted the congregation to take advantage of opportunities to praise God despite the criticisms of some who feel such activities are inappropriate in a church setting.

> Praise the Lord. Truly tonight we give the Lord thanks and praise. Tonight we are here to clap and sing and dance. Praise the Lord! When we were out in the world, we gave the devil all of our time. Praise the Lord. Look in the world and you'll see the devil singing and dancing and rejoicing. They really don't have nothing to dance about. But I'm saved and sanctified. We are the ones that are to dance and to sing and to praise the Lord. Some people, they don't want you to dance, but I know my Bible tell me that I must dance and must sing and I must clap. And whenever I get a chance to do it, I'm gonna do it for Jesus. The Bible tells us in Psalm 150, how if we read it, it tells us we must praise God with timbrel and with the dancing. Praise the Lord. So tonight, we are glad that we have the privilege to dance for Jesus Christ, because God has done so many things for us.

Testimony services at Riversdale also provide opportunities for song leaders and congregants to share personal experiences with the congregation and articulate memories of the past through musical and verbal participation. The job of the testimony service moderator is to indicate whose turn it is to testify, intersperse testimonies with appropriate songs, and monitor the length of this portion of the worship service. The testimony moderator generally starts by raising a song that encourages saints to reflect on all that God has done for them. This introductory song is usually a short chorus that is well known by most congregants, such as "When I Think of the Goodness of Jesus."

> When I think of the goodness of Jesus
> And all He has done for me,
> My soul cries out, "Hallelujah,
> Thank God for saving me."

This song prepares the way for others to open up and share stories of the Lord's "goodness." Singing that functions in this way is described by Jon Michael Spencer as a "channel" through which believers are "brought into the experience of testifying" (1990, 189). The most effective testimony moderators are familiar with a wide repository of choruses and hymns. Pastor Bryan described how she used to pick a song whose lyrics expressed sentiments corresponding to a saint's verbal testimony. For example, if someone stated, "I thank the Lord for being my friend," Pastor Bryan might raise a hymn such as "Friendship with Jesus."

> Friendship with Jesus
> Fellowship divine.
> Oh, what blessed sweet communion
> Jesus is a friend of mine.

After a testifier speaks of being rescued from a past life of sin, an astute moderator could follow up by leading the congregation in "What a Wonderful Thing."

> What a wonderful thing, a very wonderful thing
> To be free from sin and have Christ within.
> To be made a joint heir with Jesus my Lord,
> What a wonderful, wonderful thing.

Although the choice of which chorus to sing depends on the moderator's ability
to think quickly and call up an appropriate song from memory, it is the Holy
Spirit who receives credit for inspiring each selection and blessing the mind of
the moderator to recall a song that is "timely."

Five Testimonies of Conversion

Some of the most moving testimonies I recorded in Jamaica recount a conversion experience of receiving the infilling of the Holy Spirit. Let me close this
chapter by discussing five such testimonies that were given at Riversdale in
September and November 2002. It is interesting that each speaker quotes or
makes general reference to particular hymns or choruses that support the message of their testimony. Anna, Beatrice, Carol, Darlene, and Everton provide
further evidence of the interplay between spoken and sung texts in Pentecostal
settings. The memories of past events enhance the meaningfulness of Pentecostal songs, and vice versa.

Anna, age seventeen, remembers that immediately after hearing Pastor
Bryan sing the chorus, "He Touched Me," she felt a change in her life. She then
fell to the ground and subsequently found herself speaking in tongues. The lyrics of the chorus, which refer to joy that "floods my soul," continue to remind
her of her conversion experience.

Testimony by Anna, September 1, 2002, Riversdale Pentecostal Church

Tonight I'm very glad to be one of God's children. I remember when I was small
I used to say I would love to be in the heaven with God one day. And I remember
when pastor asked me did I want to [be] baptize[d] and I said yes, although I
didn't make up my mind. But I told her yes. And I [was] baptized. And I waited
one year and six months to be filled. And I remember coming from my home in
the morning, and I did something wrong and my mother was cursing me. And
I said to myself, "I wish I could die. I would love to be filled tonight and die [at
the] same time."

I came to church and I said to myself, "I'm not making any promise, but I want
to be filled tonight and die." And I remember coming to the [h]altar, and I put my

hands in the air and I [was] just asking the Lord, "Fill me. Fill me with the Holy Ghost." And I remember while I [was] standing there, I heard Pastor singing this song—I think it was "He Touched Me"—and I could feel a change in my life. And I remember then I fell. And after I fell, I came up and said to myself, "Oops, I dropped! How can it be?" And then Sister Jeannie came up and she said to me, "Don't become discouraged when you are this far." [Then she prayed,] "Please Lord, bring her closer to you." And I remember when Brother Ron, Sister Jeannie, and Sister Williams came up and said, "Seek him. Seek him. He's near. Seek him. Call on his name."

And I remember saying, "Jesus, Jesus." And it was—when I shut my eyes there was this bright light and it was coming. It was small and it become bigger and bigger and bigger until it was great. Oh! And after a few moments, I was speaking in tongues. And although I [felt] ready, I didn't want to die. I want[ed] to keep on living for him. So I thank the Lord for filling me with the Holy Ghost and making me one of his children.

In some cases it is through reflecting back on the music sung or heard during conversion that saints feel the touch of the Holy Spirit. For example, while seeking the Holy Spirit in 1995, Beatrice, age twenty-seven, recalls hearing and singing the hymn "Close to Thee," the lyrics of which are as follows:

> Thou my everlasting portion,
> More than friend or life to me.
> All along my pilgrim journey,
> Savior, let me walk with thee.

Beatrice starts to sing this hymn toward the end of her spoken testimony, reenacting her past experience. Appearing to feel overwhelmed by the presence of the Holy Spirit, she is unable to finish and begins speaking in tongues. This spurs others in the congregation to join.

Testimony by Beatrice, September 1, 2002, Riversdale Pentecostal Church

Tonight, I give the Lord Jesus thanks for filling me with the Holy Spirit. I was baptized June 4, 1995. And one night, I went to the altar and I got the anointing. Sister Wilson was sitting there for some time and every night I went home discouraged. She always encourage me and say, "Make a joyful noise unto the Lord all ye lands."

I remember the first night I speak in tongues. I went there, at the Convention, I went up to the altar and I was there kneeling down. And I feel myself reaching out even further than I used to. And I found myself speaking in tongues. After that I went home and I said, I couldn't be filled because I didn't see any angels.

I didn't see any light. And I was there on my knees all over the floor; so I said, "I shouldn't get up." So in the night, I went to church, and I testify that I almost [was] filled. Pastor Bryan said, "There's nothing as 'almost.' It's either you're filled or you're not filled." So Sunday, I said, "I'm going back to the [h]altar." I didn't see an angel, but I feel so very grateful. So Sunday in the day, I realize, well, everything Sunday, and I felt like crying. And how I felt different! I feel to shout, but I don't shout. And they were singing [sings "Close to Thee" then breaks into loud, high-pitched tongues]. And I remember that as I was singing "Close to Thee," everything just exploded. And then I said, "Lord, thanks for filling me with the Holy Spirit." [Beatrice and others begin speaking in tongues.]

The recurrence of past conversion experiences is commonplace among Pentecostals, as saints continually strive to feel manifestations of God's power. This recurrence is paralleled by the notion, expressed in the second verse of the hymn "Pentecostal Fire Is Falling," that "Pentecost can be repeated." The song draws from the biblical account of the Day of Pentecost as recorded in Acts 2. The lyrics of the second verse are as follows:

Pentecost can be repeated, for the Lord is just the same,
Yesterday, today, forever, Glory to His precious name!
Saints of God can be victorious. Over sin and death and hell;
Have a full and free salvation. And the blessed story tell.

Carol, age forty-four, references this hymn as she celebrates nearly thirty years of walking with God, pointing out that "things I used to do, I do no more." To survive over the years, she has relied on the continual outpouring of the Spirit of God for spiritual nourishment. Carol ends her testimony with an appeal to the youth to seek God. Through the repetition of the events of the Day of Pentecost, Riversdale's youth can have access to the same Holy Spirit that filled her in 1973.

Testimony by Carol, November 3, 2002, Riversdale Pentecostal Church

I was in my early teens when I answered the call of God. And you know we were just newborn babes, and so we were really thirsty for the milk of the Word, like Paul said. But when we came, there was no milk being served up! We got some big ol' bones thrown at us. Nowadays, young people have a lotta special programs set up especially for them. But back then, we didn't have that kind of thing. Yet the toughness of it helped us and encouraged us to develop a personal relationship with God and seek Him for ourselves in those early days. Being involved in the things of God meant everything to us. We used to love to come to church where we could feel the presence of God and fellowship with all the brethren. And we work hard to witness to the people and bring them in. Like Saturday evenings, we'd be in the streets of Riversdale and sometimes Linstead. Now, as a result, there is a thriving church in Linstead.

I fasted a lot in those days, and I used to pray and just seek God's face. And you know, it was very strict in those days, but I didn't feel deprived in any way because there was so much that we were getting from the Word. It changed my life completely. I used to wear fashions. Yes! Minis too, very short ones! But thank God, things I used to do, I do no more. Those things don't appeal to me any longer. People came early to church back then. You could hear the singing after 6 P.M. We were just so enthusiastic to serve the Lord. The song we sang says, "Pentecost can be repeated!" And today, I'm celebrating almost thirty years, because November 1973 I was baptized in the name of Jesus!

I just want to tell all the young people: Seek him first. And seek him with all your heart and soul and mind. Don't put school ahead of God, because he want[s] you to follow him even while you're young and then when you are [h]older you can look back and see how far you've come.

In addition to supporting personal conversion narratives, the practice of quoting song lyrics also reveals a performative aspect of Pentecostal testimonies. As Hinson (2000) notes, "the practice of lyrical citation . . . serves as a form of artful shorthand, giving speakers an effective tool for saying more by saying less" (183). Because certain songs are well known by the congregation, testifiers are able to rely on the common knowledge of a song's lyrical content to lend their discourse a feeling of coherence. For example, Darlene opens her testimony by quoting the lyrics to the hymn "Love Lifted Me." She then weaves the theme of love throughout her speech, referring to the hospitality of the saints and the kindness of Pastor Bryan as having had an impact on her coming to Riversdale. She ends by contrasting "the things of the world" with the love of God.

Testimony by Darlene, November 3, 2002, Riversdale Pentecostal Church

"I was sinking deep in sin, far from the peaceful shore. Very deeply stained within, seeking to rise no more. But the master of the sea heard my despairing cry. From the waters lifted me, now safe am I."

I [was] baptized at age eight in a little river in St. Mary. There was no pool in those days. Ten of us as children got baptized that day. I didn't want mommy to go to heaven and I didn't [go to heaven with her]. Because she was already baptized.

We didn't do the things the other children do. At Riversdale, we are three miles from home. But every Sunday, we are here on time, bright and early. I remember we had to fast even as children. Mommy would see to it that we came to prayer meeting. We grew up knowing that this is the only way. We were here on time on Sunday nights, too! The children never complained. We obeyed because we believed that the big people were directing us in the right way. We used to walk to Linstead to invite people to come to church and we were so excited about the Lord.

I couldn't understand why I couldn't get the Holy Ghost. I realize now that I didn't understand. And you know, I left the church and ended up in the world. I got married, and I never had a bed of roses out there. But the Lord never stop worrying me. My conscience was there worrying me! A friend was going to New Testament Church of God, and I used to visit but I knew I couldn't [be] baptized in that church like my friend.

And then I came [back] to Riversdale. They said, "You are married? What are you waiting for?" Pastor Bryan was the first person I met. That's why I say love met me at the gate. Praise the Lord Jesus! She used to take us home, and the brethren welcome me so much and treated me so good. And I kept coming until the Lord blessed me with the Holy Spirit. I know that love lifted me [*quoting song lyrics*] "when nothing else could help, love lifted me!" Matthew 24, verse 12 says that "because iniquity shall abound, the love of many shall wax cold." And so the things of the world is nothing good, but the love God is wonderful. The things we [used to] wear—mini-dress, (h)earrings—all of them are torment. But God is love.

Everton, age forty-five, is a deacon at Riversdale. He teaches Sunday School every week and is called upon to preach in Pastor Bryan's absence. Like his sermons, his testimony flowed smoothly and deliberately, giving me the impression that he has told his personal story several times during his Christian walk. Like the discourses of the previous testifiers, Everton's testimony shows the interdependency of song and speech as the memory of past events serves present-day Pentecostal experiences. Revisiting the time when he first sought the baptism of the Holy Spirit, Everton cites the lyrics of the chorus, "I've Got Mine."

Testimony by Everton, September 1, 2002, Riversdale Pentecostal Church

I just wanna say, yes, it's real. It's real. It's real. God's promise, God's wonderful promise, it is real. I just want to give God thanks for filling me with the Holy Spirit. I remember after I was baptized a few months, there was a chorus that we used to sing very often: "I've got mine, my brother. I've got mine, I've got the Holy Ghost and surely He is mine." I refused from singing that song. I wouldn't sing, because I said to myself, "I didn't get." They were all singing about the Holy Spirit. I remember a lot of people used to say, "Sing with faith, believing." So I start to sing, "I'll get mine, my brother. I will get mine! I will get the Holy Ghost." I couldn't sing that I have got mine. Because I used to say, "How can I say 'I've got mine' and it will still [be] something that I was seeking?"

But I'm glad that even my friends and relatives, they'd try to say, "You don't have to worry. You've got yours." My mother tried to console me. She said, "You already received the Holy Ghost, because the day you believe, God seals you with the Holy Spirit." And I could always say that I've seen that some of my brethren, my brethren have something that I don't have, and that is what I need. So I won't [be] satisfied with that which I have until I get that which I realize my brethren have. And I ask[ed] God to bless me. And as our brother and as our other sister was saying, it wasn't even in a service that God blessed me with the Holy Spirit. But I recall that day many times. I am standing at the altar. I said "hallelujah" and tried to reach out. I've tried to touch God, and as it were, I have to go home sometimes disappointed. Sister Saunders and others used to come around and say, "Hold on. Just trust God." And so I would cry all the time. But I can say that God['s] promise is sure. Because [it was during] the time when I was not even thinking honestly about the Holy Spirit. I was not even thinking about being filled.

And I remember that Monday morning I knelt in church and all I want [is] to find myself close to God. I remember saying, "God, if it mean for me to be like Lazarus, save me and let your perfect will be done." I remember the message that Sunday night was about this man Lazarus, and all I could see myself have nothing before God. And I said, "God, if it gonna take for me to be like Lazarus, just save me. I didn't even say, "Fill me." I said, "Save me and let your perfect will be done." And right there I realize I was just speakin' in tongues. There was an overshadowing. Something got a hold of me and I can just say from that wonderful day, my soul is satisfied. I'm grateful to the Lord Jesus for remembering me in my low estate and filling me with the Holy Spirit. As I'm saying, it's real. It's real. It's real!

While seeking the Holy Spirit, Everton found it helpful to change the lyrics of the chorus so that instead of reflecting back ("I've got mine"), the chorus looked ahead in faith ("I will get mine"). This enabled him to derail the frustration that was causing him to become discouraged and assert a confidence that he would receive a spiritual blessing from God. Having been filled with the Holy Spirit, he can now joyfully sing the song with its original lyrics. He expresses gratitude that he can join other saints in the creative act of remembering, through song and testimony, how God filled him with the Spirit and ushered him into the family of Pentecostal saints.

Conclusion

Cultural historian Michael Kammen reminds us that "what people believe to be true about their past is usually more important in determining their behavior and responses than truth itself" (1991, 38–39). And as Caroline Bithell (2006) notes, "It is the meaning invested in assumed memories of the past that gives present actions their rationale. The present may be unimaginable without the past, but it is the present that calls the shots" (5). The conversations and interactions I recount in this chapter, including the powerful testimonies of Anna, Beatrice, Carol, Darlene, and Everton, suggest that the past—I should say an archive of reconstituted *pasts*—comes in handy. It is a curated repository of unearthed treasures that smooths the ritual pathways of spiritual flow and empowers Pentecostals to imbue their present-day experiences with cultural and theological significance. Their testimonies also reveal what Feld and Fox (1994) refer to as the "phenomenological intertwining of music and linguistic phenomena" (29). Embedded within language about music, there lie meaningful ways of opposing the world and reaffirming religious identities. The usability of testimonies, like that of the pasts they recount, need not hinge on their "truthfulness," which as Tuleja (1997) insists "is less important, instrumentally speaking, than [their] authenticity to us as a resource for making ourselves up" (15).

I remember thinking, when I began this study, that such re-tellings of the past would be insignificant to my research goals as an ethnomusicologist. I also assumed that the nostalgic reflections of Pentecostals would not be considered "valid" enough to warrant inclusion in my research. Eventually, however, I began to consider more seriously the local construction of personal narratives as means of maintaining "containers" of social memory and historical consciousness (Fentress and Wickham 1992, 50). These narratives also offer a window into the thought processes of Pentecostals who perform their faith while standing in defiance of those who would portray them in an unfavorable light. I suggest that as saints re-member and re-experience the past, they also reassess their present-day musical practices, including the choices they make regarding appropriate musical style. By attending to the dynamic quality of sermons, testimonies, and song lyrics, I have thus come to see ethnography as an invaluable source of information about not only texts but also about the performative processes that give them spirit and vitality.

When believers speak about the past, they use phrases such as "the old-time way" or "that old-time religion" in reference to an era in which they feel Pentecostals were more committed, the manifestations of the Holy Spirit were more frequent and impactful, and Jamaican society, as a whole, was in better shape. One of the things that contributes to the appeal and efficacy of Pentecostalism in Jamaica is its ability to appropriate multiple historical narratives to serve present-day objectives. I believe the significance of Pastor Bryan's spiritual conversion and Jamaica's political one lies in more than their mere coincidence.

For Pentecostals who converted during the late 1950s and early 1960s, reflecting on that bygone era involves the selective mining of specific events from the past that are re-membered in the present to shape a self-image that is both fervently Pentecostal and staunchly Jamaican. My experiences playing for worship services at Riversdale and elsewhere put me in a unique position from which to both observe and influence the shifting boundaries between different forms of church music. I learned that in liberal worship environments, congregants flow freely from one style to another. Even at Riversdale, stylistic preferences differed. For example, Sister Sewell's children, along with most of the youth at Riversdale, have musical tastes different from those of their parents. The young people's choir, a group consisting of about eight teen girls, expressed a particular fondness for the music of contemporary African American gospel artists, whose recordings have spread even into rural areas of the island.

As becomes even more evident in chapter 5, the distinctions that saints draw between older and newer styles are sometimes expressed in terms of cultural and racial differences between Jamaican and African American gospel genres. The goals of the worship leader determine which brand of gospel music is most appropriate, and musicians well versed in several genres look for cues to guide their decision making. Verbal and bodily actions of pastors, song leaders, and congregants represent what Richard Bauman (1997) describes as the "keying of performance" (15), insofar as they establish a social and temporal frame of appropriate action. These actions also help to engender ritual cohesion and a pleasurable sense of flow (Csikszentmihalyi 1990). The spiritual flow experienced by believers such as Pastor Bryan and her congregants relies on their ability to tap into the flow of memory, as they draw connections to various pasts and imbue them with contemporary significance. As we have seen, however, flows of time and Spirit are felt to be threatened by the flows of people and expressive culture across Jamaica's boundaries. I will now examine in greater detail some of the ways that flows are defined and regulated along cultural and racial lines within Jamaican churches at home and abroad.

How do efforts to stay within the boundaries of holiness relate to the generational differences between younger and older Pentecostals? And how do notions of appropriateness vary among congregations whose leaders strive to maintain the Jamaican Pentecostal tradition? Finally, what role does African American gospel music play among Jamaican Pentecostals who embrace both a "black" American gospel sound and a Jamaican cultural identity? For Jamaican saints at home and abroad, it is through music that religious, national, and cultural identities are asserted.

CHAPTER 5

Performing Ethnicity

Style, Transcendence, and African American Gospel

One hot Saturday afternoon in August 2002, I spent some extra time hanging out in Spanish Town with several of the saints from Riversdale Pentecostal Church. We attended "Gospel Fun Day," one of several Emancipation Day events held across the island to commemorate the abolition of British slavery in 1838. At one point, the disc jockey, known as a "selector," played "Shackles," an R&B-influenced recording by African American contemporary gospel duo, Mary Mary.[1] The song speaks of spiritual bondage and deliverance while pointing metaphorically to a connection among African diasporic peoples who share a collective history of enslavement and liberation.

> Take the shackles off my feet so I can dance.
> I just wanna praise you. I just wanna praise you.
> You broke the chains now I can lift my hands
> And I'm gonna praise you. I'm gonna praise you.

This connection to a shared experience of enslavement may help to explain why gospel songs such as this are appropriated within Jamaica's Christian celebrations. Songs like "Shackles" also register as "blacker" and more progressive alternatives to classic hymns, which younger Pentecostals have described to me as "white." However, some believers see the influence of contemporary African American gospel music as a threat to the sanctity of "the old-time way." Hip-hop and R&B-influenced gospel musics are cast as too modern, too influenced by secular genres, and, therefore, too worldly for inclusion in church services.

This chapter explores the musical interplay of ethnicity, race, and Pentecostalism in Jamaica and its diaspora. Drawing on the work of Gerardo Marti (2012), I argue that Pentecostals use music to express "panethnic," "ethnic-specific," and "ethnic transcendent" transnational identities. Those who align themselves with blacks in the United States traverse an imagined boundary between Jamaican and African American church music and position themselves within a panethnic cohort of Pentecostals who nevertheless experience their worship in terms of a racialized musical aesthetic. Other saints perform identities that are shaped by a selective historical consciousness and emotional investment in the notion of an "authentic" Jamaican Pentecostal heritage. This "ethnic-specific" articulation of identity embraces Jamaican culture while holding certain "modern black" expressive cultures at arm's length.[2] An "ethnic transcendent" identity is expressed by those who champion some aspect of their Christian faith, rather than "culture," as the most important defining attribute.

Focusing on the musical flows that occur within various worship situations, I examine performances of religious ethnicity by believers who self-identify as Pentecostal, Jamaican, and, in some cases, black. These modes of self-presentation are given varying degrees of weight as saints strive to be true to themselves and protect their identities as holy worshippers. My discussion begins in Jamaica with an exploration of Jamaican and African American musical blendings that occur within four churches. I then turn to the diaspora to examine a London performance by Pentecostal gospel artist Donnie McClurkin. I conclude by highlighting musical efforts to promote unity and ethnic transcendence. Performances of identity raise intriguing questions about the role of music in regulating flow within and across the boundaries that believers construct. While these boundaries are deeply meaningful in terms of how saints portray their experiences, the collective distinctiveness that saints celebrate remains difficult to quantify. The use of "Shackles" on Emancipation Day is only the tip of the old iceberg. Jamaican Christians have long made creative use of music labeled as "black" or "African American," just as African American believers have appropriated Jamaican musics for use in gospel concerts and church settings. I believe there is much to learn from performances of racialized ethnicity that unfold onto the uncharted stages of Christian worship and play.[3] Through music-making, believers fashion a transnational religious ethnicity that, like the Pentecostal tradition on which it relies, is both real and illusory.

Although some Pentecostals in Jamaica feel that "black" (or African American) musical styles water down authentic ways of worshipping, others take pleasure in the feeling of sonic and cultural flow that musical borrowings generate. They see both "black" and "Jamaican" church music as available expressive resources that add vitality to modern-day worship. Blackness is understood here not as a static category determined by observable biological characteristics such as skin color and hair type but as one socially constructed piece of the puzzle of Jamaican ethnic identification. In short, I treat race as "a subset of ethnicity." Ethnicity is thus an umbrella term that "refers to a belief among group members and outsiders alike that it constitutes a distinctive community formation." It may also encompass "traditions, folkways, values, symbols, language, and religion" (Kivisto and Croll 2012, 11). The fluctuating tensions surrounding local and foreign musical genres call to mind what Rommen refers to as the "negotiation of proximity" (see chapter 1). However, it is sometimes the perception and attribution of *difference*, rather than a comforting sense of "at-homeness," that makes African American contemporary gospel music "more difficult to incorporate into the pristine landscape of gnostic spirituality toward which the [Jamaican Pentecostal community] aspires" (2007, 66). Ethnicity, in this sense, "takes the conscious and imaginative construction and mobilization of differences as its core" (Appadurai 1996, 14). The cultural and spiritual otherness of African American music renders it both promising and problematic for Jamaican Pentecostals.

(E)Racing Tradition at All Saints Apostolic

In chapter 4, I demonstrated how saints use music to express their love and respect for the Jamaican Pentecostal tradition. I wish now to extend this argument by positing that the re-membering of tradition is also an important means of accenting both local and transnational components of ethnic identity. These accentuations sometimes accompany heavy criticism of "outside" influences, such as black American church practices that signal a departure from the Jamaican Pentecostalism of yesteryear. According to this essentialist line of critique, the danger in embracing African American gospel music is that Jamaican Pentecostal identities are undermined and the anointed character of church worship is compromised. African American gospel music is labeled worldly and "inauthentic" for several reasons. Some believers feel that it relies on emotionalism and entertainment rather than on the Holy Spirit for its affective impact. Pastor Hermine Bryan summed up this viewpoint once by stating, "The African Americans are just having a good time. They're not really worshipping." I have also heard preachers complain that a spirit of apathy has become prevalent. They claim that too few churchgoers have kept the "Holy

Ghost anointing" that yields a desire to sing and shout praises to God even when the music isn't "entertaining." There are also saints who express consternation about the prevalence of "white" American music in Jamaican churches. The notion that local worship styles needed to be washed "whiter than snow" is decried as a symptom of degrading colonial legacies. What stands out for me here is the dialogical relation between the holy–worldly dichotomy and a self–other binary that Pentecostals map onto it.

In churches throughout the Caribbean, issues of ethnic or cultural identity have long been front and center in debates concerning musical style. During a 2007 plenary address to the Congress of Evangelicals in the Caribbean, General Secretary Rev. Gerald Seale lamented the absence of black styles in Caribbean churches. His remarks, reprinted in a Jamaican newspaper editorial, complained that "white, Southern, country and western music is still considered 'real' Gospel music and anything that sounds African or Caribbean is termed 'devilish.' Shouldn't we be able to express worship, lifestyle, discipleship from the depths of who we are as Caribbeans and not have to become white, Anglo-Saxon in culture and practice to be serious disciples of Jesus? I think so!"[4] General Secretary Seale's ascription of cultural value to gospel music on the basis of its perceived blackness lends credence to E. Patrick Johnson's assertion that "blacks around the globe cling to essentialist notions of black cultural aesthetics as a way of preserving their cultural heritage" (2003, 194). Jamaican Pentecostals sometimes articulate their experiences in terms of a binary racial opposition between white and black styles; in some circumstances, they choose to emphasize the "Jamaican" cultural attributes of the music. For those who find conventional ethnic and racial modifiers problematic, it is music's *Pentecostal* character that makes it special. I suggest that "Pentecostal" serves as an alternative ethnic marker of distinction, and it trumps considerations of blackness and Jamaicanness in idealized assessments of a given congregation's gospel music. Even Pentecostals who hear music as a racialized phenomenon at times express a desire for what we might call "color deaf" worship. They may applaud Secretary Seale's incisive critique, but they also express a hope that believers will one day move past controversies of musical style and join together as a global Pentecostal community united in Christian worship. I will revisit this issue later in my discussion of what Marti (2012) refers to as "ethnic transcendent" worship. For now, I wish to emphasize that music registers for people according to ethnic identity in ways that should not be ignored. Perceived ethnicities of musical style *matter* whether the saints want them to or not. They flavor the religious experiences of those who come to sanctuaries to be filled with the Spirit and culturally fulfilled through congregational worship and gospel music.

As I have emphasized, music by black gospel artists from the United States is pervasive in Jamaican communities. In some Pentecostal churches, however, pastors consider this genre of African American music an intrusion. They hold dear an ethnic-specific religious identity expressed through musical styles they believe to be distinctly Jamaican. This ethnic specificity denies certain forms of blackness, particularly the music and worship styles of black Pentecostals in the United States. At All Saints Apostolic Church I took note of the opinions saints articulated about the interplay of musical, racial, and cultural identity. Some of these opinions are dissenting ones expressed by those who wish church leaders would widen their embrace of "acceptable" church music to include "blacker" styles. A current All Saints musician, Byron, noted, "We definitely have white–black issues. Some say the senior choir sounds white. It's the hymn singing." Byron also described the disdain he felt about the instrumental music that accompanies the singing. He claimed that his concerns are shared by other musicians and young adult members. "We play white music, like country and western," he nodded. "If you play anything else they look at you like 'What are you playing?'" He added, however, that some church members preferred "white-sounding" music, including songs by the Gaithers, as well as those by Lanny Wolfe, whom he described as "sort of a white Andraé Crouch." A former member named Angela, now living in the United States, was even more blunt in her evaluative reflections. "You can tell the difference between white and black styles. White styles are bland, no feeling, like All Saints' choir—they sounded white. They sounded like the Chuck Wagon Gang, you know, that *old-time* singing. Black songs are more like the James Cleveland, Kurt Carr, and Kirk Franklin." Angela's inclusion of James Cleveland is telling, as his influential work of the 1960s and 1970s is more "traditional" in style than the later "contemporary" recordings of Carr and Franklin, whose careers blossomed in the 1990s.[5] For Angela and other Pentecostals, "old-time" is a modifier that may apply to church music that is "white" or "Jamaican," whereas "black" gospel musics are more likely to register as "modern," even if they are a product of a bygone era. Moreover, a racialized distinction between "old-time" and "modern" church music has hardened as a result of the more recent introduction of African American gospel musics via forms of media consumption that, prior to the 1990s, were often forbidden by conservative Pentecostal pastors (see chapter 4). Television and radio play a major role in transmitting black American styles of preaching and singing to a new generation of saints.[6]

It is important to note that the "white" style of All Saints' worship services is by no means disliked by all. Neither is it always described in terms of race. As Byron added, "People used to come to All Saints to hear an old-time sound." Its well-established reputation as a "traditional" Pentecostal church is a source of pride for its leader, Pastor Fogleson, and for most of its members. Saints who seek a style of musical worship similar to what they experienced back home in the rural areas from which they have migrated find All Saints to be a comfortable church home. As will become increasingly evident throughout this chapter, nostalgic discourses of generational decline—concerns about spiritual decay over time—are intertwined with anxieties about African American influence on Jamaican church practices. Some Pentecostal preachers in Jamaica frown upon what they described to me as the "lazy" and "stush" (uppity) style of black worship among megachurch members they see on television broadcasts, which serve as a foil for traditional Jamaican worship styles that are deemed older and better. "Give me that old-time Holy Ghost," Pastor Fogleson exhorted, "that Holy Ghost that makes me want to sing and dance and preach! I don't want the quiet one! Oh, glory! I want the one that makes me jump up and shout, 'Hallelujah! I just can't keep quiet!'" A similar message was delivered by Bishop Christie, a Jamaican minister visiting from New York, who echoed Pastor Fogleson's call for a return to old times. His expression of nostalgia was, however, for a style of worship characterized less by "emotional" musical practices that "tickle the ear" and more by the transforming power of God's anointing. He began his sermon by lamenting the changes that have moved the church away from a genuine experience of the Holy Spirit. "What we need today is not more music and emotional singing, but we need the old-time anointing. We need not more charismatic preachers, but *Holy Ghost* preachers, *anointed* preachers! The present-day church has changed! The *pastors* have changed! The *bishops* have changed! The *music* has changed! The *preaching* has changed!" Although the present generation relies heavily on musical participation to experience a feeling of transcendence, the "old-time anointing," Bishop Christie insisted, does not depend on music. He feels that the younger saints today are sacrificing a true relationship with God for the temporary pleasures of musical sound. He continued, "This generation has to make so much music because they have to create an *artificial* joy! In the old times, the people *shouted*. They didn't dance, 'cause it was the Holy Ghost! They didn't even have a lot of instruments. But when they sang 'What a Friend We Have in Jesus,' oh my! I don't need no organ to help me preach!" It is interesting that while these clergy both express a longing for a return to older Jamaican Pentecostal practices, they do so by marking different points of contradistinction to present-day African American church practices. Pastor Fogleson advocates a spiritual refreshing, an "old-time Holy Ghost" that will breathe new life into a church that has been "infected" by the apathy of modern, black American-style Pentecostalism. Bishop Christie is more concerned about a tendency to sacrifice piousness for pleasure, along with the reliance on musical entertainment instead of the "old-time anointing."

I revisit these nostalgic discourses of tradition to underscore the fact that the changes taking place in Pentecostal churches can be experienced not only as more "modern" and "inauthentic" but also as evidence of African American influence on traditional Jamaican practices. To this end, it is worth noting a few additional changes mentioned by Bishop Christie. First, he draws a significant distinction between "dancing" and "shouting," both of which index bodily movements understood to be spiritually induced. Although some Pentecostals view these terms as synonymous, "shouting" is typically used to describe a type of holy dancing that appears relatively more spontaneous, less stylized, and less controlled. Shouting is a form of bodily praise occurring during intense moments of singing and clapping that spur an individual to transcendence. Phrases such as "dancing in the Spirit" and "holy dancing" hold a worldlier connotation for Bishop Christie, who uses them to refer to a stylized dance pattern that some saints half-jokingly insist is more controlled by the dancer than by the Spirit. The use of stylized foot patterns and jig-like dance steps is more prevalent among African American Pentecostals than among Jamaican saints. Second, Bishop Christie's reference to the hymn, "What a Friend We Have in Jesus," provides evidence of a Jamaican preference for the meaningful lyrics of traditional hymns and "sober songs" with thoughtful lyrics over the simpler choruses whose appeal derives ostensibly from rhythmic or melodic elements. Although plenty of African American Pentecostals still sing hymns during worship services in the United States, I have found this practice to be more prevalent among Jamaican saints.

Finally, Bishop Christie's emphatic statement, "I don't need no organ to help me preach," refers to the collective musicality of some African American preaching, singing, and playing, particularly an organist's practice of interjecting chordal attacks and melodic riffs in between a preacher's sermonic phrases. This occurs when a preacher switches to the musical style of sermonizing that Braxton Shelley (2017) refers to as "tuning up" (173).[7] The use of the organ to complement or "help" the preacher is likewise not a common feature of the Jamaican Pentecostal churches I have attended. I encountered it only in Kingston and Montego Bay, where churches attract preachers visiting from, or influenced by, the United States. But my experiences throughout the island also suggest that no congregation is completely untouched by the sounds, concepts, and behaviors that flow through transnational networks linking Jamaicans and others around the globe. And even in the island's capital, African American styles find plenty of detractors, particularly among older saints. Tensions become all the more acute between the latter, who cling to the "old-time way," and church youth, who see African American styles as a tool for self-expression. I turn next to a discussion of three Kingston churches, Lighthouse Assembly, Bethel Apostolic Church, and Faith Fellowship. African American styles occupy different roles within these three Pentecostal congregations, as believers negotiate "tradition" and religious ethnicity.

Generational Tensions among Kingston Pentecostals

Debates concerning cultural and generational differences between worship styles are more evident in Jamaica's capital city than elsewhere on the island. Lighthouse Assembly is a five-hundred-member Pentecostal church in central Kingston. One member named Judith, age twenty, spoke to me about the frustrations of teens and young adults who are attracted to gospel music from the United States and feel they are denied opportunities to express themselves because of the conservative tastes of some church members. Older church members sometimes squirm when contemporary African American songs are performed during services, particularly when the lyrics do not meet listeners' expectations for gospel singing. Judith remembered a controversial rendition of Timothy Wright's 1998 song "Been There Done That." Some choir members refused to sing it, she explained. They complained that the song was inappropriate because of its heavy backbeat and funk-inspired groove. Other choir members felt that the song also glorified worldly living, although the lyrics do not refer to specific sinful acts. The repetition of the phrases "been there" and "done that" was seen as problematic to saints fonder of strophic hymns focusing on the goodness of God. This contemporary song's use of the first person in reference to past sins, irrespective of their renouncement, was seen as troublesome in the context of holy worship. Judith noted, "I could tell it was not well received by the congregation because people didn't stand up and sing to support us." She added that on another occasion, when the choir rendered a contemporary gospel song in a "country church" a few miles from Kingston, "the people looked at us like we were cursing!"

Aware of the controversies surrounding black gospel music from the United States, church musicians walk a fine line between celebratory musical praise and sinful musical pleasure. Crossing over into sinful sonic territory could result in getting suspended or "sat down" by the pastor, especially if musical transgressions recur. Musicians practice having fun and exercising their creativity without "creating a fuss" within the sanctuary. Judith noted that Lighthouse's instrumentalists, most of whom are under age thirty, attempt to sneak "jazz" elements into their pieces during services. These elements were the primary difference between the accompaniment played by the instrumentalists and the traditional style preferred by older church members. I asked her to describe what she meant by "jazz."

> JUDITH: Okay, it's not straight jazz, but there's a flavor of jazz in there. Like, for example, when the offering is being taken, they'll maybe put hymns like "Just a Closer Walk with You" in jazz form. It's generally traditional songs, but with a jazz taste.
>
> MELVIN: And what did the older generation think of that?
>
> J: At first they were quite resistant, 'cause, you know, anything that is not traditional is worldly.
>
> M: Well, what does "traditional" mean?
>
> J: Traditional means four-four beat, four beats to the bar, no variation, no ad-libbing, as is.
>
> M: So would they just sing a hymn or something?
>
> J: They would sing a hymn or a regular chorus, but with no twist, no flavor. Just as is, verbatim. No style. [*Laughs.*] Just straight.

Judith's parents were members of Lighthouse before she was born, and she has been attending the church for as long as she can remember. Since age five she has also been quite active in the church. Currently, Judith sings in the choir. The choir, she explains, is an outlet for youth who find congregational hymn singing stultifying. Most of the Lighthouse choristers are teens and young adults who sang in the now defunct Youth Choir, which had to disband because such a large percentage of saints relocated to the United States and England. In 2001 alone, the church lost eight of its thirty families to outmigration. Despite the preponderance of youth in the choir, Judith still feels that the choir is limited by the conservative tastes of the choir director. Although the director is only in her late thirties, she happens to be the daughter of the pastor, Bishop Wheaton, and is committed to staying within the boundaries of appropriateness determined by her father's musical preferences. Judith continued, "We have an assistant choir director who is a younger person, but there still is sort of like a muzzle on things because the main director is not very open to contemporary stuff. No, if it's not traditional, if it's gonna cause a ruption, they're not gonna listen to it. And she has the final word." Judith indicated that even traditional songs can be deemed inappropriate and "cause a ruption" if the rhythmic accompaniment does not correspond to accepted norms. She manages to find humor in the reactions of conservative-minded saints to musical selections that stray from traditional guidelines.

J: Right now, we have a song that we are in the process of practicing. It's an old song, "Saved by His Power Divine," but I'm not too sure it is going to go over very well because it has a calypso-funky beat. And I'm really nervous about it! [*Laughs.*]

M: Have you had experiences like that before?

J: Oh yes! There are times when the pastor's wife, she won't say anything but she'll start fidgeting [*imitates pastor's wife acting nervously*] and getting really uncomfortable and sitting at the edge of her seat. And that's generally how you know it's a problem. And then, she has this way of just—you see the tension. She may not say it right away. But pastor [Bishop Wheaton] will be like, "Ahhh," and you know he wants to say something, but he doesn't quite know how to come out and not offend the choir and not offend [his wife]. And the next time we choose to do the song the director will be like, "No, no, no. Do the next one," because we keep getting that response.

Bishops Christie and Wheaton both express views toward music not unlike other Pentecostals of their generation. They strive to maintain a delicate balance between allowing the use of music as a tool of transcendence and avoiding an overreliance on musical sound to experience the anointing of the Holy Spirit. These church leaders recognize the positive potential of lively musical participation, but they are careful not to mistake the pleasures of sound for the touch of the Spirit. "Emotion is not Spirit!" Bishop Wheaton proclaimed at one point during his sermon. He expounded, "When the music is played to its highest potential, it has something in it to stir the soul and touch the heart. But you've got to have the Holy Ghost that you can feel [even] when you kneel to pray, so you know it is not just the music." He thus recognizes the power of musical sound but deems it worthless apart from the Holy Spirit, who channels that power and uses it not merely to rouse emotions but, rather, to transform lives.

As is the case with All Saints Apostolic Church, the traditional style of Lighthouse attracts migrants from rural areas. Likewise, Kingston's Bethel Apostolic Church draws in migrants who are familiar with the church's musical style. Unlike All Saints and Lighthouse, which rely on word of mouth, Bethel transmits its style throughout the island via its long-running radio ministry,

"Called unto Holiness." On the air since the late 1960s, this national program features the church's senior choir rendering classic hymns, most of which are early-twentieth-century pieces found in *Redemption Songs* (see chapter 4). One minister with whom I spoke indicated that radio station administrators have insisted that the live broadcast continue to feature older, classic hymns, such as "Holiness unto the Lord," which emphasizes a lifestyle distinct from the world (see chapter 2). Classic hymns reinforce the message of Bethel's mission and reflect the church's standing as a conservative body.

While Bethel's radio broadcast helps to construct the church's identity as traditional, the congregation has continued to attract teens and young adults, who sometimes decide to maintain their membership rather than seek greener pastures under a more progressive-minded leadership. An appeal to youth comes by way of increasingly "modern" worship services in which, as Sister Marcia explained, "the people don't mind the contemporary." The junior choir she helps direct distinguishes itself from the senior choir by regularly presenting pieces recorded by contemporary African American gospel singers and choirs. It is in this regard that Bethel differs from Lighthouse. Members of Lighthouse are more apt to express nervousness about the influence of African American gospel music, and instrumentalists inject it into the service in a semi-clandestine manner, careful not to violate the stylistic boundaries imposed by church leadership. But at Bethel, contemporary gospel sounds are incorporated into the services in a more explicit way. Church leaders strive to balance musical styles so that the musical needs of a diverse congregation are satisfied. Sister Marcia's job is to ensure that the choristers have uniformity in sound and appearance, while teaching them to develop socially and spiritually. As a choir leader, she participates in "group listening sessions" in which new songs are screened and decisions are made concerning repertory. Marcia explained that the main choir director travels to the United States every few months to visit churches and family members. A highlight of these trips is the annual Gospel Music Workshop of America, where he gathers new ideas for choir songs and tips on effective ministry.

Curious about church members' feelings toward the use of gospel songs learned abroad and used in Bethel's services, I asked Marcia to comment on how she and other church members experience the use of "foreign" songs in worship. She remarked, "Kirk Franklin is like part of Jamaica. We don't really think of him so much as a black American singer. We incorporate it into our culture as though it is our own. It's the same for Donnie McClurkin." I then asked her about gospel choirs whose names situate them in a particular North

American locale, groups such as the Mississippi Mass Choir, Chicago Mass Choir, and Brooklyn Tabernacle Choir. "We do not experience these songs as foreign," Marcia explained, adding that congregants are usually unaware of songs' specific origins and the place designations in group titles. What this suggests to me is that Bethel's members eschew a bounded form of Pentecostal musical practice in favor of a fluid sense of self. Their appropriation of African American gospel music as "their own" calls into serious question the notion of a stable, island-specific "tradition" and points to the significance of a religious ethnicity nourished by flows of expressive culture across national boundaries.

I hasten to point out that while most younger members of Bethel enjoy black American gospel music, there are also youth who express a preference for traditional Jamaican choruses. Sister Marcia noted, "We still attract youthful audiences because those songs are part of Jamaican culture. And when you hear the music, you hear what your parents used to sing." As I mentioned in the previous chapter, feelings of nostalgia play a major role in congregational music-making. Bethel's youth are by no means unanimous in their acceptance of African American gospel music. Some who resist it make the cultural politics of their stance overt. They see ignorance of musical origins as discomforting evidence of U.S. cultural hegemony extending into the religious sphere. One young minister argued, "It is a spirit, you know, like the spirit of football and the World Cup. It is an American spirit, a superpower spirit. We live in a Third World mindset and don't believe we can surpass the superpower spirit and do it ourselves. The American spirit is so prevalent that if you try to stop it, it gets stronger! It is a spirit of propagation." For this minister, the most relevant and problematic element was the Americanness, rather than the perceived blackness, of the music being rendered.

As we have seen, the use of African American gospel music is controversial in churches such as All Saints, Lighthouse, and, to a lesser extent, Bethel. It is, however, the norm at assemblies led by younger, more progressive clergy. Bishop John Everett, pastor of Faith Fellowship, is a talented singer and organist. He espouses a more liberal holiness standard than that of All Saints, Lighthouse, and Bethel and allows African American music free rein in worship services. Since he started pastoring in 1994 he has made frequent trips to the United States to attend conferences. During my time in Jamaica he was a member of a pastoral fellowship headed by well-known African American televangelist T. D. Jakes. Praise and worship at Faith Fellowship's Sunday morning service featured contemporary African American gospel songs almost exclusively. The only Jamaican chorus I heard was sung at a lively "shout" tempo with a groove characteristic of black Pentecostal churches in the United States. However, the

evening service was clearly more Jamaican in tone, featuring a medley of choruses sung to a definite ska accompaniment. I believe a willingness to accept
stylistic variation, both in terms of musical sound and personal expression,
helps to attract young Pentecostals desiring a "modern" worship aesthetic,
defined partly in terms of a liturgical openness to African American gospel
music.

During my interview with Lee and Pauline, a married couple who joined Faith
Fellowship in 1996, they spoke at length about their perceptions of music in
the church. They used to attend a church where they found the praise and worship boring and bland. "I felt out of place because it's like a big deal to worship
there," Pauline explained. "You know, people look at you funny if you worship!"
Pauline felt inhibited there, as though she could not physically demonstrate her
spiritual and emotional joy without attracting unwanted stares. Eventually,
Lee and Pauline spoke candidly with their pastor, who granted them leave and
even provided them with a letter of reference to take to Bishop Everett. Paula
remarked that she is much freer at Faith Fellowship and feels "at home" singing black American gospel music. "In fact," she added, "I'd feel uncomfortable
if I went to church and the music was all Jamaican! You know, just because
our culture is Jamaican, it doesn't mean our music and worship have to be all
Jamaican." Lee shared his wife's appreciation for stylistic variety. "I have all of
Hezekiah Walker's CDs and some others too, like Kirk Franklin," he nodded.
"We do ska, reggae, and dancehall, too. There's nothing wrong with a beat,
you know!" When I asked him what he thought of the church's relatively high
percentage of African American gospel music, he replied, "So we're what you
might call 'Jamerican,' but it really doesn't bother me."

In my interview with Rayford, an eighteen-year-old member, he defended
the sentiments of Lee and Pauline, adding that gospel music occupies a special
status among cultural imports from the United States.

> M: Do you think American music is too influential sometimes? What about
> when you hear Kurt Carr's "In the Sanctuary"?
> R: That doesn't really bother me, because it is gospel. It's not like R&B or
> something else. That would be a completely different thing; but since it's
> gospel, it doesn't bother me. The only thing I don't like is the clothes. Ev-
> erybody dresses, you know, they look like Americans, all fluffed out here
> (motions to shirt sleeves) and everything. You go in town and see them.
> And the cars, too.
> M: Oh, you mean like the music-video style?
> R: Yeah!
> M: Why is it different with gospel music as opposed to other kinds of music?

R: Because gospel music reaches out to a lot of different people, you know, whereas R&B is always the same kind of thing.

Rayford makes some striking assertions in this interview. Our discussion of cultural identity prompted him to comment on both sonic and visual elements. His mention of cars and "fluffed out" clothing suggests that musical sound is considered part of a broader constellation of cultural indices. In retrospect I see that my line of questioning may have guided him toward a particular answer. But like most of the young Pentecostals I'd previously interviewed, he seemed unfazed by the abundance of African American styles. It is also noteworthy that he expressed greater discomfort with those who "look like Americans" than with the idea of sounding like them. This observation speaks to the impression that sound may be a more welcome traveler through channels of flow between the United States and Jamaica. Stated differently, it seems musical influences from abroad are more easily appropriated into Pentecostal worship services than are nonnative dress codes and other visual markers of difference.

The three Kingston churches I have discussed, along with All Saints in Spanish Town, reveal intriguing ways of grappling with black gospel music from the United States. The ratio of Jamaican to African American music is perceived differently in each congregation, as clergy and laity negotiate the relation between religious tradition and musical performances of identity. These congregations also shed light on flows of music that occur not only between the United States and Jamaica but also within particular congregations. Pentecostals ascribe meanings to musical styles that inform the ways they choose to self-identify along religious and ethnic lines. I believe performances of identity are critical to the reimagining of Jamaica's Pentecostal tradition as a protean cultural construct. To shed light on panethnic and ethnic-specific musical and religious discourses, I return now to a performance by gospel recording artist Donnie McClurkin, whom I mentioned in chapter 2. His live recording provides another example of how African American and Jamaican identities intersect and religious ethnicity is performed in the Jamaican diaspora.

Donnie McClurkin's Caribbean Gospel Medley

In October 2000, African American gospel artist and Pentecostal pastor Donnie McClurkin made his first professional trip to Jamaica. He traveled to the island to give a gospel concert at Church on the Rock, a thriving Pentecostal sanctuary in Kingston. McClurkin's visit came in the wake of his album *Donnie McClurkin: Live in London and More*, which had been recorded just months prior.[8] The recording, which is available in both audio and video formats, is McClurkin's second commercial release and was a hit among both African American and Jamaican churchgoers. Following his visit, McClurkin's popularity in Jamaica has continued to grow. Throughout my fieldwork stay in 2002, one particular track, "Caribbean Medley," was played daily on Love 101 FM, the island's gospel radio station. It gave me fodder for conversations and an abundance of questions to pose in the field: Does the fact that McClurkin himself is not Jamaican preclude him from performing a Jamaican religious ethnicity in concert? McClurkin has acknowledged that "it was Jamaicans [in New York] who taught me to sing Jamaican songs as a little boy" (Walters 2016). But he has no immediate family ties to the island. How well can an African American singer "pull off" a performance of Jamaican traditional music? The popularity of the medley among Jamaican Christians at home and abroad suggests that they connect with the piece on a musical and religious level. The young saints with whom I spoke were quite fond of it. Older Jamaicans such as Pastor Bryan were less impressed. She described it to me as "a tacky Jamaican imitation." I submit that regardless of whether this piece registers as authentic, it brings into relief the contingent nature of ethnic identities as they are refashioned within the sanctuaries of Jamaican Pentecostal worship. The following description and analysis of McClurkin's "Caribbean Medley" sheds light on Jamaican and African American religious ethnicities and the myriad ways in which they are put into dialogue through musical performance.

McClurkin's London concert takes place at Fairfield Hall before a predominantly Jamaican crowd of gospel music enthusiasts. A woman emcee introduces him and expresses pride in the fact that he has chosen London as the locale for making his live recording. McClurkin and his group then perform several selections before launching into a medley of traditional Jamaican choruses. The video version of the concert shows McClurkin first asking for applause from various African and African Caribbean ethnic groups represented in the audience. He solicits responses from Barbadians, Trinidadians, and St. Lucians before finally asking the Jamaicans, whom he apparently knows to be in the majority, to show themselves by applauding. After their overwhelming response, McClurkin introduces the medley of "Jamaican songs."

> Well, then, we gon' sing us some *Jamaican* songs! But if we sing 'em, you gotta get outta those seats. And you gotta dance like you're *really* from Jamaica, or your parents were from Jamaica, or parents' parents were from Jamaica! But I want you to be true to who you are!

McClurkin employs inflections and colloquialisms familiar to Jamaicans in the audience. He repeats the word "Jamaica" several times, drawing out and melodizing the second syllable to mimic native patois speakers. He also calls on his listeners to be "true" to themselves, suggesting that participation in Jamaican-style gospel music and dance is a way for them to assert and confirm their island identities. As he speaks, the band begins a reggae-style accompaniment with characteristic keyboard and guitar up-beats. The first piece of the medley is "I've Got My Mind Made Up." When the vocal melody begins, the bass guitar and bass drum complete the sonic approximation of classic reggae accompaniment, characterized by what is sometimes referred to as the "one drop" rhythm marked by a stress on the third beat of each measure.[9]

The second piece of the medley is "Goodbye World," the lyrics of which emphasize one's conviction to leave behind the trappings of preconversion life. The keyboards, drums, and guitar continue the reggae-style accompaniment throughout this piece, while the bass guitar rhythm becomes sparser to allow space for the new melody and chord progression. From "Goodbye, World" the group moves into "Born, Born, Born Again," which is one of the best-recognized choruses in the medley. McClurkin adopts a more strident timbre as he imitates the coarse "dub"-style vocal delivery of a contemporary dancehall artist. Against a percussive and syncopated rhythmic backdrop, he exclaims, "Born of the water, Spirit an' de blood. T[h]ank God I'm born again!"

Next, McClurkin's rhythm section returns to a classic reggae groove, which underlies a return to "I've Got My Mind Made Up" and helps to establish this chorus as the medley's unifying theme. The reggae groove is maintained as the band segues into "I Am under the Rock," followed by "Jesus Name So Sweet." The bass line varies once more, switching to a simpler arpeggio pattern that jibes with the aforementioned "one drop" rhythm and supports the sustained three-part harmonies of the background vocals. After repeating the chorus's initial couplet, the rhythm section replays the syncopated dancehall rhythm as McClurkin elicits cheers from the crowd by singing "Every rock me rock upon Jesus, Jesus name so sweet!" While most Jamaican saints are familiar with these patois lyrics, I rarely heard them during church services. Within conservative congregations, praise and worship moderators choose lyrics closer to standard English, such as "Every time I talk about Jesus, Jesus name so sweet." In response to my question about the significance of the patois version of the lyrics, one pastor scoffed, "It doesn't mean anything. It's just some words they throw together!" But this dismissive attitude hardly masks a deeper anxiety about the appearance of impropriety. For saints seeking to avoid even the slightest connotation of worldly or sexually suggestive movement, it is more acceptable to "talk about" Jesus than to "rock upon" him (see chapter 2).

McClurkin concludes the medley by returning to "I've Got My Mind Made Up." Before the final repetitions of this chorus, however, viewers witness one of the most intriguing moments of the concert. The instrumentalists suspend the classic reggae groove, and McClurkin announces, "*We* sing it like this." He then shifts gears by slowing the tempo and inserting the refrain of the gospel hymn, "Oh, I Want to See Him," composed by American Rufus H. Cornelius in 1916. McClurkin reverts to his celebrated R&B-influenced contemporary vocal style, and the rhythm section backs him with a smooth, understated accompaniment reminiscent of the sound of African American church music. McClurkin's remark, "*We* sing it like this," reveals to the audience his perception of a cultural difference between himself and the audience. Collective participation in the medley serves, however, to foreground the common spiritual ground between them. By sandwiching this hymn within the medley's reggae choruses, McClurkin appropriates the contrast between Jamaican and African American styles of gospel expression.

After a final chorus of "I've Got My Mind Made Up," McClurkin surprises the audience again by launching into "Fire, Fall on Me." As I mentioned earlier, saints understand fire as symbolic of the Holy Spirit. Consequently, this chorus, with its reference to Pentecostal fire, has the effect of heating up the spiritual atmosphere, elevating the energy of the concert until it resembles a Pentecostal worship service in which the gifts of the Spirit have free rein. Both the audio and video recordings fade out on this piece, leaving the listener (or viewer) to imagine the continuing moments of celebratory praise induced by McClurkin's "Caribbean Medley" and heightened by its final segment. McClurkin eventually introduces the next song with remarks that once again reveal his ability to manipulate cultural musical difference and evoke "place" through musical sound.

> Well, that's how you all do it in England and in Jamaica. Now I gotta take you to *my* home. I'm a-show you how we do it in Perfecting Church in Detroit, Michigan, [singing] where the pastor and founder is Marvin L. Winans!

McClurkin sings the last phrase, placing special emphasis on the church's pastor, a renowned contemporary African American gospel recording artist who later makes a guest appearance during the concert. After the short introduction, the band begins a bass-heavy funk groove, preparing the audience for McClurkin's next piece, "Hail, King Jesus." McClurkin finishes the concert with other songs that more closely match the style of African American contemporary gospel for which he is best known.

McClurkin's performance of "Caribbean Medley" is remarkable for several reasons. I believe it reveals points of dissonance between Pentecostal belief and practice and, more generally, between cultural and religious identity. There is, in fact, a curious tension surrounding McClurkin's ethnic-specific uses of music in "Caribbean Medley" to signify Jamaican and African American distinctiveness, and the manner in which saints use music to assert their distinctiveness as Pentecostals. McClurkin portrays "Hail, King Jesus" as emblematic of African American gospel expression, but the song's musical style is sometimes viewed by African American Pentecostals as too worldly because of its perceived similarity to secular hip-hop genres. In fact, the musical styles of McClurkin and other contemporary gospel artists have often been deemed inappropriate for use in Pentecostal church services. While these styles may succeed in expressing a black American racial identity, they fail to resonate with the religious identities of African American Pentecostals who fear the loss or contamination of the gospel music tradition they regard as vital to their worship experience.

Likewise, the medley's reggae groove, along with McClurkin's shift into a gruffer, dancehall-style vocal timbre, may resonate for audiences as "Jamaican," but it does not conform to the ideal aesthetic conservative Jamaican Pentecostals embrace. Those who find McClurkin's medley entertaining in a concert setting or for radio listening may disapprove of the use of such a style for actual church worship. The same choruses are sung, but the rhythmic accompaniment does not draw so obviously on a classic 1970s reggae sound, which evokes images of the contemporary dancehall, ganja smoking, and Rastafarianism. For some Jamaican saints, the fact that McClurkin is an African American rather than a Jamaican Pentecostal artist gives him creative license. He is permitted to push the envelope in his performance and render Christian songs in a style that would not otherwise be so widely embraced by Pentecostals living on the island. The "Caribbean Medley" is thus a more complicated "text" than it appears to be at first glance. I interpret it as a multifaceted performance of religious ethnicity, in which different African American, Jamaican, and Pentecostal Christian identities are foregrounded. McClurkin is a skillful plate spinner: He toys with his African American and Pentecostal identities while tossing a variety of Jamaican musical and religious identities into the mix. And to the amazement of his audience, he keeps these identities in play. In the case studies that follow, Christian artists strive to go beyond ethnic-specific and panethnic constructions in order to promote an ethnic transcendent identity. However, as we shall see, attempts to privilege Christian experience as the single marker of distinctiveness are challenged by expressions of Jamaican cultural nationalism.

Ethnic Transcendence and the Unity of Worship

"God takes pleasure in the blending of fragrances." So began another of my conversations with Pastor Hermine Bryan. On this afternoon, she was waxing poetic about the "unity of worship," describing the mixture of incense offered up as a holy sacrifice to the Lord in the Old Testament Jewish tabernacle. Burnt incense was symbolic of the praise of the saints, she explained, which draws on a multiplicity of musical styles. The upcoming Brooklyn Tabernacle Choir concert provided a convenient example for our discussion, as the ensemble was multiethnic in its composition and included only three or four members of Jamaican descent. The multiethnic makeup of the choir is emblematic of the blended congregation of Brooklyn Tabernacle itself. With a ten-thousand-member congregation in downtown Brooklyn, the church "has a unique open door to minister to the cross-cultural melting pot of New York City. The church itself includes members from all walks of life, and diverse ethnic and national origins."[10] Most of the Jamaicans with whom I spoke rave about the Brooklyn Tabernacle Choir. Some younger Pentecostals complain, however, that the group has "a white sound" that lacks that "cultural relevance" of Jamaican and African American styles. Pastor Bryan disagreed with the comments of these younger saints. Rather than discussing the choir's sound in racial terms, she preferred instead to convey her appreciation for the professionalism and sincere devotion she feels the choir displays.

As our conversation continued, Pastor Bryan opined that some African American groups lack the refinement and sincerity of the Brooklyn Tabernacle Choir. The African American singers she hears seem more skilled at entertaining than at inviting the anointing of the Holy Spirit, which she prioritized above all else. "Well, I suppose the other singers are too black for me!" she laughed. Her point, made only partly in jest, was that racial identifications along the lines of style carry less importance for her than the spiritual efficacy of the lyrics and conduciveness of the sound to authentic worship. Pastor Bryan's avoidance of musical racialization is not uncommon among Pentecostals of her generation, who define their faith in ethnic transcendent terms. In her assessments of personal and musical value, nationality and spirituality hold greater weight and validity than do racial identifications. I maintain, however, that this rhetorical position contains within it a disdain for a certain kind of "black" religious expression. For Pastor Bryan, performances of Christian music become "too black" when they place excessive emphasis on celebratory demonstrativeness in musical praise rather than on hymn singing and meditative worship. Such activities conform to a Christianity characterized by middle-class values of respectability, which Pastor Bryan learned during her Anglican upbringing. But although younger Pentecostals may count these practices as "white," the latter are described by Pastor Bryan and others of her generation as hallmarks of both a universal Christianity and an authentic "Jamaican" cultural identity. Thus, while Pastor Bryan strives for an ethnic transcendent worship—a "blending of fragrances"—she nevertheless self-identifies as "an independent Jamaican woman" and defines her cultural identity in terms of a global Christian mainstream.

Pastor Bryan does not normally attend gospel concerts, so I was delighted that she made an exception on this occasion and agreed to accompany me. Her decision to come along speaks volumes about the esteem with which she holds the Brooklyn Tabernacle Choir. Throngs of people were in attendance. This was no surprise, as the outdoor concert had been advertised on Love 101 FM for several weeks. Publicized both in Jamaica and throughout the Caribbean, it was expected to draw in listeners from several islands in the region. On this evening in late August, Pastor Bryan and I found ourselves among the thousands of fans who sat in lawn chairs or on blankets waiting in anticipation at St. Andrew's Constant Spring Golf Club for the star attraction. Two years prior, they had sent only a subset of the choir known as the Brooklyn Tabernacle Singers. This time, they were featuring all but a handful of the full 250-member ensemble. The force and volume of those voices and their tightly rehearsed arrangements had contributed to the choir's international fame. It is ironic that this would be my first time hearing the choir in person. Back home, I had walked past the Brooklyn Tabernacle on a few occasions but never entered. I'd always had my hands full with obligations at my own church, Emmanuel Temple, where Jamaican-style worship permeated worship services. It now seemed that I was witnessing another jumbling of space and place—the transportation of a Brooklyn-based sound into Jamaica.

The organizers dubbed the event "Be Glad . . . The Jamaican Worship Experience," even though the Brooklyn Tabernacle Choir's repertory includes a mix of styles. Referring to the choir's musical eclecticism, director Carol Cymbala has stated, "There's something here for everyone: black gospel, southern gospel, praise and worship, classical music . . . but more important than style, when a song blesses people, you don't really care what kind of music it is."[11] Their song "We Are United" seemed tailor made for this concert. Its shuffle groove and choppy organ up-beats indexed a classic reggae style that resonated as such among Jamaican listeners. In the months leading up to the concert, the song enjoyed a copious amount of radio airplay. At the concert, the choir rendered it twice due to audience demand. Released on their 1999 recording, *High and*

Lifted Up, the chorus emphasizes the theme of unity, which was also highlighted throughout the concert.

Although directed toward a wide swath of Christendom, "We Are United" references some of the tensions endemic to Pentecostal practice. It mentions the goals of spiritual warfare, in which saints are "soldiers of light" fighting not against humans but "principalities in the dark." The unity of the global Christian army is strengthened by virtue of its common enemy, whom the saints "crush" underfoot. Moreover, this army is "marching to one beat," ideally in lockstep with the sole purpose of victory through the divine word. Reinforcing this theme, the song leaders quoted several scriptures about the "one body" of Christ. But this notion of a shared beat also registers as a reference to musical style.[12]

While the theme of unity is applied in discourse about Christians as a global body, it is also used in a narrower sense to discuss the transorganizational ties among believers within Jamaica. A "unity service" I attended at All Saints Apostolic Church in Spanish Town was devoted to the goal of fostering a sense of togetherness among a subset of Christians in Jamaica. In this case, those called to unity were apostolic Pentecostals hailing from a variety of autonomous organizations, such as the United Pentecostal Church, Pentecostal Assemblies of the World, and Shiloh Apostolic. The emcee pointed out the need for saints to be "on one accord," referring to the events of Acts 2. It was the anointing, he insisted, that would "destroy the yoke" of division among the saints. "Accord is a musical term," a preacher subsequently explained. "We have the instruments and the voices blending together to make harmony, and that's what the Lord wants us to do as the people of God. We must be in harmony and peace with one another and in tune with what the Lord wants." He then announced that the congregation would have a unity prayer. But first, he invited a woman from one of the visiting churches to come lead the congregation in "Make Us One, Lord," a song I only later learned was composed by Carol Cymbala and featured on the Brooklyn Tabernacle Choir's 1991 recording, *Live with Friends*. The preacher's subsequent invocation called on God to "send the anointing." A manifestation of divine presence and power would entail God's blessing on the saints' efforts to break down any unnecessary barriers among them. "Oh Lord," he added, "We are expecting great things because we are in agreement." His prayer thus affirmed the unity of the saints while implicitly challenging the saints to corroborate his unity claim before God. Several repetitions of "In the name of Jesus!" sealed the prayer before a collective "Amen!" brought it to a close.

Another preacher took his turn at the podium. He continued emphasizing the unity theme but with an ostensibly broader perspective: "We have invented a cultural gospel. We have got to get rid of this mentality and preach Christ crucified." Citing 1 Corinthians 3:9, he added, "We are laborers together!" With these remarks the unity service began to emphasize the ties between Jamaican and non-Jamaican saints. His words reminded me of a conversation I'd had with Pastor Carolyn Jolley, an African American pastor who had recently relocated to Jamaica. Curious about the challenges she faced during her transition, I asked, "Was it hard to adjust to this way of life?" "No, man, not really," she replied, allowing me to detect melodic traces of the Jamaican accent she seemed to enjoy having acquired. "There is no such thing as culture shock in ministry," she added. She explained that she first visited Jamaica in June 1998, and shortly thereafter Pastor Bryan became a trusted friend. By July 1999 Pastor Jolley had sold her house in the United States and settled in Jamaica for good. "I didn't come to change anybody's culture," she assured me. Pastor Jolley applies the notion of spiritual unity to her transnational ministry and the challenges of crossing boundaries between African American and Jamaican cultural spheres. During one sermon, she cited 1 Corinthians 12:12–13.

> For as the body is one, and hath many members, and all the members of that one body, being many, are one body: so also is Christ. For by one Spirit are we all baptized into one body, whether we be Jews or Gentiles, whether we be bond or free; and have been all made to drink into one Spirit.

Notwithstanding the emphasis on unity, Pentecostal leaders are keenly aware of theological and musical differences among various Christian groups. These differences can make achieving unity difficult. Some pastors even forbid their members from worshipping with those outside of their specific folds. The most rigid boundary is that between apostolic (or "oneness") and trinitarian groups. As one Jamaican apostolic woman explained,

> Most people define "Pentecostal" by the hand clapping. Hand clapping is like a marker for society. Society calls a church "Pentecostal" if they do hand clapping, but originally the Pentecostal churches were those that baptized in Jesus's name. You might ask someone from the New Testament Church of God [a trinitarian organization] and they might say, "Yes, we're Pentecostal," but they were not originally Pentecostal.[13]

Some see biblical doctrine as the most vital defining attribute of authentic Christianity. While both trinitarian and apostolic Pentecostal groups maintain that baptism by immersion in water is essential, they disagree about how this is to be done. Song lyrics such as those found in "One God Apostolic," which I discussed in chapter 1, thus play a role in the articulation of theological differences.

The above vignettes reveal different applications of the unity theme. In the first instance, the Brooklyn Tabernacle Choir's "We Are United" emphasizes the coming together of Christians worldwide for the purposes of spiritual warfare against a common enemy. The unity theme finds a narrower application at All Saints, where it is apostolic Pentecostals who are urged to set their differences aside for the greater good. This discourse overlaps with a rebuke of a limited "cultural gospel," as members of All Saints assert spiritual kinship with non-Jamaicans who share their embrace of the apostolic doctrine. In both contexts, ethnic transcendence remains an ideal. It is an ideal exemplified by the music and multiethnic makeup of groups such as the Brooklyn Tabernacle Choir. This form of transcendence remains something toward which Jamaican believers strive rather than a pragmatic reality. Most saints accept this discrepancy between belief and practice. Part of the challenge of faith, they say, is to recognize the limitations of human existence in the world while pressing toward the radical inclusiveness of a holiness aesthetic that may be perfected only through death. While Pentecostals attempt to transcend ethnic or cultural boundaries, they do not fully escape the social and theological categorizations that inform their self-identities. Rather, they rely on these categorizations for the cultivation of musical preferences and perceptions of collective distinctiveness.

Conclusion

Articulations of religious ethnicity are unstable discursive strategies that are deployed in the service of a cultural politics of religious and national belonging. In Jamaica, members of All Saints, Lighthouse Assembly, Bethel Apostolic, and Faith Fellowship strive to maintain a critical distance from worldly musics, understanding that their Christian faith demands that they distinguish themselves from the habits of the broader society. Worldly music is understood to include the sounds of the secular dancehall, but its definition also stretches to encompass musics considered culturally "other." At stake for some is the protection of tradition and religious authenticity from what is described as the intrusiveness of foreign ritual styles. Yet as we have seen, there are plenty of Christian believers, along with artists such as Donnie McClurkin and the Brooklyn Tabernacle Choir, who revel in the fluidity of their Christian identities and underscore the value of their faith as a way of being that cuts across boundaries of denomination, ethnicity, race, and nationality. African American gospel music, along with other forms of Christian music from the United States, has been appropriated and incorporated into the worship experiences of Jamaicans. As believers redraw the lines of Jamaican Pentecostal identity to conform to their own sense of religious ethnicity, boundaries are not only transcended; they are collapsed.

This is not to say, however, that Pentecostals and other Christians are deaf to ethnic self-identifications. Quite the opposite is true. In fact, what I have argued in this chapter is that these identifications are made audible through musical performance. It is precisely this audibility that allows believers to "'transcend' their ethnic identification to promote an identity rooted in 'religion' rather than 'race'" (Marti 2012, 34). In this way, some believers express their religious identities in "ethnic transcendent" ways.[14] But we may also view religion as yet another "ethnic" marker believers choose to give primacy of place in musical and discursive performance. Religion, in this case, "serves as a particularly important aspect of ethnic identity" (Kivisto and Croll, 24). Concerts and worship services provide opportunities for musical participants to express pride in both their local culture and their connections to a broader cohort of Spirit-filled believers. Panethnic, ethnic-specific, and ethnic transcendent perspectives are never mutually exclusive. Rather, they commingle within particular congregations, concert halls, and sometimes even within individual believers.

Flows of African American music to and through Jamaican communities lend urgency to the ritual processes through which Jamaicans engender feelings of spiritual and cultural belonging. In the United States, musical participation for both Jamaicans and African Americans is a means through which each cultural group chooses to distinguish itself from the other in some situations while maintaining common status as members of the Pentecostal Christian faith. Jamaican migrants in New York and London bring with them a strong sense of their cultural distinctiveness. According to Sutton and Makiesky-Barrow (1987), they come to the United States with "foreknowledge of White attitudes of racial superiority and with experiences with problems of racial inequality. Both the problems and the achievements of West Indians are viewed by the dominant White majority, and come to be viewed by West Indians themselves in the context of Black America" (103). A "West Indian racial consciousness" thus emerges as a result of shared experiences with other nonwhite immigrants and in response to being an "invisible minority" that is lumped together into the same category as African Americans.[15] This West Indian racial consciousness is manifested in churches such as Wondrous Love and Emmanuel Temple. It also thrives in London and throughout the Caribbean diaspora where Jamaicans perform their identities and express feelings of nostalgia through musical worship.

There is a biblical notion that Christians are travelers in a strange land— "aliens" or "pilgrims" who are passing through this life en route to a heavenly home from which they are temporarily distanced. This metaphor is apropos for members of Wondrous Love, Emmanuel Temple, and other churches that include first- and second-generation migrants. These women and men work to maintain a sense of at-homeness while being doubly marginalized in the United States as "black" and "West Indian."[16] It is therefore not surprising that Jamaicans who compose a strong majority of conservative congregations keep African American gospel styles at a distance. They choose to express an ethnic-specific "Jamaican" Pentecostal identity. The title of the Brooklyn Tabernacle Choir concert, "Be Glad . . . The Jamaican Worship Experience," is revelatory. It suggests that "Jamaican" is seen and heard as an absorbent category that includes African American styles and perhaps any type of music that Jamaicans perform and enjoy. In other words, the people, not the music, define the category.

Conclusion
Identity, the Holy Spirit, and the Global Community

This book has underscored the inherent vulnerability of humanly constructed categories, subject as they are to the inward and outward flow of meanings and values. Music, I have argued, is a powerful tool for regulating this kind of flow. As stubbornly as divisions survive among Pentecostal Christians, they shrink with the musical and ritual recognition of the Holy Spirit's universality. As eagerly as boundaries are constructed between the worship styles of Jamaica and the United States, they are transcended and collapsed by the appropriation of globally circulated gospel recordings. As quickly as walls are erected between religious traditions, they are torn down by the discovery of shared repertories. As passionately as partitions are placed between the sacred and the secular, they are punctured by the creative incorporation of worldly musical styles. And yet it would be a mistake to view music as only an accelerant for flow. As I have shown, Pentecostals also use music to assert their distinctiveness vis-à-vis cultural and religious outsiders. The decision to sing an "old" Jamaican chorus instead of, say, a contemporary African American gospel piece tells us something about what an individual finds aesthetically pleasing, but it also represents an attempt to champion a collective cultural and religious identity experienced as pure and "authentic." Musical pleasure is, after all, "never just a matter of feeling; it is also a matter of judgement" (Frith 1996, 115). The rhythms of reggae and ska, the repertories of religions such as Revival and Rastafarianism, and recordings by U.S.-based gospel artists are all fraught with moral and cultural ambiguity within

Jamaica's Pentecostal churches. Judgments concerning the meaning and morality of musical genres are always contingent on the believer's social, theological, and generational positioning within Jamaica's overlapping Christian circles.

Identities are, as Stuart Hall (1996) reminds us, "points of temporary attachment to the subject positions which discursive practices construct for us" (6). Jamaican Pentecostal identities are likewise in flux, as believers define their faith through the creative use of sounds and practices whose meanings change over time, just as ideas and attitudes about gospel music evolve within arenas of Pentecostal worship and the broader society. Nevertheless, I suggest that the holy–worldly binary on which these mobile identities hinge is surprisingly resilient and complex. Throughout the preceding pages, I have peeled back the layers of this binary to expose several related dichotomies. Pentecostals map oppositional constructions of holiness and worldliness onto those of church and dancehall, past and present, white and black, Jamaican and (African) American.

I once heard a senior musicologist make an offhand remark about the supposed waning significance of "identity" as a topic of intellectual inquiry. Scholars in our discipline, he noted, have "moved on" to issues that are more "relevant." The arbitrary tone of the musicologist's proclamation stung almost as much as the cold smack of unmarked privilege, which gave him both the audacity to issue it and the luxury of believing it to be true. For whom and to whom does identity no longer matter? Who gets to decide where the boundaries of "relevant" intellectual inquiry lie? And why did no one inform me that we had "moved on"? In that moment, I could neither muster the courage to pose those questions out loud nor find the intellectual wherewithal to mount a defense of identity as a worthwhile topic. But I hope this book makes it clear that identity is, if nothing else, still "good to think with."[1] I concur with a recent assertion by Abigail Wood and Rachel Harris (2018) that "in spite of contemporary perceptions of the fluidity and performativity of identities, claims to belonging and emplacement continue to exercise considerable power over people's imaginations and aspirations" (9). There is clearly something significant at stake for Jamaican Pentecostal Christians in terms of how they see, hear, and define themselves. They care deeply about identity, and as I have shown, they adopt musical practices and codes of holy conduct to affect how they are viewed by others as well. As Spirit-filled followers of Jesus Christ, they see themselves as his ambassadors, appointed to represent and reflect God's presence in the midst of a lost world. As members of a marginalized religious and cultural community in Jamaica and the United States, these Pentecostal practitioners have little interest in "moving on" from identity. They are not finished with it yet, and neither am I.

In Jamaica and the United States, Pentecostal Christianity, like other religious traditions, has been shaped by the particular social and historical circumstances of those who practice it. It should come as no surprise that Jamaican Pentecostals sometimes embrace musical styles and repertories that feel strange and unfamiliar to African American churchgoers. Likewise, African American Pentecostals tend to enjoy gospel songs that differ from the music their Jamaican counterparts prefer. In this book, I have set out to make these differences plain while also surveying some uncharted common ground. I have discovered that Pentecostals use music to draw lines between the sacred and the profane, the church and the dancehall, and, by extension, Jamaica and the United States. The concepts of flow and transcendence help us to make sense of the blurriness of these boundaries among Pentecostals within their respective societies. The transmigration of church music connects Pentecostals in the United States and Jamaica by providing shared sonic material for use in worship services. By indexing translocal places through North American gospel songs, Jamaican believers self-identify as members of a global community and imaginatively traverse national boundaries otherwise viewed as restrictive. Music helps to support congregational singing, generate flow, invoke the Holy Spirit, facilitate praise, and usher saints into a worship mode. These ritual goals and practices are translocal insofar as they are shared by congregants residing in Jamaica and the United States. Despite, and perhaps because of, its stylistic variability, music equips saints in both cultural contexts to transcend the self and access the joy of the Holy Spirit. Pentecostal music-making is thus a vital aspect of what I have elsewhere termed a "technology of transcendence," involving the use of music to summon divine presence and facilitate ritual transformation. In Jamaica and throughout the African diaspora, religious practitioners thus "work the spirit" in ways that reflect "local manifestations of a global musico-spiritual technology" (Butler 2008, 95).[2]

In a complementary discussion of African American gospel music, Braxton Shelley (2019) applies the term "technology of transcendence" to the "gospel vamp," a musical process characterized by the "interaction of repetition and intensification" (210). I share Shelley's concern with the experience of transcendence, along with his commitment to gospel music's broader theological context. His incisive analytical project differs somewhat from mine, however, insofar as it also foregrounds details of musical form, texture, and syntax that pertain to canonical pieces of African American choral gospel. The "technology of transcendence" I have in mind applies more broadly to the interplay of gospel musics and Pentecostal rituals throughout the African diaspora.[3] It has to do with the body of biblically informed and culturally tinged principles applied within a congregation for the purpose of moving from one ritual state to another. By highlighting the musical, social, and theological dimensions of ritual technology, this book challenges definitions of technology (for example, Spier 1970) that reduce technological activities to a purely "scientific" function. As Bryan Pfaffenberger (1992) has noted, religious practices have too often been left out of such conversations. This exclusion, he claims, "forestalls any consideration of the crucial role that ritual institutions play in the coordination of labor." He advocates an approach to the social anthropology of technology based on "a principle of absolute impartiality with respect to whether a given activity 'works' (i.e. is 'technical') or 'doesn't work' (i.e. is 'magico-religious')." Such an approach will allow "the social dimensions of sociotechnical activity come to the fore" (501).

In Pentecostal church services, music-making is also form of spiritual communication through which believers attempt to feel God's presence and acquire "heavenly gifts" that will uplift and empower them. I submit, however, that it is at the level of musical sound and style that scholars and practitioners can best understand the key to a meaningful worship experience. As I have shown, saints express displeasure with church music for reasons that are complex. Sonic and stylistic unfamiliarity can make music-making feel more like a painful chore than an act of pleasurable worship. It is also not uncommon for a song that registers as too far from "home" in terms of its musical style to be blamed for the failure of a church service. When saints grumble that a service was "dry" or that "there was no anointing there," they are likely annoyed by musical choices they deem responsible for an unwanted "ebb" of the Holy Spirit. Dwindling enthusiasm for church participation, along with a lackadaisical attitude on the part of those who attend services, is often attributed to music that, for reasons having to do with stylistic familiarity and comfort, does not "speak" to the congregation. Creating and sustaining spiritual flow is more than a matter of satisfying aesthetic desires; in order to experience spiritual flow, musical foreignness must sometimes be overcome for the sake of spiritual clarity. This resonates with Simon Frith's (1996) assertion that music "constructs our sense of identity through the direct experiences it offers of the body, time and sociability, experiences which enable us to place ourselves in imaginative cultural narratives." Perhaps more often than not, "an aesthetic judgement (this sounds good) is necessarily also an ethical judgement (this is good)" (124), particularly in spaces of music, ritual, and worship. Such is the case in Jamaican Pentecostal contexts, where the success of a worship service or concert hinges on the ability of participants to get "on one accord" and create a musical atmosphere that is both pleasing to the attendees and conducive to the felt presence of the Holy

Spirit. This is precisely what is at stake in efforts to negotiate styles of gospel music and worship.

Notwithstanding doctrinal disagreements, the Holy Spirit plays a major role in shaping Pentecostal aesthetic and moral frameworks with regard to gospel music and everyday lifestyle. One of the primary goals of singing, testifying, and preaching in Pentecostal services is to encourage the saints and compel the unsaved to open their hearts and be filled with the Holy Spirit. As I have explained, believers understand that when this happens, the "overflow" of God's anointing will (super)naturally yield speech in another language. Preachers, emcees, testifiers, and song leaders commonly cite the second chapter of Acts as a way of stressing that "Pentecost can be repeated!" The challenge is simply for those present to demonstrate unity through worship, as the followers of Jesus did on the biblical Day of Pentecost.

I believe Pentecostal music-making contributes to what Simon Coleman calls a "charismatic 'habitus,' a form of embodied disposition . . . that is geared towards the transcendence of the local and yet can be articulated in specific contexts of belief and practice" (2000, 6). Understanding how this charismatic habitus is formulated in Jamaica has required a consideration of the historical and contemporary processes that give rise to Pentecostal practice not only in Jamaica but around the world. Attempts to imbue musical and verbal performances with the visual and sonic indices of the Holy Spirit are intriguing for the light they shed on how musical events are framed, in local terms, as sacred or secular. Notions of musical appropriateness have a great impact on the stylistic choices made by instrumentalists, accepted by the saints, and deemed effective by clergy. Distinctions between holy and worldly musical styles are frequently made along generational lines, such that while older Pentecostals tend to privilege styles and repertories adhering to the "tradition," teens and young adults are embracing a more "modern" sound popularized by both Jamaican and African American contemporary gospel artists. As younger religious leaders gradually replace older ones in Jamaica, Pentecostals tend to become more keenly aware of how musical repertories and styles evolve over time.

Belief in the Holy Spirit's agency also informs discourses of unity, flow, and style—key terms that encapsulate some of the critical issues that Jamaican Pentecostals negotiate as they strive to engage in effective musical worship. As a unifying agent, the Holy Spirit ties together disparate strands of Pentecostal faith, both within Jamaica and also across national boundaries. Some of the most challenging aspects of this coming together involve the reconciliation of Jamaican and "American" musical styles and worship ideals. As I have discussed, Jamaican Pentecostals, in the Caribbean and in the United States, express both an appreciation for and apprehension about African American gospel music styles.

This book has also explored questions of group identity and notions of authenticity. In this regard, I have tread on familiar ground. For example, Martin Stokes (1994) writes about the close relation between authenticity and identity. "Clearly," he states, "notions of authenticity and identity are closely interlinked." (6) He adds that authenticity "focuses a way of talking about music, a way of saying to outsiders and insiders alike 'this is what is really significant about this music,' 'this is the music that makes us different from other people' (6–7). Simon Coleman and Peter Collins (2004) note that "identity is constructed . . . through expressions of 'difference.'" Moreover, it "can never be created in a vacuum—it must always be produced in and through a set of relations with real or imagined others" (2). Likewise, Qadeer (2006) states, "Ethnic consciousness is heightened in contrast with others. . . . [It] comes to the surface when a group or an individual competes with others for economic resources, political power, and cultural or linguistic autonomy" (68). Ethnicity is also foregrounded in contexts of Pentecostal worship, where musical styles not only compete but also inform one another. Sound and spirit flow across ethnic boundaries. Musical styles influence and absorb shifting perceptions of tradition and collective strivings for spiritual flow.

I have conceptualized Pentecostal ritual in terms of several overlapping analytical frames. One frame relates music-making to its specific ritual setting—that is, within a given church service. Another analytical frame considers religious musical practices as they pertain to cultural expressions that index a particular ethnic or cultural group. Believers' notions of musical and behavioral appropriateness have been conceived against the worldly discourses concerning commercial popular music in Jamaica and, to a lesser extent, the United States. A wider frame deserving of further consideration conceptualizes Pentecostalism as a global religious movement (Martin 2002). Although scholars have begun to examine Pentecostal Christianity as global culture, there remain multiple musical manifestations of this worldwide practice that need to be distinguished according to local cultural style.[4] Even as Jamaican Pentecostals construct identities that are grounded in a sense of cultural pride, their religious expressions resonate with those of believers worldwide.

Situating Jamaican and African American Pentecostals within a global "community of practice" (Strauss 2000, 177) has interesting implications for contemporary fieldwork and reminds me of George Marcus's (1998) critical reassessment of traditional, place-based ethnography. Marcus advocates a multi-locale ethnography that effectively deals with the complex social environments in which we live and conduct fieldwork. His "multi-sited imaginary" not only entails multiple geographical locales but also implies a reflexivity whereby the commonalities between the ethnographer and his or her chosen topic are methodologically brought into play. Marcus argues that when "existing affinities between the ethnographer and the subject of study" are projected "from the realm of the more personal to the delineation of more generic social-cultural problems . . . a multi-sited canvas or space of ethnographic research emerges almost naturally" (15). Comparative analyses then stem primarily from "the fractured, discontinuous plane of movement and discovery among sites as one maps an object of study and needs to posit logics of relationships, translation, and association among these sites" (86).

This book is a "multi-sited canvas" onto which the stories of Jamaican Pentecostals sometimes overlap my own. One of the challenges I have faced involves determining the extent to which my personal experiences merit inclusion within these pages. In being open about my own religious beliefs, I run the risk of sliding down the slippery slope of reflexivity into an abyss of self-indulgence—of turning research into "mesearch." But keeping in mind Michelle Kisliuk's admonition (2000, 14) to underscore the crucial connections between myself and my Others—those whom I encounter in the fields I construct and whom I represent in the ethnographic writing I produce—I deem this risk to be manageable, if not absolutely necessary. Writing reflexively helps me to think in fresh ways about Pentecostal experience and the music-making that surrounds it through a performative lens.

Marcus's reference to the ethnographer's "existing affinities" as a conceptual bridge to understanding broader social concerns speaks to the potential value of reflexive writing. Like Gina Ulysse, I embrace the latter insofar as it "seeks to interrupt the problem of ethnographic authority that arises when the focus is only on the subject" (2008, 6; see also Herndon 1993). Rather than embrace notions of mutually exclusive "emic" and "etic" perspectives, I have tried to employ a dialogical approach to knowledge acquisition. Such an approach is similar but not identical to the "reciprocal ethnography" that Elaine Lawless identifies as "inherently feminist and humanistic." I share Lawless's (1993) desire to emphasize "dialogue as a process in understanding and knowledge retrieval," along with her disdain for epistemological hierarchies that "place the scholar at some apex of knowledge and understanding and her 'subjects' in some inferior, less knowledgeable position" (5). Yet I also reject relativisms of morality and knowledge that would deny the scholar's voice any epistemological authority whatsoever.[5] Although this book recounts a significant number of the conversations I have had with Jamaican Pentecostal Christians, I feel the need to acknowledge that it is *my* voice that is privileged. And I believe this is as it should be, not because I am somehow more "objective" or have access to "superior" forms of knowledge, but, rather, because the goal of my work is to engage, in a critical way, with a level of analysis that may be distinct from how other Pentecostals think about the topic.

Although Pentecostal beliefs and musical practices are embedded in the realm of the deeply personal, I have tried to show that they are also informed by much broader theological and cultural frames. By positing Pentecostalism as a global phenomenon, I have in mind both the worldwide Pentecostal movement as it manifests throughout Jamaica, and also the shared conception among Pentecostals of "the world as a whole."[6] This analytical frame involves an understanding of charismatic Christianity as a universal gospel and underscores the critical assertion that Pentecostals everywhere hold in common certain beliefs and experiences.[7] Karla Poewe (1994b) points out that "the significance of [charismatic Christians'] emphasis on the 'Holy Spirit' . . . is that the 'spirit' symbolizes a conception of a world or social system that crosscuts national, ethnic, and racial barriers, ignores barriers of communication and language, cross-cuts professionals and laborers, the rich, the poor, and diverse denominations" (239). Global elements of Pentecostalism are reinforced by international organizations, which have codified biblical practices and conceptions of the divine. Another one of my challenges has been to keep hold of what is particular to the local settings in which Pentecostal religion and music are practiced. This book's focus on musical practice has demanded attention to the local, as songs are experienced in different ways according to the contexts in which they unfold.

Pentecostals profess a faith described by one scholar as "a repertoire of recognizable spiritual affinities which constantly breaks out in new forms" (Martin 2002, 176). These "new forms" make it unreasonable to posit Pentecostalism as a static belief system that is shared among a globally united contingent of practitioners. However, U.S.-based organizations such the Pentecostal Assemblies of the World, the United Pentecostal Church, and the Church of God are global in reach and have historically exerted a strong proselytizing force in Jamaica. These missions were instrumental in popularizing teachings that are held in common by Pentecostals in Jamaica and the United States. As I discussed in chapter 5, it is also true that Jamaicans are major contributors to worship services in black churches within the United States. Moreover, Jamaican musical styles and repertories influence recordings by African American gospel artists. With the proliferation of global mass media, gospel music repertories from Jamaica and the United States have blended. In Jamaica, this has facilitated the widespread use of African American gospel styles that are sometimes controversial.

These pages have explored the vital role of musical sound and performance in Pentecostal identity constructions as they are unfolding within and flowing beyond Jamaica's transnational arena. In making observations about early-twenty-first-century Pentecostalism, I have drawn on an array of scholarly and ethnographic texts to argue that gospel music is a fundamental means through which Jamaican believers index both a global cosmology and the local and transnational contexts they traverse. While witnessing the flow of identities and the overstepping of boundaries music facilitates, I inhabited the enlivened spaces of Pentecostal worship, transcended boundaries of my own, and found ways to make myself at home among Jamaican Christian families. The ambiguous frontiers of field and home are sources of inspiration from which the book has taken shape. Along the way, this ethnography has also become a more intimate story of the challenges in conducting fieldwork while flowing between worlds of musical, spiritual, and critical encounter.

Notes

Introduction

1. Gidal's notion of "musical boundary-work" reformulates Thomas Gieryn's (1983) theory of "boundary-work," which aimed to buttress an epistemological claim about the distinctiveness of science as an area of academic inquiry. Gieryn's focus was on scientists' "attribution of selected characteristics to the institution of science . . . for purposes of constructing a social boundary that distinguishes some intellectual activities as 'non-science.'" (781). Fredrik Barth's (1969) foundational study on ethnic group differentiation, Pierre Bourdieu's (1984) classic work on "taste" as an aesthetic and politicized marker of social class, and Anthony Cohen's (1985) theories of symbolic boundary construction are also noteworthy predecessors to Gidal's discussion. My interest in boundary crossing also applies to the conventional distinctions between "musicological" and "ethnomusicological" methods and topics, and I agree with Shelemay (1996) concerning the "need to explore, and cross, long-standing boundaries" within the music-centered arenas of historical musicology, music theory, and ethnomusicology (22). There may be much to gain, for example, from a "music theory" paradigm that supplies a detailed analysis of the rhythms, harmonies, and timbres characterizing Jamaican Pentecostal music-making. However, such an approach lies outside the scope of this book, which relies more on a disciplinary blend of ethnomusicology, anthropology, and religious studies than on data mined from "the borderlands of musical scholarship" (20).

2. This definition comes from the Center for Black Music Research website. https://www.colum.edu/cbmr/Resources/style-genre-definitions.html.

160 · *Notes to Introduction*

3. See Rommen (2007, 73–74) for an analogous discussion of how "gospel music" is defined in Trinidad and Tobago.

4. Burnim (1985) identified musical and cultural elements of gospel music that comprise a "black aesthetic." See also Jackson (1979), Burnim (1983), and Wise (2002) for surveys of gospel music literature and overviews of twentieth-century definitions.

5. In accordance with Jamaican parlance, I use "chorus" and "song" interchangeably to denote a short, nonstrophic piece of music that typically features the repetition of two to eight lines of text. A "chorus" can also designate the recurring section of a hymn known as the refrain. A "hymn" is distinct from a "Jamaican song" or chorus in that it contains several stanzas of text, each of which is set to the same melody and harmony. Hymns, unlike choruses, also tend to be of known authorship by writers from Europe and the United States.

6. For a fuller discussion of the use of "riddims" as part of a studio production method in Jamaica, see Stolzoff (2000, 91) and Manuel and Marshall (2006). In Trinidad and Tobago, Timothy Rommen explores sacred-secular controversies among members of Full Gospel and Pentecostal churches (2007). In the United States, debates concerning the meaning of black gospel music have centered on artists who cross over from sacred to secular forms of popular music. Mellonee Burnim (2017) explains that "many African Americans are both passionate and unwavering in their support or condemnation of such musical border crossings." She concludes that "constructs of race, culture, and, by implication, religion, are critical variables in defining how gospel music is perceived, produced, and marketed not only among African Americans but within the broader national music industry as a whole" (80).

7. The command to "worship the Lord in the beauty of holiness" appears in 1 Chronicles 16:29, 2 Chronicles 20:21, Psalm 29:2, and Psalm 96:9 of the Authorized (King James) Version of the Old Testament Bible. For ethnographic analysis of both performative and rhetorical contexts of Christian worship music in the United States, including a discussion of how "worship experiences can be produced, packaged, and sold," see Ingalls (2018, 42).

8. A full exposition of Appadurai's theory of "scapes" lies beyond the scope of this book. Moreover, there has been an abundance of writing devoted to critiquing his account of global cultural flows. Eric Zolov (1999) complains that Appadurai's theories of flow "dehistoricize sociocultural change" (264). Matthew Sparke (2004) employs Appadurai's theories with the caveat that they overemphasize these flows' "deterritorializing impacts" (92). Likewise, Maria Koundoura (1998) critiques Appadurai's "acceptance of the imperial dominance of the single integrated market orchestrated by the USA," adding that such an approach "offers no means of negotiating for different kinds of national projects or for a revolutionary restructuring of one's own nation-state" (85). While emphasizing cultural flow and the fluidity of Jamaican Pentecostal identities, I also maintain that individual Jamaicans hold on to their Jamaicanness, not simply as a figment of their ethnic imagination but as

tied to their "place" on the island and to a national identity in which they are deeply invested. See Stokes (2004) for a review of ethnomusicological and anthropological theories of globalization. Further discussions may be found in White (2012) and Krüger and Trandafoiu (2014).

9. In her comprehensive sociohistorical exploration of Pentecostalism in Jamaica, Diane Austin-Broos (1997) argues persuasively that this religion has become indigenized as Jamaicans have adapted North American Pentecostal practice to fit their cultural needs. Nicole Toulis (1997) focuses on how Jamaicans in England negotiate their identities through Pentecostalism. But John Hopkin's short essay (1978) has remained the only existing music-centered study of Pentecostal church music in Jamaica.

10. Although the labels "Protestant" and "Pentecostal" are sometimes used interchangeably, "Pentecostal" Christians tend to celebrate an apostolic lineage that began on the biblical Day of Pentecost (Acts 2) but extends primarily from the 1906 Azusa Street revival to the modern day. See Spittler (1994), Hollenweger (1997), and Burgess and van der Maas (2002) for exhaustive surveys of the topic. Birgitta Johnson's (2015) ethnographic work uncovers a worthwhile problematization of such labels, demonstrating that music is an indispensable ingredient in one African American Baptist church's theological transformation into a "Bapticostal Charismatic nondenominational church" (163). Notwithstanding doctrinal and musical shifts and debates, the Bible serves as a strong unifying text among the Pentecostal Christians I discuss, and the teachings and interpretations derived from scripture and handed down since the early twentieth century have remained fundamentally in place.

11. John Pulis's (1999) painstaking review of refugee transportations to Jamaica from Georgia, South Carolina, Florida, and New York chronicles "a series of evacuations that transported approximately 200 black Loyalists, upwards of 2,000 white Loyalists along with 5,000 slaves, and perhaps as many as 65,0000 African Americans seized as contraband" (183).

12. The British had established the Anglican Church in Jamaica after winning control of the former Spanish colony in 1655. Most white planters refused to share their religion with enslaved persons, deeming them too unsophisticated for Christian conversion. Whites also feared that religious instruction would contribute to feelings of equality and entitlement among the blacks (Barrett 1997, 17). George Simpson (1978) reports that "for nearly a hundred years after Britain acquired Jamaica . . . no missionary work was carried on in the island" (112). But by 1738, an evangelical revival had begun in England, and this religious fervor inspired a movement, led by John Wesley, to reform the Anglican Church. The Wesleyan Methodist movement soon spread to the New World, where missionaries in Jamaica began to make attempts at Christianizing the enslaved population (Barrett 1997, 20; Sherlock and Bennett 1998, 177). In 1754 the Methodist presence in Jamaica was supplemented by the United Brethren, or Moravians, who arrived from Germany (Sherlock and Bennett 1998, 177). However,

the Moravian Church had only limited success, baptizing fewer than one thousand enslaved persons by 1800 (Simpson 1978, 33).

13. Anthropological studies of Jamaican Revival include Simpson's early study (1956), as well as works by Moore (1953), Seaga (1969), and Chevannes (1978).

14. The New Testament Church of God, a trinitarian group, is the largest Pentecostal organization in Jamaica in terms of membership. My fieldwork in Jamaica and New York City was conducted among Pentecostals adhering to both apostolic and trinitarian doctrines. See Austin-Broos (1997, 91–101) for a detailed historical discussion of Pentecostalism's installation in Jamaica. She notes that the Holiness Church of God, an important predecessor to the Jamaican Pentecostal movement, arrived on the island in 1908 and is mentioned in several articles in the *Jamaica Daily Gleaner* from the 1920s. "Pentecostal" and "Holiness" churches were difficult to distinguish early on because the Jamaican census conflated these two categories. In 1918 A. J. Tomlinson, founder of the Pentecostal Church of God in Cleveland, Tennessee, sent an evangelist, J. S. Llewellyn, to Jamaica. This trinitarian church changed its name to the New Testament Church of God and is now the largest Pentecostal organization in Jamaica. In the 1920s, there were also notices in the *Gleaner* concerning Pentecostal groups such as the Apostolic Church of God, the Church of God in Christ, and the Pentecostal Assemblies of the World. It was this latter organization that experienced the most rapid growth in Jamaica during this time, largely through the efforts of George and Melvina White. In an article published in the *Gleaner*, Clinton Chisholm comments on the 2011 census, noting that after Seventh-Day Adventists, the "next largest denomination is the nebulous group called 'Pentecostal' at 295,195, significantly up from the 2001 figure of 247,452. Next in line is another unclear group, 'Other Church of God,' at 246,838, up from the 2001 membership of 215,837. The New Testament Church of God follows with 192,086, swelling from its 163,912 following in 2001."

15. Throughout this book, pseudonyms are used for interviewees whom I quote at length, with the exception of Pastors Tommy Seals and Hermine Bryan, who gave me permission to use their actual names.

16. I draw on Catherine Bell's concept of "ritualization" to discuss the "various culturally specific strategies for setting some activities off from others, for creating and privileging a qualitative distinction between the 'sacred' and the 'profane,' and for ascribing such distinctions to realities thought to transcend the powers of human actors." The concept of ritualization effectively captures the intentionality of believers, whose actions serve "to distinguish and privilege what is being done in comparison to other, usually more quotidian, activities" (Bell 1992, 74).

17. As professor and ordained minister Michael Eric Dyson (2003) states, "There are some tremendous difficulties in maintaining one's commitment to a religious tradition that says, 'We know by faith and not by sight,' while maintaining habits of critical inquiry that rest on relentless interrogation of the warrants, grounds, bases, and assertions of truth put forth in all sorts of intellectual communities, including religious ones" (12).

18. See Gupta and Ferguson (1997, 12–15) for a fuller discussion of how the concepts of "field" and "home" have been historically constructed in anthropology and related disciplines.

19. I thank Kyra Gaunt for suggesting this term to connote the sometimes-imperceptible boundary between fieldwork and the activities of "real" world everyday life. Val Colic-Peisker (2004) also uses "homework" to describe her position as a sociologist conducting research within "her own" minority Croatian community in Australia. "Introspection thus became an important part of my work," she remarks, "reflecting the apparent tension between the roles of the detached observer and engaged participant" (83). While I drew on the common denominator of Pentecostal faith, Colic-Peisker found that "shared language"—her ability to speak the same Croatian dialect as her interviewees—"helped to turn 'fieldwork,' with its wintry connotations of exposure and venturing out, into cozy and sheltered 'homework'" (87). I believe conducting "homework" instead of "fieldwork," and conceptualizing ethnographic work in terms of the former, is a way to engage with a "politics of location" that critically refocuses the anthropological gaze inward toward peoples and practices that are less epistemologically stable than scholars have traditionally assumed (see Visweswaran 1994, 101–4; Lavie and Swedenburg 1996, 21).

20. The studies of Larry Ward (1997) and Mellonee Burnim (1980) merit comparison with this book, not only because they, too, are ethnomusicological treatments of Pentecostal church music, but also because each author stands in a distinct relation to his or her topic. Ward, a white nonbeliever, is seen as a cultural and religious outsider. He devotes a full chapter to a discussion of the tensions caused by his outsider status during fieldwork, even describing his own "ethnographic naïveté" in presuming he could "quietly observe worship without being actively drawn into the event" (1997, 375). Burnim's African American Methodist background led her informants to view her as a cultural insider and a religious outsider.

21. Deborah Thomas (2004) notes that "bitter divides of color, class, and culture" fuel skepticism that the promise of Jamaica's motto, "Out of Many, One People," can ever be fulfilled in the long term. She argues that moments of national pride and unity "are few and far between in Jamaica" and that the consolidation of such moments "often requires the appearance of an external threat" (263–64). I suggest that the aforementioned holy–worldly dichotomy, along with the rhetoric of spiritual warfare, lends itself to a strategic mobilization of oppositional Jamaican Pentecostal identities through which believers define themselves as both culturally and spiritually triumphant over "worldly" enemies. In chapter 5 I discuss narratives of ethnicity and race as vital to negotiations of Jamaican Pentecostal identity.

22. See Hobbs (2014) for a cultural history of racial "passing" from the mid-nineteenth to the mid-twentieth century, where African Americans in the United States crossed the color line to take on white identities. Karla Slocum (2001) discusses the challenges that arise for researchers whose "outsider" identities are constructed by those with whom we engage during fieldwork. She writes, "Attempting to downplay

differences of class, education, or even gender does not allow us to circumvent the outsider part, if for no other reason than that our informants will not let us forget who we are." However, our differences may themselves hold the key to "connect[ing] the field experience with our politics" (147). In other words, politically minded scholars "can interrogate the local categories of identity construction in the places where we do our research, but we need not see the categories as obstacles. Rather, as we analyze how we differ from those we study and consider the impact of such differences on our research goals, we can still identify a set of responsibilities to which we will adhere in our work and which we hold toward the people who participate in our research" (146).

23. See, for example, Samarin (1970), Goodman (1972), and Austin-Broos (1997). Of the existing research on black church music in the United States, relatively little is written by scholars who claim membership in the religious community they study. To my knowledge, William Dargan's dissertation (1983) represents the earliest comprehensive study of Pentecostal church music written by a Pentecostal. In his later work (2006), he allows his church upbringing to inform his descriptions of congregational hymn singing. Guthrie Ramsey (2003) writes "from the strength of [his] own subject position" to provide an eloquent account of his conversion from a traditional Protestant denomination to a Pentecostal church (43). He also discusses the sacred-secular tensions he experienced as a church keyboardist and aspiring jazz musician (10–14).

24. There is an extensive body of scholarship devoted primarily to African American sacred practice. See, for example, Waterman (1951), Frazier (1964), Williams (1974), Paris (1982), Sanders (1996), Sernett (1997), Raboteau (2001), and Best (2005). See also DuPree (1994) for an annotated bibliography of works on African American Pentecostalism. These general studies complement numerous music-centered writings on the topic, of which the following are also only a short sample: Lincoln (1974), Williams-Jones (1975), Ricks (1977), Jackson (1979), Walker (1979), Marks (1982), Burnim (1985), DjeDje (1989), Costen (2004), Dargan (2006), Spencer (1992), Harris (1992), Lincoln and Mimaya (1990), Allen (1991), Reagon (1992), Boyer (1995), Ward (1997), Maultsby (1999), Hinson (2000), Reed (2003), Jackson (2004), Smith (2004), Darden (2005), and Marovich (2015).

25. Exemplifying what Elizabeth Puttick (1997) calls "an increasingly common situation" (6), it was only after I had already begun graduate work in ethnomusicology that I began to envision Pentecostal practice as a possible research topic. Religion scholar Jo Pearson (2002) describes this type of situation in terms of "going native in reverse," noting, "I do not consider myself to have broken the anthropological taboo against 'going native,' for I was a 'native' already" (105). Similarly, in her research among Spanish transmigrants, Sarah Pink (2000) notes, "It is difficult to pinpoint precisely when 'fieldwork' began. The research developed in a context of friendship and shared lifestyle with different Spanish people in England. Initially, I did not situate the practices of my social life as research, but rather as a way of locating myself in a social world, communicating with people with whom I sense a 'common ground.' At

an indeterminable point I began to imagine how these experiences might be written up as anthropology" (47).

Chapter 1. Boundaries and Flows

1. I heard this axiom in Jamaica on more occasions than I can recount. Most of those who repeated it posited it as an indisputable fact supported by *The Guinness Book of World Records*. Glasceta Honeyghan (2000) states that "90% of Jamaican households are religious, and that there are more churches per square mile than anywhere else in the world" (411). Honeyghan does not provide a source for this assertion, and I have not been able to corroborate it. Nonetheless, the endurance of this bold narrative is, in itself, a remarkable feature of Jamaican social discourse. Irrespective of their veracity, claims of Christian piety help to create, among Jamaicans and non-Jamaicans alike, a sense of the island nation's distinctiveness vis-à-vis other Caribbean countries and the United States.

2. The line "Pentecost can be repeated" is a catchphrase for those who emphasize the contemporary relevance of early Church practices. To my knowledge, it was first used in the hymn "Pentecostal Fire Is Falling," composed in 1912 by George Bennard. I discuss this hymn in chapter 4.

3. Jamaicans began arriving in the United States in particularly large numbers after 1965, with the passage of the Immigration and Nationality Act (Foner 1987, 117).

4. I discuss West Indian and African American musical interactions at Emmanuel Temple in greater detail elsewhere (Butler 2000).

5. Todne Thomas Chipumuro (2012) discusses the work of Aaron Powell and other Bahamian missionaries who established black evangelical congregations throughout the U.S. South in the 1950s. Highlighting the interactions of West Indian and African American churchgoers in an Atlanta suburb, Chipumuro identifies a "tradition of black Atlantic evangelical Protestantism in which Afro-diasporic religious participants forged shared religious institutions through religious migrations" (607).

6. Gerardo Marti's discussion of ethnicity (2012), which I discuss in detail in chapter 5, provides a useful lens through which to view this interaction of identities. See also Maultsby's useful discussion (1994) of "ethnicity" as it relates to African American popular music-making in the United States.

7. The Authorized (King James) Version of the Bible is used throughout this text. The biblical account of Holy Spirit baptism is found in Acts 2:1–4.

8. See Walston (2005) for a more in-depth discussion of the speaking-in-tongues controversy.

9. See, for example, Chang and Chang (1998, 31–37) and Kauppila (2006).

10. Thomas Turino (2008) describes three types of "transstate cultural formations": cosmopolitan formations, immigrant communities, and diasporas. The latter two types apply well to Jamaican Pentecostals in the United States. As an immigrant community, they "associate with each other on the basis of 'original home' identity and operate within community networks in the host country to a significant degree, such

that the community forms an enclave and supplies prominent models for socialization." As a diaspora, they "combine habits from the original home and their new home *and* are influenced by the cultural models from other places in the diaspora" (118; italics in the original). McAlister's work (2012) challenges us to consider "some of the *limits* of the concept of national and ethnic diaspora to understand how Caribbean groups form networks and imagine themselves to be situated." Pentecostals do not, by themselves, constitute a "diaspora" in the conventional sense. But as McAlister demonstrates, the musical sounds of Caribbean faith communities can serve as "sonic points on a cognitive compass that orients diasporic people in time and space" and helps them to "conceive of their 'spiritual lineage,' their past and their future, in ways that mirror a 'classic' diasporic consciousness" (27; italics in the original).

11. Lance Appleton first recorded this piece on his 1975 recording, *One God Apostolic*. See http://www.freelancemusic.net/onegod.htm.

12. See Austin-Broos (1997, 114–15) for a discussion of racial tensions among black and white Pentecostal organizations in Jamaica and the United States.

13. See Hopkin (1978) for a fuller description of hand-clapping patterns in Jamaican Pentecostal churches. His musical transcriptions of these patterns corroborate what I observed in the churches I attended.

14. In biblical parlance, believers will be "caught up together" (1 Thessalonians 4:17); they will not actually "fly away." Therefore, some Christians see these choruses as theologically incorrect. I believe this doctrinal dissonance tells us something important about the *performance* of faith. Indeed, the study of expressive culture can reveal inconsistencies between deeply held beliefs and the practices through which individuals choose to articulate them. Nevertheless, I contend that the latter are worthy of scholarly investigation. By shining light on those inconsistencies, we gain a more thorough appreciation of what makes both faith and action special human endeavors.

15. Rastafarianism gets its name from Ras Tafari, who adopted the name Haile Selassie after being crowned King of Ethiopia in 1930. He then became the driving force behind the new religious sect. Rastafari viewed Selassie as a black Messiah whose rise to power represented a fulfillment of biblical prophecy. See Sherlock and Bennett (1998, 395–98). Braithwaite (1978) and Chevannes (1994) have also researched *Kumina* and Rastafarianism, respectively. Diane Austin-Broos (1997) draws useful comparisons between Rastafarianism and Pentecostalism in Jamaica (239–42).

16. Jamaican scholars Barry Chevannes and Olive Lewin provide useful discussions of Revival tunes that Rastafari have appropriated. Chevannes identifies "Fly Away Home" as "a very popular Revival song" that Rastafari "adopted with a change of words." He notes that while the use of "Zion" actually accords with the earlier Revivalist version, the substitution of "work" for "life" reflects a more recent Rasta emphasis on "salvation in the here and now of this life as against the postponement into the next" (1998, 28). Lewin (2000) describes another piece, "O Let the Power Fall on Me, My

Lord," as a "popular Revival chorus" that was likewise "'captured' by the Rastas" and lyrically modified to suit their beliefs (205).

Chapter 2. Perfecting Holiness

1. See Thomas Turino's discussion (2008) of cultural cohorts united by a set of habits and practices.

2. I discovered the lyrics to this hymn, "The Promised Land," in *Redemption Songs*, number 619. It was composed by Joshua Gill in 1886 (Jones 1974, 44).

3. The hymn "Holiness unto the Lord" is found in *The Best of All*, p. 32. See also Blumhofer 2006, 980.

4. According to a recent survey, tourists from North America made up the largest number of overnight visitors to Jamaica in 2017, with 1.51 million from the United States and more than 400,000 from Canada. (Jamaica Tourist Board: Annual Travel Statistics 2017, 18–22, https://www.statista.com/statistics/375841/leading -source-countries-for-overnight-tourist-arrivals-to-jamaica.)

5. *How Stella Got Her Groove Back* (1996) is a bestselling novel by Terry McMillan. It was adapted into a feature film in 1998.

6. Christians' anxieties about the moral transgressions of tourists are part of a more widely expressed set of concerns about dysfunctional cultural values, an upsurge in violence, and the supposed negative effects of foreign media and "cultural exchange" on Jamaican youth. In *Exceptional Violence*, Deborah Thomas (2011) problematizes the role of policymakers who assign blame for Jamaica's social problems solely to the United States without accounting for "the continued legacy of British imperial violence" or attending to the motivations of youth who "produce visions of transnational cultural practice that resonate for them" (105–6).

7. According to most Pentecostals I met in Jamaica, visible evidence of Holy Spirit infilling includes modest styles of dress. However, they also distinguish this evidence from "proof" of the Holy Spirit's presence. One may thus adopt the "form and fashion" of holiness while still having a sinful attitude or lifestyle (see also Hinson 2000, 230–41). As I mentioned in the Introduction, audible evidence of Holy Spirit infilling includes speaking in tongues.

8. Although I am concerned here with holiness–worldliness boundaries as they pertain to the opposition that Jamaican Pentecostal churchgoers express toward dancehall music, this phenomenon is intimately related to the history of perceived incompatibility between the music of black churches in the United States and secular genres such as blues, jazz, R&B, and rap, which were, at times, considered "the devil's music." Writing about the social experiences of early twentieth-century blues artists in the United States, Giles Oakley (1997) notes that "for a large portion of the [African American] community, the blues was still the devil's music, the music of immorality, licentiousness, eroticism, whisky-drinking, juke joints, low life, violence, [and] a source of corruption and . . . social disruption" (196–97; see also Reed 2003, 89–112).

And even within the "sacred" realm of black musical expression, there is controversy over stylistic appropriateness, as gospel music draws from an ever-changing pool of expressive resources. Thus, while I draw attention to these debates as they occur in Jamaican churches, they are far from unprecedented among African diasporic communities. As Guthrie Ramsey (2003) explains: "Thomas Dorsey's mix of blues and gospel in the 1920s and 1930s; Rosetta Tharpe's blend of jazz and gospel during the 1940s; Edwin Hawkins's and Andre Crouch's pop-gospel of the late 1960s; and the Winanses' smooth-soul gospel of the 1980s were all seen as hybrid—and quite controversial in their day" (191).

9. Although the generic category of "dancehall music" is relatively new, having been widely used only since the late 1980s, Stolzoff (2000) maintains that "Jamaican masses have been creating cultural counterworlds through secular music and dance performances in the 'cultural spaces' known as dancehalls for more than two centuries" (3–4; see also Erlmann 1991, 18).

10. Personal interview, Liliput (St. James), Jamaica, March 25, 2002.

11. "Kanye West Sings Gospel . . . or Does He?," September 13, 2004. https://www .today.com/popculture/kayne-west-sings-gospel-or-does-he-wbna5993983.

12. "Stellar Awards Press Release: September 24, 2004." http://www.gospelflava .com/stellar/stellarpressreleasesept2004-kanyewest.html.

Chapter 3. The Anointing Makes the Difference

1. As I discuss in this chapter, the spiritual labor of women is critical to the worship experiences of Pentecostal churchgoers throughout Jamaica. Although I conducted much of my fieldwork in churches affiliated with the Pentecostal Assemblies of the World Inc., scholars of religion have shown that the practices I describe apply to other U.S.-based Pentecostal organizations as well. See, for example, Anthea Butler's historical study (2007) of women in the Church of God in Christ, as well as Judith Casselberry's ethnography (2017), which underscores the "contours of labor" performed by women in the Church of Our Lord Jesus Christ of the Apostolic Faith. Pentecostal performances of anointing and holiness also bear similarity to religious practices in some Islamic societies, where, as Nieuwkerk argues, "the gendered nature of performing piety and the centrality of the body and the senses are central issues" (2013, 11).

2. Personal interview, Emmanuel Temple, Brooklyn, New York, October 19, 1999.

3. Elder Delton McDonald, Refuge Temple Apostolic Church, Kingston, Jamaica, August 14, 2002.

4. Personal interview, Spanish Town, Jamaica, August 18, 2002.

5. Each of the four Gospels of the Bible's New Testament provides an account of a woman using her hair to wash the feet of Jesus. See Matthew 26:6–13, Mark 14:3–9, Luke 7:36–50, and John 12:1–8.

6. Several Bible verses discuss gender roles in the church and home, including Ephesians 5:22–24, 1 Corinthians 11:3, 1 Corinthians 14:34, 1 Timothy 2:11–14, Colossians 1:18, 1 Peter 3:1–2.

7. In African American churches, the pursuit of racial justice has often failed to address gender inequities that limit women's access to leadership positions. Sandra Barnes (2006) notes, "One might assume that a history of racial oppression would sensitize African Americans, both women and men, relative to other forms of discrimination and actually increase the likelihood of support for gender equity. But based on the historic mistreatment of African-American men, their counterparts are often expected to 'stand by her man,' thereby supplanting concerns of sex/gender inequality for issues of racism" (382). Writing from "womanist" theological perspectives, Gilkes (2001), Riggs (2003), and Turman (2013) provide compelling analyses of sexism and patriarchy in black churches. Turman (2015) offers a comparative critique of an "Afro-patriarchy" that dehumanizes black women, not only in Christian churches but also in the Nation of Islam. She concurs that "gender injustice is a reality in African American religion, even in contexts where Black religion is situated as a justice-making endeavor" (145).

8. Acts 2:38 states, "Then Peter said unto them, Repent, and be baptized every one of you in the name of Jesus Christ for the remission of sins, and ye shall receive the gift of the Holy Ghost." Apostolic Pentecostals cite this Bible verse to underscore the necessity of baptism in water and Holy Spirit infilling.

9. Elder Noel Facey, "I Am Armed and Extremely Dangerous" (sermon, Riversdale Pentecostal Church, August 21, 2002).

10. Melinda Weekes (2005) provides a historical analysis of contemporary gospel music as it relates to the efforts of African American pastors to keep youth involved in church. She argues that present-day concerns about the "secularization" of church worship are part of a recurring cycle that began with Thomas Dorsey in the 1920s. In chapters 4 and 5, I discuss objections to "contemporary gospel" music in greater detail.

11. The song "In the Sanctuary" is featured on Kurt Carr's recording, *Awesome Wonder* (2000).

12. Borrowing Halbwachs's argument regarding social and personal memory formation, Connerton (1989) states, "Most frequently, if I recall something that is because others incite me to recall it, because their memory comes to the aid of mine and mine finds support in theirs. Every recollection, however personal it may be, even that of events of which we alone were the witnesses, even that of thoughts and sentiments that remain unexpressed, exists in relationship with a whole ensemble of notions which many others possess: with persons, places, dates, words, forms of language, that is to say with the whole material and moral life of the societies of which we are part or of which we have been part" (36).

13. Connerton expands on Halbwachs's research by emphasizing the fact that "to study the social formation of memory is to study those acts of transfer that make remembering in common possible" (39). Connerton focuses on commemorative ceremonies and bodily practices in order to argue that "images of the past and recollected knowledge of the past are conveyed and sustained by (more or less ritual) performances" (40).

14. Exhortation by Youth president, Refuge Temple Apostolic Church, August 21, 2002, 2K Greenwich Road, Kingston.

15. I am influenced here by the work of performance theorists Gregory Bateson (2000), Erving Goffman (1974), and Richard Bauman (1984). All three scholars view performance as a mode of communication that establishes an interpretive frame through which actions derive their meaning. Performative frames are, Bauman says, "communication about communication" (15), or what Bateson calls "metacommunicative" (188) insofar as they provide instructions for how messages are to be understood. Drawing on Goffman's landmark study, *Frame Analysis*, Bauman discusses some of the cultural conventions that serve to "announce" performative frames and provide "keys" to their interpretation. These keys may include linguistic codes and formulae, appeals to tradition, and even denials that a performance is taking place (15–16). Conventional statements such as, "We're not here to entertain you," along with attempts to reframe the concert (performance) as a church service (ministry), represent "disclaimers of performance." Bauman adds that these disclaimers have less to do with an unwillingness to prove performative competence than with a desire to conform to "standards of etiquette and decorum, where self-assertiveness is disvalued. In such situations, a disclaimer of performance serves both as a moral gesture, to counterbalance the power of performance to focus heightened attention of the performer, and a key to performance itself" (22).

Chapter 4. The Old-Time Way

1. Cultural theorist Mieke Bal (1999, xi) provides a useful definition of nostalgia, paraphrased by Averill (2003, 14) as "an emotionally charged form of cultural memory in which the past is idealized and invested with a present longing."

2. I draw here from Tad Tuleja's (1997) discussion of "usable pasts," which presents itself as a healthy alternative to Hobsbawm and Ranger's (1983) "invented traditions." The latter term refers to "a set of practices, normally governed by overtly or tacitly accepted rules and of a ritual or symbolic nature, which seek to inculcate certain values and norms of behaviour by repetition, which automatically implies continuity with the past" (1983, 1). Tuleja's critique is that Hobsbawm and Ranger have in mind primarily "ostensibly stable" or larger-scale practices, albeit ones that are not as vintage as they seem. By contrast, Tuleja's mission—and it is one that I share—is to stay grounded in the concrete practices of "relatively small, subnational entities" where "local knowledge" is generated. He argues that the term "invented," along with the similarly used word "constructed," is too fraught with negative connotations and "has come to smack of falsity, inviting the delicious glee of the scholarly debunker" (1997, 4).

3. "Lining out" refers to the song leader's act of singing or speaking each line of a hymn just before the congregation repeats it. This is helpful when congregants do not have hymnals or when an unfamiliar song is being introduced. The practice of lining out may have stemmed from the Church of England and was brought to Britain's New World colonies by the 1640s (Boyer 1995, 7).

4. Tarrying services may derive from the conversion practice of sitting on the "mourners' bench," which began in black churches in the United States during the nineteenth century. For historical discussions of the mourners' bench (or "moaners' bench") as it relates to the practice of tarrying for the Holy Spirit during conversion, see Daniels (2001, 280) and Raboteau (1978, 254–55).

5. Proverbs 23:10–11 states, "Remove not the old landmark; and enter not into the fields of the fatherless: For their redeemer is mighty; he shall plead their cause with thee."

6. See Curwen Best's discussion of how the Caribbean region's gospel music industries and church theologies were "systematically transformed" after 2000 via the global circulation of televangelism and gospel music programming from the United States (2004, 83).

7. Personal interview, November 7, 2003.

8. In African American churches, what scholars such as Davis (1985) and Spencer (1987) call the "chanted sermon" is more commonly referred to as moaning, tuning, humming, or whooping. See Simmons (2010, 864) and Shelley (2017, 175). Musicologist Braxton Shelley (2017) synthesizes much of the extant scholarly literature on the topic. He uses the concept of "tuning up" to theorize multiple "forms of homiletical musicality" that extend beyond preaching to encompass performances of gospel music (175). I return to the topic of "chanted sermons" in chapter 5.

9. See Gordon (2008) and Frederick (2016, 146–54) for insightful discussions of Jamaica's radio and television networks and their struggles to stay afloat amid a sea of global competitors, particularly the U.S.-based Trinity Broadcasting Network and the Word Network, with whom Jamaican broadcasters compete for advertising dollars.

10. Although terms such as *indigenization*, *contextualization*, and *inculturation* connote similar types of cultural practices, I believe the term *musical localization* more aptly describes Jamaican Pentecostals' use of musical genres from the United States. In this regard, I follow Ingalls, Reigersberg, and Sherinian (2018), who define musical localization as "the process by which Christian communities take a variety of musical practices—some considered 'indigenous,' some 'foreign,' some shared across spatial and cultural divides; some linked to past practice, some innovative—and make them locally meaningful and useful in the construction of Christian beliefs, theology, practice, or identity" (13).

11. F. James Davis (1991) and Joel Williamson (1995) describe how whites in the United States enforced a "one-drop" rule and codified a black–white racial binary in the mid-nineteenth century. Sharon Placide (2010) situates this binary in relation to a Jamaican "color hierarchy" that is more fluid and complex.

Chapter 5. Performing Ethnicity

1. The group Mary Mary is composed of two sisters, Erica and Tina Atkins-Campbell. The song "Shackles" is on their debut recording, *Thankful* (2000), and is stylistically influenced by the album's R&B and hip-hop producer, Warryn Campbell.

2. Deborah Thomas (2004) argues that since the 1990s, Jamaica has witnessed a remarkable shift away from the "creole multiracial nationalism," which intellectual elites of the 1960s put forth as an emblem of Jamaican distinctiveness, and toward a "racialized vision of citizenship," which she refers to as "modern blackness" (11–12). The "ethnic-specific" expressions of Pentecostal identity to which I refer entail a rejection not only of the blackness associated with African Americans but also of the blackness tied to poor and working-class Jamaican popular musics such as dancehall reggae.

3. I use "black" and "African American" here as synonymic designations of a "racialized ethnicity" (Kivisto and Croll 2012, 11) operative in the United States. Likewise, some Jamaican Pentecostals with whom I spoke use "black" and "African American" interchangeably, particularly when referencing styles of Christian music. There are, however, other ways that "black" and "African American" are employed. For example, Jamaicans also draw a significant local distinction between the two terms, using "black" in reference to the popular culture of darker-skinned Jamaicans presumed to be of African descent. They also use the identity marker "black" to denote a panethnic transnational community of African-derived peoples.

4. Gerald Seale, "Our Environment in Making Disciples," Congress of Evangelicals in the Caribbean, Centre for Excellence, Tunapuna, Trinidad October 22–25, 2007. http://www.caribbeanevangelical.org/conecar2007reports/plenarypapers.htm. Reprinted in "Mind and Spirit: A Theologian Does Not a Leader Make," *Gleaner*, November 17, 2007, http://www.jamaica-gleaner.com/gleaner/20071117/news/news6.html.

5. See Burnim (2015, 189–212) for a helpful discussion of "traditional" and "contemporary" as they apply to the aesthetic and historical development of gospel music performance.

6. Marla Frederick (2016) explores in detail the transmission of religious programming from the United States to Jamaica. She notes that while U.S.-based televangelists such as T. D. Jakes, Creflo Dollar, Paula White, and Juanita Bynum have become household names among the island's Pentecostals, Jamaicans are also "pushing back on American religious broadcasting by establishing their own religious networks," such as Mercy and Truth Ministries Network and Love Television (163).

7. There is extensive literature on the musicality of African American preaching. See, for example, Jackson (1981), Davis (1985), Spencer (1987), Rosenberg (1988), Turner (1988), Pitts (1993), Smith (2004), Simmons (2010), Martin (2014), and Shelley (2017). As a style of musical preaching, "tuning up" is more common among African American preachers than the Jamaican ones I have heard. But according to Shelley, "tuning up" is not limited to preaching or other "musical techniques." The latter are but "one side of the complex of sound and belief that constitute 'the gospel imagination'" (190). In describing the recorded sermons of Rev. Ford Washington McGhee, Lerone A. Martin (2014) notes that the "chanted sermon" was advertised in the 1920s as a crucial part of the "frenzy" of Pentecostal practice, in which "the expressive worship of the congregation, and the chanted sermon all merged to create

an ecstatic worship experience." He adds, "Pentecostals believed this brand of euphoric experience was a must for true Christian experience. Profits from the media ministry indicated that many consumers agreed" (115). Thérèse Smith (2004) provides detailed transcriptions of chanted preaching, calling it "the most powerful expression of the African American church" (204). Describing a situation similar to what I found in Jamaica, she explains that controversy stems from the perception of chanted preaching as overly emotional. It is important to note that her ethnography is based on fieldwork among black Baptists in northern Mississippi, evidencing the fact that all sorts of Christians engage in these kinds of ritual practices and that "tuning up" is not unique to those who identify as Pentecostal.

8. See "Rocking Gospel" (2000).

9. Not to be confused with the "one-drop" ideology of racial classification (see chapter 4), the term "one drop" refers to a drumming pattern that emerged in the late 1960s as a distinguishing feature of the popular dance music known as rocksteady (Katz 2003, 67; Veal 2007, 31). Kenneth Bilby (2010, 9) offers a broader definition of "one drop" as "a rhythmic principle that appears in various guises in several of the major stages through which Jamaican popular music has gone, from ska and rocksteady [through] the Rasta cultural explosion of the 1970s, where it came into its own as a defining feature of so-called roots reggae."

10. http://www.brooklyntabernacle.org/the-church.

11. http://www.cbn.com/cbnmusic/artists/btc.aspx.

12. The notion that saints must "be united" is articulated through repetition of other key verses in the New Testament. For example, Ephesians 4:3–6, which emphasizes a spiritual oneness that binds believers, is cited to reinforce the notion of unity among Pentecostals: "Endeavoring to keep the unity of the Spirit in the bond of peace. There is one body, and one Spirit, even as ye are called in one hope of your calling; One Lord, one faith, one baptism, One God and Father of all, who is above all, and through all, and in you all."

13. Personal interview, Montego Bay, Jamaica, April 11, 2002.

14. Gerardo Marti describes the "ethnic transcendent" identity as a newer alternative to "panethnic" and "ethnic-specific" identity formations that are expressed among Latino Christian congregations in the United States (2012, 25–35). Marti's observations apply well to Jamaican Pentecostals.

15. Milton Vickerman (2001) writes that "whereas Jamaicans define 'blackness' loosely, Americans adhere to a much stricter definition." He adds that Jamaicans "often do not realize what it means to be 'black' until they migrate to America; this, of course, refers to the stronger negative sentiments attached to African ancestry in [the United States] compared to Jamaica" (211).

16. For helpful explorations of the experiences of Caribbean immigrants in the United States, see Carolle Charles's (2003) essay "Being Black Twice" and Candis Watts Smith's book (2014) on the complex political strategies of black ethnic groups in the United States.

Conclusion

1. I borrow this turn of phrase from an English translation of Claude Lévi-Strauss's *Totemism* (1963, 89).

2. See Murphy (1994) for discussion of how ritual practitioners "work the Spirit" in several different African diasporic locales.

3. Theories of a "technology of transcendence" have also been applied to experiences and practices beyond the African diaspora. See, for example, Walsh (1993, 130).

4. It took scholars until the 1990s to devote serious attention to the worldwide Pentecostal movement. Karla Poewe (1994a), Walter Hollenweger (1997), and Simon Coleman (2000) provide comprehensive overviews of Pentecostalism as it has spread, since the 1906 Azusa Street revival, from scant numbers of devotees to approximately five hundred million adherents across the globe. Coleman's study differs from my own in that he is primarily concerned with "Word of Faith" churches that emphasize obtaining financial prosperity through faith and sacrificial giving.

5. Glenn Hinson (2000), for example, goes so far as to accuse some ethnographers of deploying "strategies of disbelief" and resorting to a kind of "ontological colonialism," whereby "supernatural experience is . . . consigned to a reality apart, a realm where the 'real' is defined only within the narrow parameters of belief" (330). Hinson's critique is leveled most strongly against academics' "implicit claims to a fuller knowledge and a more real reality" (330). Similar critiques have targeted "traditions of disbelief" (Hufford 1982, 47), particularly when scholars wield power by pitting "official knowledge" (Foucault 1977, 219) against the "counterknowledge" (Fiske 1994, 192) that is sometimes cultivated within marginalized communities for survival and self-determination.

6. Roland Robertson (1992) uses the concept of globalization to refer to "both the compression of the world and the intensification of consciousness of the world as a whole" (8). Simon Coleman (2000) argues that charismatic Christians "construct a place of their own, a specific arena of action and meaning, within the shifting, liminal, chaotic space of the global." He also cautions, "The orientations towards the world displayed by these Christians involve not merely a set of ideas, but also engagement in certain physical and material activities, including the development of a spiritually charged aesthetic that encompasses ritual movements, media consumption, linguistic forms and aspects of the external environment" (5–6).

7. In this analytical context, "Pentecostal" connotes a sect of Spirit-filled Christians of the twentieth and twenty-first centuries, whereas "charismatic Christian" works for me in a broader, diachronic sense, referring to believers of any era who embrace gifts and manifestations of the Holy Spirit. Writers also distinguish "Pentecostal" and "charismatic" in other ways, using the latter to denote a mid-twentieth-century "charismatic movement" within congregations that maintained self-designations such as Baptist, Methodist, or even Catholic.

Bibliography

Allen, Ray. 1991. *Singing in the Spirit: African-American Sacred Quartets in New York City.* Philadelphia: University of Pennsylvania Press.

Amit, Vered. 2000. "Introduction: Constructing the Field." In *Constructing the Field: Ethnographic Fieldwork in the Contemporary World*, edited by Vered Amit, 1–18. London: Routledge.

Appadurai, Arjun. 1996. *Modernity at Large: Cultural Dimensions of Globalization.* Minneapolis: University of Minnesota Press.

Austin-Broos, Diane J. 1997. *Jamaica Genesis: Religion and the Politics of Moral Orders.* Chicago: University of Chicago Press.

Averill, Gage. 2003. *Four Parts, No Waiting: A Social History of American Barbershop Harmony.* New York: Oxford University Press.

Bal, Mieke. 1999. "Introduction." In *Acts of Memory: Cultural Recall in the Present*, edited by Mieke Bal, Jonathan Crewe, and Leo Spitzer, vii–xvii. Hanover, N. H.: University Press of New England.

Barnes, Sandra L. 2006. "Whosoever Will Let Her Come: Social Activism and Gender Inclusivity in the Black Church." *Journal for the Scientific Study of Religion* 45, no. 3: 371–87.

Barrett, Leonard E. 1997. *The Rastafarians.* Boston: Beacon.

Barth, Fredrik. 1969. "Introduction." In *Ethnic Groups and Boundaries: The Social Organization of Culture Difference*, edited by Fredrik Barth, 9–37. Boston: Little, Brown.

Bateson, Gregory. 2000. "A Theory of Play and Fantasy." In *Steps to an Ecology of Mind: Collected Essays in Anthropology, Psychiatry, Evolution, and Epistemology*, 177–93.

Chicago: University of Chicago Press, 2000. Originally published as "A Theory of Play and Fantasy," *Psychiatric Research Reports* 2 (1955): 39–51.

Bauman, Richard. 1984. *Verbal Art as Performance*. Prospect Heights, Ill.: Waveland.

Beckford, Robert. 2006. *Jesus Dub: Theology, Music and Social Change*. New York: Routledge.

Bell, Catherine. 1992. *Ritual Theory, Ritual Practice*. New York: Oxford University Press.

Bence, Evelyn. 1997. *Spiritual Moments with the Great Hymns: Devotional Readings That Strengthen the Heart*. Grand Rapids, Mich.: Zondervan.

Best, Curwen. 2004. *Culture @ the Cutting Edge: Tracking Caribbean Popular Music*. Kingston, Jamaica: University of the West Indies Press.

Best, Wallace D. 2005. *Passionately Human, No Less Divine: Religion and Culture in Black Chicago, 1915–1952*. Princeton, N.J.: Princeton University Press.

Bilby, Kenneth. 2016. "Distant Drums: The Unsung Contribution of African-Jamaican Percussion to Popular Music at Home and Abroad." *Caribbean Quarterly* 56, no. 4: 1–21.

Bithell, Caroline. 2006. "The Past in Music: Introduction." *Ethnomusicology Forum* 15, no. 1: 3–16.

Blumhofer, Edith. 2006. "Women Hymn Writers." In *Encyclopedia of Women and Religion in North America*, edited by Rosemary Skinner Keller, Rosemary Radford Ruether, and Marie Cantlon, 974–86. Bloomington: Indiana University Press.

Bourdieu, Pierre. 1984. *Distinction: A Social Critique of the Judgement of Taste*. London: Routledge / Kegan Paul.

Boyer, Horace C. 1973. "An Analysis of Black Church Music with Examples Drawn from Services in Rochester, New York." PhD diss., University of Rochester.

Boyer, Horace C., and Lloyd Yearwood. 1995. *How Sweet the Sound: The Golden Age of Gospel*. Washington, D.C.: Elliot and Clark.

Braithwaite, Edward Kamau. 1978. "Kumina: The Spirit of African Survival in Jamaica." *Jamaica Journal* 42: 45–63.

Burgess, Stanley M., and Eduard M. van der Maas, eds. 2002. *The New International Dictionary of Pentecostal and Charismatic Movements*. Grand Rapids, Mich.: Zondervan.

Burnim, Mellonee. 1983. "Gospel Music: Review of the Literature." *Music Educators Journal* 69, no. 9 (May): 58–61.

Burnim, Mellonee V. 1980. "The Black Gospel Music Tradition: Symbol of Ethnicity." PhD diss., Indiana University.

——. 1985. "The Black Gospel Music Tradition: A Complex of Ideology, Aesthetic, and Behavior." In *More than Dancing: Essays on Afro-American Music and Musicians*, edited by Irene V. Jackson, 147–76. Westport, Conn.: Greenwood.

——. "Gospel." 2015. In *African American Music: An Introduction*. Second Edition, edited by Mellonee V. Burnim and Portia K. Maultsby, 189–212. New York: Routledge.

——. 2017. "Crossing Musical Borders: Agency and Process in the Gospel Music Industry." In *Issues in African American Music: Power, Gender, Race, Representation*, edited by Portia K. Maultsby and Mellonee V. Burnim, 79–89. New York: Routledge.

Burton, Richard D. E. 1997. *Afro-Creole: Power, Opposition, and Play in the Caribbean*. Ithaca, N.Y.: Cornell University Press.

Butler, Anthea D. 2007. *Women in the Church of God in Christ: Making a Sanctified World*. Chapel Hill: University of North Carolina Press.

Butler, Melvin L. 2000. "Musical Style and Experience in a Brooklyn Pentecostal Church: An 'Insider's' Perspective." *Current Musicology* 70 (Fall): 33–60.

———. 2005. "Songs of Pentecost: Experiencing Music, Transcendence, and Identity in Jamaica and Haiti." PhD diss., New York University.

———. 2008. "In Zora's Footsteps: Experiencing Music and Pentecostal Ritual in the African Diaspora." *Obsidian* 9, no. 1: 74–106.

Carradine, Beverly, Charles J. Fowler, and William J. Kirkpatrick, eds. N.d. *The Best of All*. Indianapolis: Christ Temple.

Casselberry, Judith. 2017. *The Labor of Faith: Gender and Power in Black Apostolic Pentecostalism*. Durham, N.C.: Duke University Press.

Cassidy, Frederic Gomes, ed. 1961. *Jamaica Talk: Three Hundred Years of English Language in Jamaica*. London: Macmillan.

Chang, Kevin O'Brien, and Wayne Chang. 1998. *Reggae Routes: The Story of Jamaican Music*. Philadelphia: Temple University Press.

Charles, Carolle. "Being Black Twice." 2003. In *Problematizing Blackness: Self-Ethnographies by Black Immigrants to the United States*, edited by Percy Claude Hintzen and Jean Muteba Rahier, 169–80. New York: Routledge.

Chevannes, Barry. 1978. "Revivalism: A Disappearing Religion." *Caribbean Quarterly* 24, no. 3/4: 1–17.

———. 1994. *Rastafari: Roots and Ideology*. Syracuse, N.Y.: Syracuse University Press.

———. 1998. "New Approach to Rastafari." In *Rastafari and Other African-Caribbean Worldviews*, edited by Barry Chevannes, 20–42. New Brunswick, N.J.: Rutgers University Press.

Chipumuro, Todne Thomas. 2012. "Breaking Bread with the Brethren: Fraternalism and Text in a Black Atlantic Church Community." *Journal of African American Studies* 16, no. 4: 604–21.

Chisholm, Clinton. 2012. "Religion and the 2011 Census." *Gleaner*, November 4, 2012. http://jamaica-gleaner.com/gleaner/20121104/focus/focus4.html.

Clarke, Denise. 2002. "Stepped-up Security: Spring Breakers Get Increased Protection." *Gleaner*, March 21, 2002. http://old.jamaica-gleaner.com/gleaner/20020321/cornwall/cornwall1.html.

Cohen, Anthony P. 1985. *The Symbolic Construction of Community*. London: Horwood / Tavistock.

Coleman, Simon. 2000. *The Globalisation of Charismatic Christianity: Spreading the Gospel of Prosperity*. Cambridge: Cambridge University Press.

Coleman, Simon, and Peter Collins. 2004. "Introduction: Ambiguous Attachments: Religion, Identity and Nation." In *Religion, Identity and Change: Perspectives on Global*

Transformations, edited by Simon Coleman and Peter Collins, 1–25. Aldershot, U.K.: Ashgate.

Colic-Peisker, Val. 2004. "Doing Ethnography in 'One's Own Ethnic Community': The Experience of an Awkward Insider." In *Anthropologists in the Field: Cases in Participant Observation*, edited by Lynne Hume and Jane Mulcock, 82–94. New York: Columbia University Press.

Columbia College Chicago. N.d. "Definitions of Styles and Genres." *Center for Black Music Research*. https://www.colum.edu/cbmr/Resources/style-genre-definitions .html.

Connerton, Paul. 1989. *How Societies Remember*. Cambridge: Cambridge University Press.

Conway, Dennis, and Ualthan Bigby. 1994. "Where Caribbean Peoples Live in New York City." In *Caribbean Life in New York City: Sociocultural Dimensions*, edited by Constance R. Sutton and Elsa M. Chaney, 70–78. New York: Center for Migration Studies of New York.

Cooley, Timothy J., and Gregory Barz. 2008. "Casting Shadows: Fieldwork Is Dead! Long Live Fieldwork!" In *Shadows in the Field: New Perspectives for Fieldwork in Ethnomusicology*, edited by Gregory Barz and Timothy J. Cooley, 3–24. New York: Oxford University Press.

Costen, Melva Wilson. 2004. *In Spirit and in Truth: The Music of African American Worship*. Louisville: Westminster John Knox.

Creech, Joe. 1996. "Visions of Glory: The Place of the Azusa Street Revival in Pentecostal History." *Church History* 65, no. 3: 405–24.

Csikszentmihalyi, Mihaly. 1990. *Flow: The Psychology of Optimal Experience*. New York: Harper and Row.

———. 1975. *Beyond Boredom and Anxiety*. San Francisco: Jossey-Bass.

Daniels, David, III. 2001. "African-American Pentecostalism in the Twentieth Century." In *Century of the Holy Spirit: 100 Years of Pentecostal and Charismatic Renewal, 1901–2001*, edited by Vinson Synan, 265–91. Nashville: Thomas Nelson.

Darden, Robert. 2005. *People Get Ready: A New History of Black Gospel Music*. New York: Continuum.

Dargan, William T. 1983. "Congregational Gospel Songs in a Black Holiness Church." PhD diss., Wesleyan University.

———. 2006. *Lining Out the Word: Dr. Watts Hymn Singing in the Music of Black Americans*. Berkeley: University of California Press.

Davis, F. James. 1991. *Who Is Black? One Nation's Definition*. University Park: Penn State University Press.

Davis, Gerald L. 1985. *I Got the Word in Me and I Can Sing It, You Know*. Philadelphia: University of Pennsylvania Press.

DjeDje, Jacqueline. 1989. "Gospel Music in the Los Angeles Black Community: A Historical Overview." *Journal of Black Music Research* 9, no. 1: 35–79.

Dueck, Jonathan. 2011. "Binding and Loosing in Song: Conflict, Identity, and Canadian Mennonite Music." *Ethnomusicology* 55, no. 2: 229–54.

DuPree, Sherry Sherrod. 1994. *African-American Holiness Pentecostal Movement: An Annotated Bibliography*. New York: Garland.

Durkheim, Émile. 1915. *The Elementary Forms of the Religious Life*. Translated by Joseph Ward Swain. London: Allen and Unwin.

Dyson, Michael Eric. 2003. *Open Mike: Reflections on Philosophy, Race, Sex, Culture and Religion*. New York: Basic Civitas.

Eliade, Mircea. 1959. *The Sacred and the Profane: The Nature of Religion*. Translated by Willard R. Trask. San Diego: Harcourt Brace Jovanovich.

Erlmann, Veit. 1991. *African Stars: Studies in Black South African Performance*. Chicago: University of Chicago Press.

Feld, Steven. 1984. "Communication, Music and Speech about Music." *Yearbook for Traditional Music* 16: 1–18.

Feld, Steven, and Aaron Fox. 1994. "Music and Language." *Annual Review of Anthropology* 23: 25–53.

Fentress, James, and Chris Wickham. 1992. *Social Memory: New Perspectives on the Past*. Oxford, U.K.: Blackwell.

Finley, Stephen C. 2007. "Real Men Love Jesus? Homoeroticism and the Absence of Black Heterosexual Male Participation in African American Churches." *Council of Societies for the Study of Religion Bulletin* 36, no. 1 (February): 16–19.

Fiske, John. 1994. *Media Matters: Everyday Culture and Political Change*. Minneapolis: University of Minnesota Press.

Foner, Nancy. 1987. "The Jamaicans: Race and Ethnicity among Migrants in New York City." In *New Immigrants in New York City*, edited by Nancy Foner, 195–217. New York: Columbia University Press.

Foucault, Michel. 1977. "Revolutionary Action: 'Until Now.'" In *Language, Counter-Memory, Practice*, edited by Donald F. Bouchard, 218–33. Ithaca, N.Y.: Cornell University Press.

Frazier, Edward Franklin. 1964. *The Negro Church in America*. New York: Shocken.

Frederick, Marla F. 2003. *Between Sundays: Black Women and Everyday Struggles of Faith*. Berkeley: University of California Press.

———. 2016. *Colored Television: American Religion Gone Global*. Stanford, Calif.: Stanford University Press.

Frey, Sylvia R., and Betty Wood. 1998. *Come Shouting to Zion: African American Protestantism in the American South and British Caribbean to 1830*. Chapel Hill: University of North Carolina Press.

Frith, Simon. 1996. "Music and Identity." In *Questions of Cultural Identity*, edited by Stuart Hall and Paul du Gay, 108–27. London: Sage.

Gaunt, Kyra D. 2002. "Got Rhythm? Difficult Encounters in Theory and Practice and Other Participatory Discrepancies in Music." *City and Society* 14, no. 1: 119–40.

Gidal, Marc. 2016. *Spirit Song: Afro-Brazilian Religious Music and Boundaries*. New York: Oxford University Press.

Gieryn, Thomas. 1983. "Boundary-Work and the Demarcation of Science from Non-Science: Strains and Interests in Professional Ideologies of Scientists." *American Sociological Review* 48: 781–95.

Gilkes, Cheryl Townsend. 2001. *"If It Wasn't for the Women…": Black Women's Experience and Womanist Culture in Church and Community*. Maryknoll, N.Y.: Orbis.

Goffman, Erving. 1974. *Frame Analysis: An Essay on the Organization of Experience*. London: Harper and Row.

Goodman, Felicitas D. 1972. *Speaking in Tongues: A Cross-cultural Study of Glossolalia*. Chicago: University of Chicago Press.

Gordon, Lewis R. 2000. *Existentia Africana: Understanding Africana Existential Thought*, New York: Routledge.

Gordon, Nickesia S. 2008. *Media and the Politics of Culture: The Case of Television Privatization and Media Globalization in Jamaica (1990–2007)*. Boca Raton, Fla.: Universal.

Guest, Matthew. 2002. "'Alternative' Worship: Challenging the Boundaries of the Christian Faith." In *Theorizing Faith: The Insider/Outsider Problem in the Study of Ritual*, edited by Elisabeth Arweck and Martin D. Stringer, 35–56. Birmingham, U.K.: University of Birmingham Press.

Gupta, Akhil, and James Ferguson. 1997. "Discipline and Practice: 'The Field' as Site, Method, and Location in Anthropology." In *Anthropological Locations: Boundaries and Grounds of a Field Science*, edited by Akhil Gupta, James Ferguson, 1–46. Berkeley: University of California Press.

Halbwachs, Maurice. 1976. *Les Cadres Sociaux de la Memoire*. Paris: Mouton.

———. 1992. *On Collective Memory*. Chicago: University of Chicago Press.

Hall, Stuart. 1996. "Introduction: Who Needs 'Identity'?" In *Questions of Cultural Identity*, edited by Stuart Hall and Paul du Gay, 1–17. London: Sage.

Harris, Michael W. 1992. *The Rise of Gospel Blues: The Music of Thomas Andrew Dorsey in the Urban Church*. New York: Oxford University Press.

Hebdige, Dick. 1987. *Cut 'n' Mix: Culture, Identity and Caribbean Music*. London: Routledge.

Herndon, Marcia. 1993. "Insiders, Outsiders: Knowing our Limits, Limiting our Knowing." *World of Music* 35, no. 1: 63–80.

Hinson, Glenn. 2000. *Fire in My Bones: Transcendence and the Holy Spirit in African American Gospel*. Philadelphia: University of Pennsylvania Press.

Hobbs, Allyson. 2014. *A Chosen Exile: A History of Racial Passing in American Life*. Cambridge, Mass.: Harvard University Press.

Hobsbawm, Eric, and Terence Ranger, eds. 1983. *The Invention of Tradition*. Cambridge: Cambridge University Press.

Hollenweger, Walter J. 1997. *Pentecostalism: Origins and Developments Worldwide*. Peabody, Mass.: Hendricks.

Honeyghan, Glasceta. 2000. "Learning from the Cultures of Home Literacy." *Language Arts* 77, no. 5: 406–13.

Hopkin, John B. 1978. "Music in the Jamaican Pentecostal Churches." *Jamaica Journal* 12: 23–40.

Hufford, David J. 1983. "Traditions of Disbelief." *New York Folklore Quarterly* 8: 47–55.

Ingalls, Monique M. 2018. *Singing the Congregation: How Contemporary Worship Music Forms Evangelical Community*. New York: Oxford University Press.

Ingalls, Monique M., Muriel Swijghuisen Reigersberg, and Zoe C. Sherinian. 2018. "Music as Local and Global Positioning: How Congregational Music-Making Produces the Local in Christian Communities Worldwide." In *Making Congregational Music Local in Christian Communities Worldwide*, edited by Monique M. Ingalls, Muriel Swijghuisen Reigersberg, and Zoe C. Sherinian, 1–31. New York: Routledge.

Jackson, Irene. 1979. *Afro-American Religious Music: A Bibliography and a Catalog of Gospel Music*. Westport, Conn.: Greenwood.

Jackson, Jerma A. 2004. *Singing in My Soul: Black Gospel Music in a Secular Age*. Chapel Hill: University of North Carolina Press.

Jackson, John L., Jr. 1998. "Ethnophysicality; or, An Ethnography of Some Body." In *Soul: Black Power, Politics, and Pleasure*, edited by Monique Guillory and Richard C. Green, 172–90. New York: New York University Press.

Jackson, Joyce M. 1981. "The Black American Folk Preacher and the Chanted Sermon: Parallels with a West African Tradition." In *Discourse in Ethnomusicology II: A Tribute to Alan P. Merriam*, edited by Caroline Card, Jane Cowan, Sally Carr Helton, Carl Rahkonen, and Laura Kay Sommers, 205–22. Bloomington, Ind.: Ethnomusicology Publication Group.

Jebbinson, Andre. 2018. "Lester Lewis: Pioneer of Gospel Reggae Style." *Gleaner*, December 15, 2006. http://old.jamaica-gleaner.com/gleaner/20061215/ent/ent1.html.

Johnson, Birgitta. 2015. "This Is Not the Warm Up Act! Praise and Worship Expanding Liturgical Traditions, Theology, and Identities in an African American Megachurch." In *The Spirit of Praise: Music and Worship in the Pentecostal-Charismatic Tradition*, edited by Monique M. Ingalls and Amos Yong, 117–32. University Park: Pennsylvania State University Press.

Johnson, E. Patrick. 2003. *Appropriating Blackness: Performance and the Politics of Authenticity*. Durham, N.C.: Duke University Press.

Jones, Alisha Lola. 2015a. "'Are All the Choir Directors Gay?': The Policing of Black Men's Gender and Sexuality in Gospel Performance." In *African American Music: An Introduction*, edited by Mellonee V. Burnim and Portia K. Maultsby, 216–36. New York: Routledge.

———. 2015b. "Pole Dancing for Jesus: Negotiating Masculinity and Sexual Ambiguity Gospel Performance." In *Esotericism in the Africana Religious Experience: There is a Mystery*, edited by Stephen C. Finley, Margarita Simon Guillory, and Hugh R. Page Jr., 314–30. London: Brill.

Jones, Charles Edwin. 1974. *Perfectionist Persuasion: The Holiness Movement and American Methodism, 1867–1936*. Boston: Scarecrow.

Kammen, Michael. 1991. *Mystic Chords of Memory: The Transformation of Tradition in American Culture*. New York: Knopf.

Katz, David. 2003. *Solid Foundation: An Oral History of Reggae*. New York: Bloomsbury.

Kauppila, Paul. 2006. "'From Memphis to Kingston': An Investigation into the Origin of Jamaican Ska." *Social and Economic Studies* 55, no. 1: 75–91.

Kernodle, Tammy L. 2006. "Work the Works: The Role of African-American Women in the Development of Contemporary Gospel." *Black Music Research Journal* 26, no. 1: 89–109.

Kidula, Jean Ngoya. 2010. "'There Is Power': Contemporizing Old Music Traditions for New Gospel Audiences in Kenya." *Yearbook for Traditional Music* 42: 62–80.

Kisliuk, Michelle. 2000. *Seize the Dance! BaAka Musical Life and the Ethnography of Performance*. New York: Oxford University Press.

Kivisto, Peter, and Paul R. Croll. 2012. *Race and Ethnicity: The Basics*. New York: Routledge.

Knowles, Caroline. 2000. "Here and There: Doing Transnational Fieldwork." In *Constructing the Field: Ethnographic Fieldwork in the Contemporary World*, edited by Vered Amit, 62–78. London: Routledge.

Koundoura, Maria. 1998. "Multiculturalism or Multinationalism?" In *Multicultural States: Rethinking Difference and Identity*, edited by David Bennett, 69–87. New York: Routledge.

Krüger, Simone, and Ruxandra Trandafoiu, eds. 2014. *The Globalization of Musics in Transit: Music Migration and Tourism*. New York: Routledge.

Lamont, Michele, and Virag Molnar. 2002. "The Study of Boundaries across the Social Sciences." *Annual Review of Sociology* 28: 167–95.

Lange, Barbara R. 2003. *Holy Brotherhood: Romani Music in a Hungarian Pentecostal Church*. New York: Oxford University Press.

Lavie, Smadar, and Ted Swedenburg 1996. "Introduction: Displacement, Diaspora, and Geographies of Identity." In *Displacement, Diaspora, and Geographies of Identity*, edited by Smadar Lavie and Ted Swedenburg, 1–25. Durham, N.C.: Duke University Press.

Lawless, Elaine J. 1993. *Holy Women, Wholly Women: Sharing Ministries of Wholeness through Life Stories and Reciprocal Ethnography*. Philadelphia: University of Pennsylvania Press.

Lévi-Strauss, Claude. 1963. *Totemism*. Translated by Rodney Needham. Boston: Beacon.

Lewin, Olive. 2000. *Rock It Come Over: The Folk Music of Jamaica*. Kingston: University of West Indies Press.

Lincoln, C. Eric. 1974. "Black Religion and the Black Church: Mode, Mood and Music—Humanizing the Social Order." In *The Black Experience in Religion*, edited by C. Eric Lincoln, 1–65. New York: Anchor.

Lincoln, C. Eric, and Lawrence H. Mamiya. 1990. *The Black Church in the African American Experience*. Durham, N.C.: Duke University Press.

Manuel, Peter, and Wayne Marshall. 2006. "The Riddim Method: Aesthetics, Practice, and Ownership in Jamaican Dancehall." *Popular Music* 25, no. 3: 447–70.

Marcus, George E. 1998. "Introduction: Anthropology on the Move." In *Ethnography through Thick and Thin*, edited by George E. Marcus, 3–30. Princeton, N.J.: Princeton University Press.

Marks, Morton. 1982. "'You Can't Sing Unless You're Saved': Reliving the Call in Gospel Music." In *African Religious Groups and Beliefs: Papers in Honor of William R. Bascom*, edited by Simon Ottenberg, 305–31. Meerut, India: Archana.

Marovich, Robert M. 2015. *A City Called Heaven: Chicago and the Birth of Gospel Music*. Urbana: University of Illinois Press.

Marti, Gerardo. 2012. "The Diversity-Affirming Latino: Ethnic Options and the Ethnic Transcendent Expression of American Latino Religious Identity." In *Sustaining Faith Traditions: Race, Ethnicity, and Religion among the Latino and Asian American Second Generation*, edited by Carolyn E. Chen and Russell Jeung, 25–45. New York: New York University Press.

Martin, David. 2002. *Pentecostalism: The World Their Parish*. Oxford: Blackwell.

Martin, Lerone A. 2014. *Preaching on Wax: The Phonograph and the Making of Modern African American Religion*. New York: New York University Press.

Maultsby, Portia K. 1994. "Ethnicity and African American Popular Music." *Bulgarian Musicology* 18, no. 1: 50–58.

———. 1999. "The Impact of Gospel Music on the Secular Music Industry." In *Signifyin(g), Sanctifyin', and Slam Dunking: A Reader in African American Expressive Culture*, edited by Gena Dagel Caponi. Amherst: University of Massachusetts Press.

McAlister, Elizabeth. 2012. "Listening for Geographies: Music as Sonic Compass Pointing toward African and Christian Diasporic Horizons in the Caribbean." *Black Music Research Journal* 32, no. 2: 25–50.

Migge, Bettina. 2010. "Negotiating Social Identities on an Eastern Marron Radio Show." *Journal of Pragmatics* 43, no. 6: 1498–511.

Mills, Claude. 1998. "Country Music's Popularity Growing." *Gleaner*, September 7, 1998. https://gleaner.newspaperarchive.com/kingston-gleaner/1998-09-07/page -16.

Moore, Joseph G. 1953. "The Religion of Jamaican Negroes: A Study of Afro-American Acculturation." PhD diss., Northwestern University.

Murphy, Joseph. M. 1994. *Working the Spirit: Ceremonies of the African Diaspora*. Boston: Beacon.

Nieuwkerk, Karin van. 2013. *Performing Piety: Singers and Actors in Egypt's Islamic Revival*. Austin: University of Texas Press.

Oakley, Giles. 1997. *The Devil's Music: A History of the Blues*. New York: Da Capo.

Otto, Rudolf. 1923. *The Idea of the Holy*. Translated by John W. Harvey. London: Oxford University Press.

Paris, Arthur E. 1982. *Black Pentecostalism: Southern Religion in an Urban World*. Amherst: University of Massachusetts Press.

Pearson, Jo. 2002. "'Going Native in Reverse': The Insider as Researcher in British Wicca." In *Theorizing Faith: The Insider/Outsider Problem in the Study of Ritual*, edited by Elisabeth Arweck and Martin D. Stringer, 97–113. Birmingham, U.K.: University of Birmingham Press.

Pfaffenberger, Bryan. 1992. "Social Anthropology of Technology." *Annual Review of Anthropology* 21: 491–516.

Pink, Sarah. 2000. "Informants Who Come Home." In *Constructing the Field: Ethnographic Fieldwork in the Contemporary World*, edited by Vered Amit, 96–119. London: Routledge.

Pitts, Walter F. 1993. *Old Ship of Zion: Afro-Baptist Ritual in the African Diaspora*. New York: Oxford University Press.

Placide, Sharon E. 2010. "Navigating Racial Boundaries: The One-Drop Rule and Mixed-Race Jamaicans in South Florida." PhD diss., Florida International University.

Poewe, Karla. 1994a. "Introduction: The Nature, Globality, and History of Charismatic Christianity." In *Charismatic Christianity as a Global Culture*, edited by Karla Poewe, 1–32. Columbia: University of South Carolina Press.

———. 1994b. "Rethinking the Relationship of Anthropology to Science and Religion." In *Charismatic Christianity as a Global Culture*, edited by Karla Poewe, 234–58. Columbia: University of South Carolina Press.

Pritchard, Elizabeth A. 2019. "Introduction." In *Spirit on the Move: Black Women and Pentecostalism in Africa and the Diaspora*, edited by Judith Casselberry and Elizabeth A. Pritchard, 1–23. Durham, N.C.: Duke University Press.

Pulis, John W. 1999. "Bridging Troubled Waters: Moses Baker, George Liele, and the African American Diaspora to Jamaica." In *Moving On: Black Loyalists in the Afro-Atlantic World*, edited by John W. Pulis, 183–222. New York: Garland.

Puttick, Elizabeth. 1997. *Women in New Religions: In Search of Community, Sexuality and Spiritual Power*. London: MacMillan.

Qadeer, Mohammed. 2006. *Pakistan: Social and Cultural Transformations in a Muslim Nation*. New York: Routledge.

Raboteau, Albert J. 1978. *Slave Religion: The "Invisible Institution" in the Antebellum South*. New York: Oxford University Press.

———. 2001. *Canaan Land: A Religious History of African Americans*. New York: Oxford University Press.

Ramsey, Guthrie P. 2003. *Race Music: Black Cultures from Bebop to Hip-Hop*. Berkeley: University of California Press.

Reagon, Bernice Johnson. 1992. *We'll Understand Better By and By: Pioneering African American Gospel Composers*. Washington, D.C.: Smithsonian Institution Press.

Redemption Songs. N.d. London: Pickering and Inglis.

Reed, Teresa L. 2003. *The Holy Profane: Religion in Black Popular Music*. Lexington: University of Kentucky Press.

———. 2012. "Shared Possessions: Black Pentecostals, Afro-Caribbeans, and Sacred Music." *Black Music Research Journal* 32: 5–25.

Rice, Timothy. 1994. *May It Fill Your Soul: Experiencing Bulgarian Music*. Chicago: University of Chicago Press.

———. 2007. "Reflections on Music and Identity in *Ethnomusicology*." *Muzikologija/Musicology* (Journal of the Serbia Academy of Sciences and Arts) 7: 17–38.

Ricks, George Robinson. 1977. *Some Aspects of the Religious Music of the United States Negro: An Ethnomusicological Study with Special Emphasis on the Gospel Tradition*. New York: Arno.

Ricoeur, Paul. 1981. *Hermeneutics and the Human Sciences*. Cambridge: Cambridge University Press.

Riggs, Marcia Y. 2003. *Plenty Good Room: Women versus Male Power in the Black Church*. Cleveland, Ohio: Pilgrim.

Robertson, Roland. 1992. *Globalization: Social Theory and Global Culture*. London: Sage.

"Rocking Gospel." *Gleaner*, October 23, 2000. http://old.jamaica-gleaner.com/gleaner/20001023/star/star1.html.

Rommen, Timothy. 2007. *"Mek Some Noise": Gospel Music and the Ethics of Style in Trinidad*. Berkeley: University of California Press.

Rosenberg, Bruce A. 1988. *Can These Bones Live? The Art of the American Folk Preacher*. Revised edition. Urbana: University of Illinois Press.

Ruether, Rosemary Radford. 2014. "Sexism and Misogyny in the Christian Tradition: Liberating Alternatives." *Buddhist-Christian Studies* 34: 83–94.

Samarin, William J. 1970. *Tongues of Men and Angels: The Religious Language of Pentecostalism*. New York: Macmillan.

Sanders, Cheryl. 1996. *Saints in Exile: The Holiness-Pentecostal Experience in African-American Religion and Culture*. New York: Oxford University Press.

Seaga, Edward. 1969. "Revival Cults in Jamaica: Notes toward a Sociology of Religion." *Jamaica Journal* 3: 3–13.

Seale, Gerald. 2007. "Our Environment in Making Disciples." Congress of Evangelicals in the Caribbean, Centre for Excellence, Tunapuna, Trinidad. October 22–25, 2007. http://www.caribbeanevangelical.org/conecar2007reports/plenarypapers.htm. Reprinted in "Mind and Spirit: A Theologian Does Not a Leader Make." *Gleaner*, November 17, 2007. http://old.jamaica-gleaner.com/gleaner/20071117/news/news6.html.

Sernett, Milton C. 1997. *Bound for the Promised Land: African American Religion and the Great Migration*. Durham, N.C.: Duke University Press.

Shelemay, Kay Kaufman. 1996. "Crossing Boundaries in Music and Musical Scholarship: A Perspective from Ethnomusicology." *Musical Quarterly* 80, no. 1: 13–30.

———. 2008. "The Ethnomusicologist, Ethnographic Method, and the Transmission of Tradition." In *Shadows in the Field: New Perspectives for Fieldwork in Ethnomusicology*, edited by Gregory F. Barz and Timothy J. Cooley, 141–56. New York: Oxford University Press.

Sheller, Mimi. 2003. *Consuming the Caribbean: From Arawaks to Zombies*. London: Routledge.

Shelley, Braxton D. 2017. "Sounding Belief: 'Tuning Up' and 'the Gospel Imagination.'" In *Exploring Christian Song*, edited by M. Jennifer Bloxam and Andrew D. Shelton, 173–93. Lanham, Md.: Lexington.

———. 2019. "Analyzing Gospel." *Journal of the American Musicological Society* 72, no. 1: 181–243.

Sherlock, Philip, and Hazel Bennett. 1998. *The Story of the Jamaican People*. Kingston: Randle.

Simmons, Martha. 2010. "Whooping: The Musicality of African American Preaching Past and Present." In *Preaching with Sacred Fire: An Anthology of African American Sermons, 1750 to the Present*, edited by Martha Simmons and Frank A. Thomas, 864–84. New York: Norton.

Simpson, George Eaton. 1956. "Jamaican Revivalist Cults." *Social and Economic Studies* 5: 321–403.

———. 1978. *Black Religions in the New World*. New York: Columbia University Press.

Slocum, Karla. 2001. "Negotiating Identity and Black Feminist Politics in Caribbean Research." In *Black Feminist Anthropology: Theory, Praxis, Poetics, and Politics*, edited by Irma McClaurin, 126–49. New Brunswick, N.J.: Rutgers University Press.

Smith, Candis Watts. 2014. *Black Mosaic: The Politics of Black Pan-Ethnic Diversity*. New York: New York University Press.

Smith, Thérèse. 2004. *"Let the Church Sing!": Music and Worship in a Black Mississippi Community*. Rochester, N.Y.: University of Rochester Press.

Sparke, Matthew. 2004. "Nature and Tradition at the Border: Landscaping the End of the Nation State." In *The End of Tradition?*, edited by Nezar Alsayyad, 87–115. New York: Routledge.

Spencer, Jon Michael. 1987. *Sacred Symphony: The Chanted Sermon of the Black Preacher*. New York: Greenwood.

———. 1990. *Protest and Praise: Sacred Music of Black Religion*. Minneapolis, Minn.: Fortress.

———. 1992. *Black Hymnody: A Hymnological History of the African-American Church*. Knoxville: University of Tennessee Press.

Spier, Robert F. G. 1970. *From the Hand of Man: Primitive and Preindustrial Technologies*. Boston: Houghton Mifflin.

Spittler, Russell P. 1994. "Are Pentecostals and Charismatics Fundamentalists? A Review of American Uses of These Categories." In *Charismatic Christianity as a Global Culture*, edited by Karla Poewe, 103–16. Columbia: University of South Carolina Press.

Spradley, James P. 1980. *Participant Observation*. New York: Holt, Rinehart and Winston.

Stokes, Martin. 1994. "Introduction: Ethnicity, Identity and Music." In *Ethnicity, Identity and Music: The Musical Construction of Place*, edited by Martin Stokes, 1–27. Oxford, U.K.: Berg.

———. 2004. "Music and the Global Order." *Annual Review of Anthropology* 33: 47–72.

Stolzoff, Norman C. 2000. *Wake the Town and Tell the People: Dancehall Culture in Jamaica*. Durham, N.C.: Duke University Press.

Strauss, Sarah. 2000. "Locating Yoga: Ethnography and Transnational Practice." In *Constructing the Field: Ethnographic Fieldwork in the Contemporary World*, edited by Vered Amit, 162–94. London: Routledge.

Sutton, Constance R. 1987. "The Caribbeanization of New York City and the Emergence of a Transnational Cultural System." In *Caribbean Life in New York City: Sociocultural Dimensions*, edited by Constance R. Sutton and Elsa M. Chaney, 15–30. New York: Center for Migration Studies of New York.

Sutton, Constance R., and Susan Makiesky-Barrow. 1987. "Migration and West Indian Racial and Ethnic Consciousness." In *Caribbean Life in New York City: Sociocultural Dimensions*, edited by Constance R. Sutton and Elsa M. Chaney, 92–116. New York: Center for Migration Studies of New York.

Tedlock, Barbara. 1991. "From Participant Observation to the Observation of Participation: The Emergence of Narrative Ethnography." *Journal of Anthropological Research* 47, no. 1: 69–94.

Thomas, Deborah A. 2004. *Modern Blackness: Nationalism, Globalization and the Politics of Culture in Jamaica*. Durham, N.C.: Duke University Press.

———. 2011. *Exceptional Violence: Embodied Citizenship in Transnational Jamaica*. Durham, N.C.: Duke University Press.

Toulis, Nicole R. 1997. *Believing Identity: Pentecostalism and the Mediation of Jamaican Ethnicity and Gender in England*. Oxford, U.K.: Berg-Oxford International.

Tuleja, Tad. 1997. *Usable Pasts: Traditions and Group Expressions in North America*. Logan: Utah State University Press.

Turino, Thomas. 2008. *Music as Social Life: The Politics of Participation*. Chicago: University of Chicago Press.

Turman, Eboni Marshall. 2013. *Toward a Womanist Ethic of Incarnation: Black Bodies, the Black Church, and the Council of Chalcedon*. New York: Palgrave Macmillan.

———. 2015. "'The Greatest Tool of the Devil': Mamie, Malcolm X, and the PolitiX of the Black Madonna in Black Churches and the Nation of Islam in the United States." *Journal of Africana Religions* 3, no. 1: 130–50.

Turner, William C. Jr. 1988. "The Musicality of Black Preaching: A Phenomenology." *Journal of Black Sacred Music* 2, no. 1: 21–34.

Ulysse, Gina Athena. 2008. *Downtown Ladies: Informal Commercial Importer, a Haitian Anthropologist and Self-Making in Jamaica*. Chicago: University of Chicago Press.

Veal, Michael E. 2007. *Dub: Soundscapes and Shattered Songs in Jamaican Reggae*. Middletown, Conn.: Wesleyan University Press.

Vickerman, Milton. 2001. "Jamaicans: Balancing Race and Ethnicity." In *New Immigrants in New York*, edited by Foner Nancy, 201–28. New York: Columbia University Press.

Visweswaran, Kamala. 1994. *Fictions of Feminist Ethnography*. Minneapolis: University of Minnesota Press.

Walker, Daniel E. 1999. "Pleading the Blood: Storefront Pentecostalism in James Baldwin's 'Sonny's Blues.'" *College Language Association Journal* 43, no. 2: 194–206.

Walker, Wyatt Tee. 1979. *"Somebody's Calling My Name": Black Sacred Music and Social Change.* Valley Forge, Penn.: Judson.

Walsh, Roger. 1993. "Phenomenological Mapping and Comparisons of Shamanic, Buddhist, Yogic, and Schizophrenic Experiences." *Journal of the American Academy of Religion* 61, no. 4: 739–69.

Walston, Rick. 2005. *The Speaking in Tongues Controversy: The Initial Physical Evidence of the Baptism in the Holy Spirit Debate.* Eugene, Ore,. Wipf and Stock.

Walters, Aldane. 2016. "Donnie's Good Deeds." *Jamaica Observer*, July 26, 2016. http://www.jamaicaobserver.com/Entertainment/Donnie-s-good-deeds_68217.

Ward, Larry F. 1997. "Filled with the Spirit: The Musical Life of an Apostolic Pentecostal Church in Champaign-Urbana, Illinois." PhD diss., University of Illinois at Champaign-Urbana.

Waterman, Richard. 1951. "Gospel Hymns in a Negro Church in Chicago." *International Folk Music Journal* 3: 87–93.

Weekes, Melinda E. 2005. "This House, This Music: Exploring the Interdependent Interpretive Relationship between the Contemporary Black Church and Contemporary Gospel Music." *Black Music Research Journal* 25, no. 1/2: 43–72.

White, Bob W. 2012. "Introduction: Rethinking Globalization through Music." In *Music and Globalization: Critical Encounters*, edited by Bob W. White, 1–14. Bloomington: Indiana University Press.

Williams, Melvin D. 1974. *Community in a Black Pentecostal Church.* Pittsburgh: University of Pittsburgh Press.

Williams-Jones, Pearl. 1975. "Afro-American Gospel Music." *Ethnomusicology* 19: 373–85.

Williamson, Joel. 1995. *New People: Miscegenation and Mulattoes in the United States.* Baton Rouge: Louisiana State University Press.

Wise, Raymond. 2002. "Defining African American Gospel Music by Tracing Its Historical and Musical Development from 1900 to 2000." PhD diss., Ohio State University.

Wood, Abigail, and Rachel Harris. 2018. "Introduction: Sharing Space? Sharing Culture? Applied Experiments in Music-Making Across Borders." *World of Music* 7, no. 1/2: 7–16.

Zolov, Eric. 1999. *Refried Elvis: The Rise of the Mexican Counterculture.* Berkeley: University of California Press.

Index

influence on Jamaican Pentecostalism,
8; Pentecostals from United States, 157
Mississippi Mass Choir, 136
Montego Bay: New Testament Church of
God, 33–36; tourism in, 48
multi-sited ethnography, 155–56
"musical boundary-work," 2, 159n1
musical instruments, role of: in African
American churches, 111; in the Bible,
63, 116; in gender socialization, 57; in
gospel concerts, 140; at the Jamaican
Convention, 107; in large Jamaican
churches, 102; in preaching, 84, 130–31;
in studio production, 5; in tarrying
services, 103
musical style: African American, 131–32;
"black" and "white," 113, 126, 128–29,
144; country-and-western-influenced,
101, 114; cultural politics of, 58, 136;
dancehall-influenced, 54, 60, 140, 142;
debates concerning, 40, 128, 136, 142; at
Emmanuel Temple, 22–26; evolution of,
25, 111; funk-influenced, 132; gendered,
77; generational differences and, 25, 30,
154; "home" indexed by, 32, 34, 39–40;
hymn-performance and, 24; identity
and, 14, 50, 132, 138, 155; Jamaicanness
symbolized by, 26, 32; jazz-influenced,
20, 133; negotiations of, 20, 23–24, 123,
135, 154; at New Testament Church of
God, 35; "praise" and "worship" distinguished by, 5; preaching as a, 172n7;
racialization of, 112–14, 128–29, 143–44,
172n3; reggae-influenced, 59–60, 140;
rhythm-and-blues-influenced, 31, 35,
125–26, 141; rock-influenced, 5; ska-
influenced, 31, 35, 91, 109, 137; strategies
of, 19; traditional Pentecostal, 133–34;
unity and, 143–45

"negotiation of proximity" (Rommen), 40,
127
Nelson, Grace, 84
New Testament Church of God, 33–35,
121, 146, 162n14. *See also* Pentecostal
organizations
Ninjaman, 66
nostalgia, 26, 99–100, 110, 130, 170n1

Oakley, Giles, 167n8
obeah, 70
"observant participation," 11
"Old Landmark," concept of the, 104, 171n5
"old-time way," the: authenticity of, 34, 101;
contemporary gospel versus, 125, 132;
as an invented tradition, 100; nostalgia
and reverence for, 14, 99, 112; singing in,
104–5, 129
"one drop" rhythm, the, 140, 173n9
"one-drop" rule, the, 114, 171n11
"One God Apostolic" (Lance Appleton),
29–33, 41, 166n11
"one-liners," 24–25
oneness: apostolic doctrine of, 30, 146;
spiritual unity as, 109–10, 112–13,
173n12
oneness Pentecostalism. *See* Pentecostalism: apostolic
Otto, Rudolf, 42

"panethnic" identity (Marti), 15, 126, 148,
173n14
Papa San, 4
patois, 21, 59–60, 109, 140
patriarchy, 55, 79, 169n7
Patterson, Percival James, 82
Paul, Les, 88
PAW. *See* Pentecostal Assemblies of the
World
Pearson, Jo, 164n25
Peart, Allan, 106–7
Pentecost, Day of, 21, 106, 119, 154, 161n10
Pentecostal Assemblies of the World, 8,
106–13, 145; establishment in Jamaica,
162n14; global influence, 157; International Convention, 79–80, 107; Jamaican
Convention, 106–13, 118; New York
State-Ontario district, 20; women's
roles, 70
Pentecostalism: apostolic, 30–33, 146–47;
beliefs and practices of, 1–3, 98, 146–47;
charismatic Christianity and, 15, 157,
174n6; conservative forms of, 45, 112,
132–34, 142; globalization of, 11, 155,
157; history in Jamaica, 7–8, 15; in New
York, 9; and Protestantism, 161n10; stig-
matization of, 70

MELVIN L. BUTLER is an associate professor of musicology at the Frost School of Music at the University of Miami and a saxophonist with Brian Blade and the Fellowship Band and many other artists.

AFRICAN AMERICAN MUSIC IN GLOBAL PERSPECTIVE

The University of Illinois Press
is a founding member of the
Association of University Presses.

―――――――――――――――――

Composed in 10.25/13 Marat Pro
with Trade Gothic Condensed display
by Kirsten Dennison
at the University of Illinois Press
Cover designed by Jim Proefrock
Cover illustration: Pentecostal church members on
Jamaica's northern coast. Photo by Melvin L. Butler.

University of Illinois Press
1325 South Oak Street
Champaign, IL 61820-6903
www.press.uillinois.edu